The Use of Instructional Technology in Schools

LESSONS TO BE LEARNED

Mal Lee and Arthur Winzenried

ACER Press

First published 2009
by ACER Press, an imprint of
Australian Council for Educational Research Ltd
19 Prospect Hill Road, Camberwell
Victoria, 3124, Australia

www.acerpress.com.au
sales@acer.edu.au

Edited by Ronél Redman
Cover design by Polar Design Pty Ltd
Text design based on design by mightyworld
Typeset by Polar Design Pty Ltd
Printed in Australia by Hyde Park Press

Cover photographs (l to r): images 1–3 courtesy Peter Dalwood; image 4
courtesy Camberwell High School (photograph by Guy Lavoipierre);
image 5 courtesy Promethean, Inc; image 6 by Stockbyte.

National Library of Australia Cataloguing-in-Publication entry

Author:	Lee, Malcolm, 1944-
Title:	The use of instructional technology in schools : lessons to be learned/Mal Lee, Arthur Winzenried.
ISBN:	9780864318886 (pbk.)
Notes:	Includes index. Bibliography.
Subjects:	Educational technology--Australia. Teaching--Australia--Aids and devices.

Other Authors/Contributors:
          Winzenried, Arthur, 1949-

Dewey Number: 371.330994

CONTENTS

FIGURES AND TABLES

Figures

Tables

ACKNOWLEDGEMENTS

The authors would like to thank the many people who have assisted in the researching of this book, and in particular those who agreed to be interviewed.

Barrett, T.	Harvey, R.	O'Brien, D.
Beamish, P.	Hay, L.	O'Brien, M.
Bellenger, J.	Hodgkinson, J.	Paton, I.
Bonanno, K.	Hughes, P.	Price, B.
Boyle, M.	Joliffe, K.	Richardson, K.
Brewster, D.	Kent, P.	Robinson, P.
Burfitt, H.	King, G.	Sandery, P.
Cribb, P.	King, S.	Schnetker, P.
Croft, M.	Knowlton, N.	Shanley, J.
Dalwood, P.	Lambert, P.	Shaw, A.
Dillon, K.	Langford, T.	Shaw, D.
Duffle, P.	Lee, B.	Simpson, D.
Dunnett, C.	Leo, G.	Smith, C.
Elliot, C.	Lowe, A.	Shanley, J.
Finger, G.	Macarthur, J.	Tolley, R.
Flannery, D.	Macaulay, V.	Walker, G.
Grantham, C.	Meally, L.	Webb, I.
Griffin, J.	Messenger, C.	Wharton, S.
Hounsell, D.	Morrow, J	Williams, M.
Jones, B.	Muirhead, B.	Wright, G.

FOREWORD

It is a special pleasure to write this foreword for *The Use of Instructional Technology in Schools*, a book whose message is very timely. Education everywhere is under pressure, seeking to find more effective means of meeting the diverse needs of individuals and of societies. In such a search, this book has an important message. Mal Lee and Arthur Winzenried, from their diverse experience, are ideally placed to handle such a theme. Appropriately for this task they combine varied and long experience in schools and education systems with a genuine familiarity with the technology of which they write so relevantly. I have had the pleasure in the past of working with Mal Lee in helping to build a new education system in Canberra and admire his capacity to contribute in all aspects of such systems.

What makes my task even more pleasant is that this book will make a significant contribution to an aim that is of real urgency: to achieve a successful education for all students at a period when such success is vitally important to their lives and to their societies.

AN UNRESOLVED PARADOX

There is a paradox in educational technology that needs to be resolved urgently. Education is the source of technological advance, providing the knowledge and the people so necessary for that purpose. At the same time, the basic processes for schooling remain largely unaffected by that advance. Technology has altered irrevocably the means of operation of most social agencies, governments, hospitals, libraries, shops and factories, entertainment and the media. Schools, however, operate now in much the same way as they have always done, with the teacher and the classroom as the setting for learning and with technology playing only a minimal role.

This book addresses that paradox, recognising the failure of past many attempts to make major differences in the operation of schools and classrooms, and pointing to developments that promise real advances.

THE URGENT NEED FOR EFFECTIVE EDUCATION FOR ALL PEOPLE

This issue is of paramount importance. Education is the key to successful development, whether that development is individual or national. The United Nations (UN) has included Education For All (EFA) in the eight Millennium Development Goals to be achieved by 2015. The UN has assigned the task of achieving EFA to the United Nations Educational, Scientific and Cultural Organization (UNESCO) as its major priority for the immediate future. The reason for this priority is not difficult to see. Education is one of the great human enablers: those individuals with an effective education are more likely to be successful in diverse aspects of life, their work, their contribution to the wider society, their health and their personal development. On the contrary, those people who miss out on an effective education suffer long-term disadvantage in all these aspects. The importance of education to individuals is repeated on the large scale for nations: those nations with effective and efficient education systems have the strongest basis for their progress, their prosperity and their wellbeing.

THE SEARCH FOR IMPROVEMENT

As emphasised earlier, while almost every other major social agency has changed fundamentally in their means of operation, schools have not done so. A hospital today would be unrecognisable to Florence Nightingale; however, if Jean Jacques Rousseau were to return to observe schools, he would see essentially the same pattern that he criticised more than 200 years ago. Schools are one of the oldest forms of organisation in our societies—from their origins many thousands of years ago to achieve religious and cultural aims, to today's current role as agents for universal education. The processes for the operation of schools remain fundamentally the same: communication from an individual teacher to a group of students.

The Use of Instructional Technology in Schools demonstrates vividly that this essential sameness is not a matter of intent. Education has been willing—perhaps even too willing—to try new technological approaches and new teaching approaches. From the traditional blackboard, the focus has moved to film, to radio, to teaching machines, to television and, more recently, to computers. Schools and their administrators have not been unwilling to try new developments. Nor have other institutions. The Australian Broadcasting Commission (ABC) was itself a major player in earlier attempts to assist teachers by bringing technology into the classroom. The ABC had a significant education section with many permanent staff plus other seconded educators, beginning with radio in the 1930s and continuing with television in the 1960s. Their regular programs were used in primary and secondary schools throughout the country. This initiative was dropped by the ABC. The Commonwealth Secondary Schools Libraries Program was introduced in the 1970s, sponsored by the Australian Government, and made a major effort to provide school libraries that could act as centres for the use of books and technology in schools. That strong emphasis has faded, at least for the time being. Currently, with the arrival of computers in accessible forms, all schools are involved in the search to find ways in which this new technology can fundamentally assist education, as it is helping so many other areas of our society. However, as revealed by research in many countries (much of it referenced in this book), the new media have not yet materially altered the work of schools and teachers.

THE URGENCY

The lack of impact of technology in schools would not be a problem if there were not an urgent need for the successful education of all students. We now know the extent of loss, for the individuals concerned and for the societies to which they belong, from an education that does not work for all. This is the most important area where education must improve, both in Australia and more widely. In Australia, research by the Business Council of Australia shows that 35 000 students every year leave school without the qualifications to enable them to take a useful part in society. This is an enormous penalty for them and a heavy burden for the wider society. Schools need to have available to them every means by which education can be improved for all students, including those who currently do not succeed.

Can technology help in this search? The answer might well have been negative, given our past experience. Technology as yet has not made the hoped-for impact. There are real indications provided in this book of effective options for the future. It points out that schools are now at a critical decision time in their processes for using technology.

By 2008, there was a wide and growing divide between the extent of the digital technology and its use in the home and the classroom. Schools and education authorities had largely chosen to ignore the technological development of the young in their homes, particularly in the period 1995–2008, and have rarely factored that development into any holistic or networked educational development. Schools and education authorities have invariably continued to work on the assumption that the only 'real' education occurs in the classroom. (pp. 223–4)

What is encouraging in this book is that the argument does not stop at this depressing conclusion, but points the way ahead for uses of technology that will take account of the realities of schools and classrooms. It also recognises the potential bounty from such technology as the interactive whiteboard (IWB) that can accommodate the needs of schools and also of students and can fit so powerfully into the regular classroom.

The authors have not been content to merely point out the failings and go no further, they have used the experience from many case studies that show the prospect of real change. It is significant that the schools featured in the case studies in Chapter 17 have all chosen a whole-school approach that focuses centrally on enhancing the teaching and simultaneously addresses a range of variables that relate to whole-school development.

REAL HOPE FOR THE FUTURE

Mal Lee and Arthur Winzenried point out the great disjunction between the use of technology in the home and in the classroom. One reason they give is that all the instructional technology introduced in the last 50 years in teaching has, with one major exception, been available for use in the home, and indeed was designed originally for home use. That major exception is the IWB. This offers real promise to provide a major breakthrough if linked in a whole-school effort. The authors see the school library, revitalised, as playing a central role in the provision of resources that can be a major factor in utilising the potential of the IWB. Whole-school information management and information services are also a vital part of the process recommended. Most essentially, the authors see the teacher as the key to any advance: 'The teacher is the gatekeeper who has to be convinced. In fact, it is every teacher, whether working full-time or part-time in the school, who has to be convinced' (p. 226). It is this whole-school approach, combined with recognition of the power of the individual teacher, that they see as breaking the logjam that has prevented technology in the past from making the impact that is necessary.

This book is not a remote study of the problem. It is a major achievement through its use of the experience that has accumulated in many schools over the past seven years. It is also powerful in its understanding of the possibilities of technology in that setting. I can only recommend it strongly to all those who wish to see major advances for education in the future. Currently in Australia, education has become a major political priority and technology features strongly in that priority. The authors provide invaluable directions for the use of technology in schools, directions that can make the political priority a real benefit to those schools and, through them, to Australian society.

Phillip Hughes
Australian National University

CHAPTER 1

INTRODUCTION

The desire to use technology to enhance teaching and learning has been evident at least since the early years of the Industrial Revolution, if not earlier. Since then, numerous moves have been made to use different types of technology to markedly enhance teaching and, in particular, student learning. Over the last century, particularly since the introduction of electricity into schools, there have been concerted efforts to use the emerging technology to revolutionise teaching.

With the advantage of hindsight it is now apparent that none of those revolutions occurred and that only in the last few years have any significant breakthroughs been made and the way forward identified. What we now know is that in the twentieth century teachers were not provided with electric or electronic instructional technology which they could readily use to assist their everyday teaching. Nor, in general terms, did the school, education authority or government leadership provide the desired direction setting or support required to ensure that the instructional technology was used to best educational advantage.

It was not until the start of the twenty-first century that a confluence of technological and human developments enabled a group of pathfinding and visionary schools, education authorities and governments to finally begin harnessing the undoubted capacity of the digital instructional technology in order to provide teachers with the tools and support they required to enhance their teaching and improve student learning.

It is also disturbing—as will become increasingly apparent—that in 2008 the combination of astute leadership and appropriate technology was limited to a relatively small proportion of situations. The most commonly used instructional technologies—that is, 'any device available to teachers for use in instructing students in a more efficient and stimulating manner than the sole use of the teacher's voice' (Cuban, 1986, p. 4)—throughout the developed world were still the pen, paper and teaching board. That said, in different parts of the world there were schools and education authorities finally using digital instructional technology in everyday teaching to enhance student learning, with insights into what is required for everyone to use that technology successfully.

In the early 2000s, a small group of pathfinding schools finally succeeded in getting all their teachers and students to use digital technologies as a normal part of everyday teaching. Most of those schools opted for an approach that built upon the placement of interactive whiteboards (IWBs) and a complementary suite of digital technologies in every classroom. Virtually overnight, the teachers in those schools moved from occasionally using the technology as a supplement to their paper-based teaching to a mode of teaching that was predominantly digitally based. Indeed, so dramatic and rapid were the uptake and everyday use of the interactive whiteboards that the authors have referred to the phenomenon and the surge in use as a 'digital take-off' (Chapter 16). After decades of the purported disinclination by teachers to embrace all manner of electronic instructional technology, it was suddenly common in these schools to see all the teachers and students not only using the interactive whiteboards but also other digital tools.

In the mid 1990s, a similarly small, prescient group of national governments recognised the vital importance of preparing their young people and schools for a digital future and embarked on a concerted plan of action to use the digital technology and the networked world to assist in enhancing national economic productivity.

By 2008 it was apparent that the proactive pathfinding schools, education authorities and governments had not only begun to successfully use the digital technologies to enhance teaching, student learning, school efficiency and productivity, they could also provide an important set of lessons for others wanting to embark on the same quest.

However, while individual pathfinders were showing the way forward, the majority of schools and education authorities were still tinkering with the technology and had not adopted comprehensive strategies to use the digital instructional technologies to enhance national productivity. Rather, a suite of indicators suggested most were still providing the traditional paper-based schooling and falling further behind their more proactive competitors.

It is still very early to postulate the existence of the divide and the likely implications if no concerted actions are taken, and it is appreciated that the hypothesis does need to be researched more fully, but at a time when the educational opportunities associated with the digital and networked world are emerging at such a pace, those still embracing traditional schooling stand to continue to fall further behind and to disadvantage their students' life chances. As will become evident throughout this study, the signs point to growing digital divides between:

- homes and schools
- pathfinding and traditional schools
- proactive and reactive governments and education authorities.

The message that is becoming clearer in the twenty-first century is that the longer it takes governments, education authorities and schools to appreciate the fundamental importance of successfully using the emerging instructional technology, to build on the lessons of history and the pathfinders, the further they will fall behind those who have opted to take advantage of the digital world. What was evident in 2008 with those who had embarked in the mid 1990s on the path to provide an education for a digital future, and ultimately enhance national productivity, was that they were beginning to reap the rewards of their decade's investment and had positioned their societies to thrive in the future.

The importance of this development in the overall history of the use of instructional technology in schools is significant. While it will become apparent that some governments did endeavour to use the emerging instructional technology to enhance teacher productivity in the 1950s and 1960s, their efforts were to little avail, and it was not until the 1990s that a small number of governments and education authorities began adopting concerted and well-reasoned strategies that would enable teachers to use instructional technologies that would ultimately enhance national productivity.

While in the end the onus will be on each school to achieve the desired whole-school use of the instructional technology, the school's task is made that much easier in situations where there is a clear national vision and an appropriate support strategy.

This book is designed to provide educators, particularly in leadership roles, with an in-depth appreciation of how history with its successes and failures can contribute to identifying the way forward. History cannot provide all the answers, but it can most assuredly provide an insight into patterns, trends and ways in which instructional technologies have and have not impacted on teaching and learning.

What this study of the last century can do is to identify what has and has not succeeded, and what is required for the appropriate technology to have the desired positive impact on both student learning and, increasingly, on national productivity. Historically, it is very timely in 2008—as education authorities across the developed and developing world contemplate the digital future—to reflect on the ways of the past and consider why no significant breakthrough was made until the early 2000s.

In 1992, Lewis Perelman in *School's Out* maintained that:

> In the wake of the hyperlearning revolution, the technology called 'school' and the social institution commonly thought of as 'education' will be as obsolete and ultimately extinct as dinosaurs. (p. 50)

While Perelman's projected solution was extreme, misunderstood the realities of schooling and was never likely to be accepted, he nonetheless foresaw how the then emerging digital technology could be used to enhance teaching and economic productivity. Sixteen years after that observation, the digital technology remains remarkably underused in schools despite the global surge in its everyday use and the transformation it has brought to commerce worldwide.

Probably the most telling statement on the low-level use made of technology in teaching at the time of writing is to contrast the use of the various digital technologies by the young in their homes with the use of those same technologies in the classroom. In the home, young people have embraced all manner of digital technology and they use it very skilfully to communicate, learn, create and entertain themselves. PCs, Web use, iPods, USB drives and multifunction phones are part of their daily existence. Significantly they have seemingly opted at home for a strongly constructivist, collegial, play-oriented approach to learning. In contrast, in most classrooms the same young people have been invariably obliged to rely on the teaching tools of the nineteenth century, to listen to the teachers talk and to play the formal education game if they want to secure society's credentials. Occasionally—and only occasionally—have they been able to use the technology that is an integral part of their lives.

> Kids lead high-tech lives outside school and decidedly low-tech lives inside school. This new 'digital divide' is making the activities inside school appear to have less real world relevance to kids.

> (Illinois Institute of Design, 2007, p. 24)

In 2008, few schools appear to have endeavoured to learn what was happening with the students' use of the technology in the home, let alone try to integrate that learning into the school's activities. Indeed, in the mid to later 2000s, one saw a significant number of schools and education authorities introducing considerable constraints on the use of the emerging digital technologies. By the mid 2000s it was apparent that the divide between the learning in the home and in the classroom was widening at a pace that had the facility to markedly diminish the place of the school in the future education of young people.

Why has formal schooling reached that stage and not used the tools of the digital era?

Why this is so is one of the underlying questions we address in this study. However, before addressing that question several points need to be made.

In choosing to examine the use of instructional technology, the authors are not for a moment advocating the adoption of a technology-driven model of teaching; others have over the years, but we do not. Good teachers have always used (and should always use) a variety of approaches and tools in their teaching, some of which will have been around for years and others that are new. A well-told story can be as effective as a quality interactive multimedia presentation. Pens, paper and whiteboards have an important and continuing role to play in teaching for some time yet. The teaching board—be it black, green or white—has undoubtedly been one of the most successful of all instructional technologies. Teachers have used the boards across the world for over 200 years. In many respects the teaching board defines the classroom. Interestingly, an analysis of the reasons for the boards' continuing near-universal use provides an important insight into what is needed with the other technologies if they are to achieve such widespread acceptance and use.

That said, in contemporary society there are compelling reasons for making significantly greater use of digital teaching resources, and indeed digital student administration and communication systems. The digital can enrich the teaching, make the learning more relevant, engage all manner of students, individualise much of the teaching, enhance the efficiency of the teaching, open new unexplored worlds, reduce teachers' workload, and when successfully used across the schools of the nation can assist to enhance national productivity in knowledge-based economies.

The traditional paper-based mode of teaching has long since maximised its impact. A predominantly digitally based mode of teaching has only just begun to realise its potential.

As the title indicates, this study focuses on the use made of instructional technology by teachers and students, education authorities and governments in the past, primarily with a view to assisting schools make wise educational use of the appropriate technology in the future. It is not overly concerned with the amount of technology in the schools or the monies expended on it, but rather how the technology was used in everyday teaching. If teachers do not use the technology, it does not matter how much there is or how effective it might be in theory.

That is not to suggest that the effectiveness of the technology should not be a concern for decision makers and researchers, but simply that in 2008 the authors believe it is timely to adopt a different approach to help explain why the various technologies have had such a limited impact on teaching and learning over the past century despite the considerable investment and effort made.

The other point is that macro studies on the limited impact of technology—and in particular ICT—on teaching and learning have already been published, with those by Higgins and Moseley (2002), Balanskat, Blamire and Kefala (2006) and Becta (2007) providing excellent overviews. However, while those studies touch upon the plethora of variables potentially impacting upon the effectiveness of using ICT, the authors believe it was important to use history to assist in identifying and fleshing out the key variables that need to be borne in mind when:

- framing a national, authority or school instructional technology strategy
- selecting the appropriate instructional technology
- implementing one's strategy
- making the best use of the technology, conscious that in an integrated, networked school community the same technology will (and ought to be) used for a range of reasons—some educational while others might be administrative, logistical or for communication or enjoyment
- researching the effectiveness of the digital technologies, aware again of their likely multiple uses.

We have chosen—in contrast to Larry Cuban's seminal study in 1986, *Teachers and Machines*—to analyse all the major instructional technologies. Where Cuban opted only to examine film, radio, educational television and computers in his quest to 'explain the degree of teacher use of these technologies since the 1920s' (Cuban, 1986, p. 6), and then only in the United States of America, the authors suspected that telling information could be divined by exploring the use of all the major technologies, across the developed world.

We did, however, restrict the study to only the major instructional technologies. As you will appreciate, there have been many other technologies that have been tried and found wanting by teachers over the century. Over those years, there has been a plethora of distinct technology-like teaching machines and epidiascopes, and indeed forms of the core technology like Philips video and Sony's Beta-format VCR, that secured little acceptance. There has, moreover, been the specialist instructional technology intended for use in a particular teaching niche. Considerable use was undoubtedly made of the slide rule, computer-aided drawing (CAD) programs, electronic keyboards, language laboratories and the computerised sewing machines, but the belief was that an examination of them would not contribute any more than a consideration of the main technologies. In Australia, for example, the School of the Air has made excellent use of specialist technologies. Formed in 1951 to cater for the children of the outback, the School of the Air has variously used pedal-generated radios, two-way radio, aerial patrols, four-wheel drive vehicles and, more recently, laptops, email and the Web (http://www.assoa.nt.edu.au/_HISTORY/history.html). However, this was a niche group of students requiring particular solutions, with little to inform mainstream schooling.

All the main lessons can be derived from a consideration of the use of the major technologies.

We will be concentrating on general teacher- and student-usage patterns. Throughout the research and interviews, regular references were made to pathfinding teachers' very effective use of the various technologies and the impact that the use of these tools had on student learning. Over the years there have undoubtedly been many wonderful teachers who have made excellent use of all the technologies, but in retrospect those teachers have constituted but a small fraction of the teaching force. Historically, the early adopter teachers and the pathfinding schools have received considerable coverage. With all the new technology the media has focused on the pathfinders. The reality is that there has always been a considerable gap between the usage patterns of the early adopters and the middle and late adopting teachers who constitute the vast majority of teachers, with the gap appearing to grow wider by the day.

LIFE CYCLE OF THE TECHNOLOGY

In examining the introduction and use made of each of the instructional technologies it soon became apparent that all had experienced a common life cycle, and that few schools or education authorities have factored this information into their development strategies, technology selection or budgeting.

All the technologies had been launched into the schools' market with great hype. All were characterised by remarkably common patterns of use. And ultimately all had a finite life. Be it film, radio, television, and more recently personal computing in its many forms, all were proclaimed as the magic panacea. But in the end none were widely used by most teachers or integrated into everyday teaching. They either became occasional supplementary aids or vanished into history.

In searching for the reasons for the poor uptake by schools of technology that was used extensively by the general populace, it is important to examine the common elements of their life cycles and to identify the lessons upon which future educational leaders can build.

THE BUSINESS OF INSTRUCTIONAL TECHNOLOGY

It is also important at the outset to recognise that a very basic market force—the desire by technology companies to make a profit—has been behind the introduction of all the instructional technologies. One should never forget that basic drive in considering the history of the use of the technologies; something that does appear to have been neglected in all previous studies.

With the exception of the interactive whiteboard (IWB) (Chapter 15), all of what educators view as instructional or educational technologies were in fact products developed for sale to the wider consumer market. While both the companies concerned and many educators believed they could be used to enhance teaching and learning, the reality is that none of the major technologies of the twentieth century were designed specifically for teaching. Basically, teachers had to make do with products designed for the general consumer or office markets (Chapter 3).

The prime drivers behind each of the new electric or electronic technologies were technology companies, be they primarily entertainment, broadcasting or consumer electronics corporations. Their desire was to convince the key educational stakeholders—and in particular the financial decision makers and the major vested interests—of the wisdom of buying the particular technology.

It should therefore come as no surprise that in the introduction of each of the new technologies the focus has been on a particular piece of technology, and with it came the assertion that it alone was the magic panacea. Scant mention was made of the desirability of using the particular technology in conjunction with other teaching tools until at least the latter part of the 1990s. One thus finds periods where the 'in' technology was film, school radio broadcasts, educational television, computer-aided learning, laptop programs, interactive multimedia CD-ROMs or the 'information superhighway'.

With the introduction of each of the new technologies one finds governments, senior educational bureaucrats and invariably some tertiary educators seeking to improve their situation by supporting the introduction of the new technology. Undoubtedly, the vast majority of the technology corporation personnel and the vested interests genuinely believed in the potential of the new technology, but experience would also suggest that some—particularly governments and senior bureaucrats—used the 'latest bandwagon' to further their interests.

School leaders and teachers, particularly the early adopters, were not immune from seeking to harness the educative power of the new technology, and were invariably willing to make a concerted effort to use what was new to enrich their teaching.

What came as a surprise in our analysis was the ongoing acceptance of each of the new technologies, and the general failure by educational leaders to question the intended use of each, particularly when it was apparent by the 1980s that most teachers were not using them. One struggles to find educational decision makers asking if the new technology was intended for occasional use or whether it was to be used as an integral part of a teacher's delivery. While from the outset education authorities put in place rigorous buying procedures to select the desired brand, they did not appear to question the choice of the technology until well into the 1990s.

Allied to the focus on the broader consumer market, and to education being a secondary player, all the electric and electronic technologies used as instructional tools in the past century—except one—have been extensively used by the wider society. It has probably been the mass market's increasing acceptance of the various technologies that has gradually inclined schooling to the stage where teachers were willing to begin using the tools of a digital world.

On reflection, the level of ownership and use of 'educative' electronic technology by the average home has always exceeded that of the average classroom. Be it film, radio, hi-fi, TV, telecommunications, video and audio recorders, computers, PDAs or Internet access, the facilities available in the average classroom have always lagged well behind what has been available in the average household.

While the digital forms of the instructional technology might not have been used extensively in many classrooms, ironically by the mid 1990s the digital technology was invariably being used extensively in school administration and by most teachers in the preparation of their lessons (Cuban, 2001; Balanskat, Blamire & Kefala, 2006, p. 4). By the 2000s, the vast majority of schools in the developed world were making extensive use of the digital technology in most facets of their school's operations except the teaching.

THE VARIABLES

Anyone who has been associated with major organisational change appreciates that no single factor, such as a particular type or brand of technology, will bring about sustained change. Rather, a host of interrelated variables need to be addressed. The authors' analysis of the history reveals that this is very much the case with the use of instructional technology in everyday teaching.

In considering the use made of the technologies over the last century, nine major factors became apparent, as did the general failure to address those interrelated variables.

1 Teacher acceptance

The first—and clearly the most important—was the gaining of teacher acceptance to use the technology. Time and time again throughout the twentieth century no apparent effort was made to understand why the vast majority of teachers were not prepared to use the emerging technologies in their teaching. Indeed, the situation was still to be found in more 'reactive' schools and education authorities in 2008.

Cuban makes the telling observation that teachers were—and still are—the gatekeepers to what technology is used in the classroom (Cuban, 1986, pp. 66, 70–71). When teachers close their classroom doors, they are in control of what happens. That basic fact would appear not only to have been forgotten; one notes the concerted efforts made by the 'scientific' educators in the middle decades of the twentieth century to decide what was best for teacher productivity, and indeed to 'teacher proof' the use of the new technologies. What will become evident as one examines the technology introduced in the twentieth century was that virtually all of it obliged the teachers to dramatically change their style of teaching if they were to make extensive use of the technology. Rather than teachers being provided with tools that would assist their teaching, teachers were obliged to change their ways to suit the tools on offer.

Little wonder therefore that all the schools featured in the case studies in Chapter 17 succeeded because they:

- consciously aimed to provide technology that would assist the existing teaching, and
- ensured that they secured teacher acceptance of the new technologies.

Unless the teachers believe the technology will enhance the students' education, feel comfortable using the technology and are able to use the technology as an integral part of their everyday teaching, they will generally not use it.

2 Working with the givens

Related to securing teacher acceptance has been the failure to give due consideration to the conditions within which teachers work. While there have been critics and educational theorists over the years wanting to change many of the givens, most have been in place for centuries, and are likely to remain so for some time yet.

The kind of 'givens' that were invariably forgotten when selecting the appropriate instructional technology are:

- Teachers are allocated class groups to teach.
- Teachers are expected to manage those classes.
- Classes are allocated to a teaching room or two.
- Classrooms have been designed to accommodate the class groups and little more. The rooms have limited space.
- At the front of virtually every teaching room is a black, green or whiteboard.
- Teachers want to create their own lessons, or at least incorporate their professional insights into each lesson.
- Teachers have only limited teaching time to teach a crowded curriculum.
- Teachers want tools that can assist their teaching in their classrooms.

3 Teacher training and teacher developmental support

If teachers are to use the new and increasingly sophisticated technologies wisely and appropriately, not only do they need to be comfortable and competent in their use, they must also understand how best to use the tools to improve their teaching. In brief, they need training and ongoing developmental support.

However, history constantly reveals that this need has largely been forgotten except in the more astute education authorities and schools. As the technology changes in nature more rapidly, becomes more sophisticated and converges with other technologies, so the need for appropriate and timely development grows. By the late 1990s the challenge in even the more forward-thinking situations was considerable.

Time and again schools and education authorities have not accorded ongoing teacher development the requisite support or funding.

4 Nature and availability of the technology

Somewhat surprisingly, over the history of the use of instructional technology little analysis has been undertaken on the nature of the technology, its applicability for use in classrooms where teachers are obliged to work within the aforementioned givens, or indeed the availability of appropriate technology. What is even more surprising is the fact that the technologies used were not designed for teacher use and as such their suitability should have come under greater scrutiny.

Ironically, if one was examining the history of the use of the tools of a wood turner or a plumber, one would automatically consider the nature of the tools and their appropriateness for the desired task. One would also not contemplate focusing on one tool as the magic panacea but rather on an appropriate suite of tools. For some reason, that has not happened with teachers' tools. Teachers need tools they can integrate into their teaching. As will become apparent, it was not until the start of the twenty-first century that one saw—with the interactive whiteboard—the development or availability of such tools.

On reflection, it was not until the early 2000s that teachers had ready access to a suite of digital technologies that could be integrated into their everyday teaching. The vast majority of the earlier technologies had (as will be seen in the following pages) major shortcomings and could at best be used as supplementary teaching aids.

One could argue that it was not until mid 2008 and the release of the second-generation iPhone that secondary students finally had a portable handheld digital technology with the functionality needed that everyone could use.

5 Appropriate content/software

A key factor is the need for teachers to have ready access to the appropriate quality content and software to use with the emerging technology.

Film projectors, television sets, video recorders and interactive white-boards are somewhat limited unless teachers have the appropriate content or programs. To be widely used, the technology needs programs or content of immediate value that can be accessed readily. These programs and content took nearly as long a time to assemble as did the provision of the hardware. It was not until very recently that teachers had the ready access to the technology—other than the teaching board—that allowed them to construct lessons in conjunction with the class group.

6 Infrastructure

All electric and electronic instructional technology needs some infra-structure in place before it can be used in teaching. Not least is the access to reliable and appropriate electrical power, and the facility to secure the teaching materials to use with the instructional technology.

In more recent years the increasingly sophisticated digital and net-worked technology has heightened the fundamental importance of having equally sophisticated underpinning infrastructure and support. Without it digital schools simply cannot operate.

As will again be apparent in the following pages, historically the underlying infrastructure has been lacking and, once again, it is not until recently that schools have begun to be equipped adequately. Without reliable, inexpensive high-speed broadband access within every teaching room there will be major limitations to what teachers can do with the instructional technology.

7 Finance

Special mention needs to be made at this point of the limited monies that have been (and are today) available to schools to finance the requisite technology and associated support and training. School education budgets have always been based on a traditional, paper-based mode of schooling where the vast proportion of the recurrent funding is allocated to staff salaries. While undoubtedly there will be some variation across the OECD nations, in general terms salaries have consumed approximately 85–90 per cent of the recurrent allocation to schools. The remaining 10–15 per cent of the monies has to pay for all the other annual expenses, be it cleaning, utilities, books or instructional technology. Capital works monies are usually handled separately.

It needs to be stressed—as Atkinson et al. found for the UK-based NFER in 2005 (Atkinson, 2005)—that there is a major dearth of published analyses of the nature of school budgets and in particular of the proportions allocated for the various operational commitments. Anderson and Becker did, however, undertake an in-depth analysis of the 1998 US education budget and found that only 2.7 per cent of that budget was spent on ICT (Anderson & Becker, 1999, p. 5).

That very small proportion of the total budget is consistent with the authors' own experience with Australian school education budgets in the 1970s, 1980s and 1990s. Interviews with former senior educational administrators reinforce the authors' recollections and suggest that the same kind of allocations occurred in the 1960s.

What will become apparent as one explores the use made of each of the technologies is that there has been an ongoing shortage of monies to spend on instructional technology and an ever-increasing challenge put to the schools to find the monies for the technology.

Up until the 1960s, and probably even the 1970s, the small allocation did not have a marked impact on the school's acquisition of instructional technology, particularly as the supporting infrastructure needs were not extensive. Most schools' contribution was supplemented by some kind of central audiovisual or A/V unit.

However, from the 1980s onwards, the pressure kept increasing as the technology developed and the required infrastructure grew. Other demands like photocopying and media centres placed pressures on the same limited pool of money, and education authorities did away with the central A/V units. By the 1990s, the obligation to install increasingly sophisticated and extensive networks and to markedly improve the computer-to-student ratio placed immense strain on the limited resource allocation.

Schools turned increasingly to parents for the monies, while governments occasionally recognised the desirability of providing one-off infusions of monies or 'seeding' grants. By the mid 1990s, the more prescient nations that appreciated the importance of national investment in their future productivity began providing substantial supplementary funding for ICT. Mention will be made of the kind of investment made in the UK, Singapore, South Korea, the Clinton–Gore Administration in the US, and New Zealand.

That said, in 2008 the authors could not find (with the possible exception of Singapore) any OECD nation that had fundamentally changed its traditional paper-based mode of school funding. The OECD itself notes:

Financing has been identified as a central aspect of modernising school education. The last Joint Report pointed out that 'the necessary reforms cannot be accomplished within current levels and patterns of investment'. (2006, p. 110)

It would appear that schools were still largely expected to fund their burgeoning digital technology requirements from the same minuscule allocation as 50 years earlier or to seek supplementary funding. Reference is made below (and also in particular in Chapter 17) to a group of pathfinding schools that have adopted a model of using instructional technology throughout the school with monies from the existing recurrent funding; however, they have been able to do so only at the expense of other activities.

As will become increasingly apparent, school education is —as Perelman (1992) suggests—one of the last of the dinosaurs to undergo restructuring for the use of digital technology to enhance productivity. In the concluding chapter, the authors return to this vital issue and suggest some ways forward. There is an undoubted need for detailed comparative international research on this vital issue.

8 School and education authority leadership

For schools and education authorities to achieve and sustain the successful school-wide use of instructional technology across all the nation's schools, it will become increasingly evident that it is imperative that the leadership in the schools and education authorities appreciate the underlying vision, have a macro understanding of the digital technologies and the supporting infrastructure, and are highly conscious of addressing the key human and technological variables of the type examined by Lee and Gaffney (2008) in *Leading a Digital School*.

The role of the school principal has always been vital (and is even more so today) to any whole-school use of instructional technology.

As one reads of the efforts made in the past century to use the various instructional technologies in teaching, one is struck by the general lack of leadership displayed at both the school and education authority level. As always, there have been major exceptions, but the lack of high-level understanding revealed in recent analyses like that of Kathryn Moyle (2006) has been evident for the past century.

It was not until the 1990s that some of the pathfinding school and education authority leaders and national governments questioned the appropriateness of the technology on offer, identified what was desired by the teachers and students and took the lead in specifying what was required in the instructional technology.

9 Implementation

Closely allied to the provision of appropriate leadership is the desirability of using systematic, well-researched, practical, holistic education authority and school implementation strategies. Some began to appear in the latter 1990s, but they were still uncommon in the 2000s.

What one will see with the introduction of each of the emerging technologies is a surprising lack of implementation strategies with an underlying educational vision and building on the very considerable research on organisational change. The successful holistic implementations were the exceptions. Rather, what one finds are implementation strategies that focus on the technical, with scant regard for the human change component.

Interestingly, the authors found in the literature on each of the technologies little specific mention of the desire to have all teachers use the instructional technology in their everyday teaching. That total use is implied, and critics of the teachers' failure to use the technology also assume all of them should be doing so. It is not until the late 1990s and 2000s that one begins to see explicit concerted efforts to have all staff using the technology. In an interview with one of the main interactive whiteboard providers, mention was made of the company's concern in the mid 2000s of governments' preoccupation with rolling out the equipment, paying lip-service to the human change component and, as a consequence, seeing the technology sit idle.

RELATEDNESS OF THE KEY VARIABLES

In analysing each of the instructional technologies in the following chapters and reflecting on how they might have been used better, it will soon become apparent that even in 2008 many lessons had still to be learned and that any successful total teacher use of digital instructional technology requires schools to simultaneously address all the afore-mentioned variables.

To illustrate the growing complexity of the challenge, one of the authors consulted in 2007 on the development of a large, independent secondary girls' school as a digital school, where the teaching resources and the administration and communication systems were predominantly digital. The school had:

- a visionary principal who was strongly committed to using the digital technology to educate the girls for the contemporary world
- excellent leadership staff
- a high-speed network linking every classroom to the Net, and a support structure that had ensured the network had been working uninterrupted for eighteen months
- made a major commitment to staff development
- a desktop computer-to-student ratio of 1:2
- four large PC laboratories.

However, most teaching rooms had no digital technology that could be used integrally in everyday teaching. The majority of the teachers relied on the pen, paper and the whiteboard. The students on average used the computers less than an hour a week. The school of 940 students had only four digital cameras. The school still relied on the use of personal computers as largely discrete instructional tools. While it had successfully addressed most of the aforementioned variables, it had yet to address several key ones, namely the availability of appropriate instructional technology in every teaching room.

We suspect that school is not unrepresentative of many schools in the developed world in 2008 as it relates to the use of instructional technology. Indeed, it may well be ahead of many.

THE CHALLENGE

The above case study also illustrates succinctly the challenge that has faced schools, education authorities and national governments as they have sought to significantly increase the teacher use of instructional technology and, in turn, the effectiveness of its use in teaching and learning.

For most of the twentieth century few schools made extensive use of the instructional technology. That challenge appeared—and until this day still appears—virtually insurmountable. However, hindsight (and a little historical research) tells us that the widespread teacher use of instructional technology is easy to achieve at the individual school level if several key points are observed.

First and foremost is the necessity to secure teacher acceptance of the appropriate instructional technology. Due consideration then has to be accorded a set of educational givens. It is then essential to:

- select technology appropriate for everyday teaching
- provide the requisite content and software
- give the teachers the ongoing training, development and support to best use those tools in their teaching
- ensure the arrangements are in place to enable the desired ready use of the technology
- provide the requisite finance
- have knowing school and education authority leaders who are able to provide teachers and students with the required direction and support
- use appropriate whole-school implementation and development strategies.

And the fundamental importance of the school principal cannot be over-emphasised.

History also informs us that in the past, little regard has been paid to many or most of these factors.

While in many respects the securing and sustaining of total teacher and student use of the technology are now relatively simple at the individual school level, the challenge is that much greater at the education authority and national government levels, particularly at the latter: the challenge is immense at the national level to ultimately have every school and teacher using the appropriate instructional technology as a normal part of everyday teaching and learning.

It may well be too great a challenge for most governments within the present structures, and as Lew Gerstner et al. (1995) suggests later in this study, it might be necessary to release the operation of schools from the tight control of the educational bureaucrats.

CHAPTER **2**

INSTRUCTIONAL TECHNOLOGY— THE NOMENCLATURE

Over the years the mystique—and indeed the jargon—associated with the instructional technology and the associated infrastructure has grown. It is therefore important to pause briefly to clarify the terms that will be used throughout the study and reiterate what the publication will and will not address.

USAGE

As previously indicated, this book is very much about a history of the use of instructional technology by both teachers and students in the classroom.

Most will be aware that the use of instructional technology in teaching over the last century has at best been limited. While homes and businesses have embraced all manner of technology, and in particular digital technology, in their everyday operations, the vast majority of teachers in the developed world have used little technology in their teaching; and what they do use, teachers have used for centuries. The questions that have to be asked are why after all this time is the use of the newer instructional technology so low and what lessons can contemporary educators learn from the history.

Interestingly, very little has been written about the low-level classroom use of instructional technology in schools worldwide. One can read at length about the wonderful initiatives by governments and industry over the last half century in introducing superb technology in schools, the task forces that have been created, the projects mounted and the many in-depth studies of the educational benefits of the latest technology, but there is little mention of the extent of use made of that 'superb' technology in the classroom.

Not surprisingly, therefore, most parents would believe their school is well served by the latest technology and, indeed, many would have contributed to the purchase of that technology. Unfortunately, the rhetoric is a long way from the reality. The tools might be in the school but most have limited use in the classroom. The bottom line is that if the instructional technology is not being used, it has little chance of enriching teaching or improving learning.

Over the decades, many a discussion has taken place on the educational merits of a particular type of technology or of particular brands. The authors have sat through many such discussions. The same discourse can be found on today's mailing lists or blogs. In the end, all that discussion counts for little if most teachers continue to use pen, paper and the board.

While ultimately consideration does have to be made about the impact of the various instructional technologies on student learning in the first instance, it is vital to get all the teachers using the appropriate tools as an integral part of everyday teaching.

EVERYDAY TEACHING VERSUS SUPPLEMENTARY USE

In selecting the term *everyday teaching*, we wanted a term teachers and educational leaders could readily understand. We also wanted a loose term that recognised the flexibility needed in good teaching, in that on certain days—or indeed in certain blocks of study—the teachers and the students might make extensive or minimal use of the instructional technology, depending on the desired learning.

In using the expression *making integral use in their everyday classroom teaching*, we have in mind that the way teachers use the instructional technology will be akin to their use of a pen or a book—the use has been normalised and indeed the technology has been de-mythologised. There will be teaching where a particular piece of instructional technology will be used up-front and extensively, another where it might be used incidentally, and yet another where it will not be used at all. One should not affix a particular time period.

The other term that is used extensively is *supplementary use*. One finds many teachers over the years have used particular tools to supplement their every teaching. Film, video and more recently DVDs have typically been used to supplement the teaching, with teachers occasionally showing a total program to enrich their teaching.

INSTRUCTIONAL TECHNOLOGY

After much consideration, the authors found Larry Cuban's definition of instructional technology that he coined in *Teachers and Machines* in 1986 to be the best. Cuban defines instructional technology as:

> *any device available to teachers for use in instructing students in a more efficient and stimulating manner than the sole use of the teacher's voice. (p. 4)*

Over the years, various terms have been used to describe the technology used in the classroom; indeed, with each of the terms there was a body of professionals and often formal associations that came together to support the advancement of that form of technology. Interestingly, the terms used generally reflected the state of the technology of the time, and as the technology morphed into a new form, so the names changed. One of the advantages of the Cuban definition is its facility to accommodate those changes and, most significantly, the shift from the use of discrete technologies to integrated suites of technologies.

In the early 1920s, one finds terms like 'visual education', 'graphic education' and 'audio education'—and with each, supporting professional associations such as the Virtual Instruction Association of America. In the later 1930s and in particular the 1940s onwards, one finds the term 'audiovisual' or 'A/V education' being used. One notes 'A/V centres' being set up by education authorities throughout the developed world to support the use of this technology in schools. In time, schools created their own A/V cells and appointed 'A/V officers', often within the library staff. In brief, the term reflected the shift to the integrated use of both sound and film, be it still or moving (Saettler, 1990; Cuban, 1986).

In the 1950s and in particular the 1960s, with the growing interest in the media and the societal belief in the power of science, one saw in addition to the term 'A/V' nomenclature like 'media education', 'mass media education', 'mass communication' and 'educational technology' being used to describe all or some portion of the instructional technology.

With the introduction of computers in the late 1970s and early 1980s 'computer education' became the 'in' term, and with it came the emergence of the computer education associations. Once again, the name reflected the nature of the use of the technology and indeed the focus on the use of computers as discrete tools. The 1970s and 1980s also saw a significant growth in media studies as a subject taught in schools, the study and creation of films, videos and radio, and the emergence of teacher mass media associations.

With the development in the 1990s of the multimedia tools, and more significantly with the emergence of the Internet, one saw the term 'computer education' being superseded by the terms 'information technology' (IT) and 'information and communications technology' (ICT). At the same time, the school librarians began shifting away from book-related terms like 'the library' (from the Latin *librarius* meaning 'book') and began to provide 'information services' and 'knowledge management', while advocating the development of 'information literacy'. In some cases, 'research centres' or 'resource centres' replaced libraries.

In the 2000s, with the societal shift to all manner of digital technology, and the pathfinding schools' use of an extensive suite of digital technologies, one sensed the term 'ICT' was struggling and that another term associated with the digital element was needed.

The more the authors analysed the various nomenclature, and in particular looked at the range of digital technologies that could be used to assist student instruction, the more we became concerned about the term 'ICT'. We found it limiting and increasingly dated. The term was used synonymously with the term 'personal computers' even in 'official' publications like the OECD's *Are Students Ready for a Technology-rich World?* (OECD, 2005). An even greater problem is that the term covered all manner of analogue information and communications technology, be it television, radio, phone or video. Most importantly, the term did not emphasise the vital element—the digital—and the associated facility for ready digital convergence.

Others have mirrored the authors' concerns. Marc Prensky uses the term 'digital technology' throughout his writings on digital natives and digital immigrants (Prensky, 2006, 2007). The Illinois Institute of Design think-tank on digital schooling (referred to earlier), which involved thinkers of the calibre of Charles Handy and Gary Hamel, opted to use the term 'digital media' (Illinois Institute of Design, 2007, p. 5). The Australian Communications and Media Authority in its report, *Media and Communications in*

Australian Families 2007, chose to use the expressions 'technology' and 'electronic media' to refer to the range of digital technologies used by young people in their homes (ACMA, 2007, p. 2).

The important points to note with all the above terms is the emphasis on the digital nature, the facility to readily converge digital functions and the ever-expanding range of digital developments that teachers and students can use in the teaching and learning at home and in the classroom. A tool like Apple's iPhone exemplifies that kind of digital convergence and near impossibility of categorising it under any of the existing categories. While labelled a phone, it can handle not only the normal telephony but also work as a web browser, handle email and operate as a digital camera, an iPod, a computer games console or a digital storage facility, to name but a few of its functions.

The authors have thus chosen the more inclusive term *digital technology* in preference to the expression 'ICT'.

The 2000s also saw a very significant shift in focus from the technology to the teaching and the adoption of the term 'e-learning'. Indeed, for probably the first time in the history of the use of instructional technology the nomenclature focused on the teaching and not the technology. The following definitions of e-learning reflect that shift.

> ... learning that is facilitated by the use of digital tools and content. Typically, it involves some form of interactivity, which may include online interaction between the learner and their teacher or peers.

(New Zealand Digital Strategy, 2008)

> Learning facilitated and supported through the use of information and communications technology, e-learning can cover a spectrum of activities, from supported learning, to blended learning (the combination of traditional and e-learning practices), to learning that is entirely online. Whatever the technology, however, learning is the vital element.

(University of Bath, 2008)

EDUCATIONAL TECHNOLOGY

Particular mention needs to be made of the term *educational technology*, as it has become associated with an international group of educators and with particular tertiary educators seeking to make the best educational use of technology.

This school of thinking emerged out of the behaviourist movement of the 1950s and was extensively involved in the promotion of the various types of computer-based or computer-assisted learning (CAL). One of the major advocates was Paul Saettler. In *The Evolution of American Educational Technology* (1990), Saettler notes:

> Ely (Donald) makes a clear distinction between devices and equipment or the physical science of educational technology and the behavioral science of educational technology and considers process as the how to knowledge and skills (the art and craft of the Greek concept of techne) and product as the equipment and materials used in the process …

> Heinrich et al. adapted John Kenneth Galbraith's definition of technology and, applying it to instruction, defined instructional technology 'as the application of our scientific knowledge about human learning to the practical tasks of teaching and learning'. Thus, technology of instruction is 'a particular, systematic arrangement of teaching/learning events designed to put our knowledge of learning into practice in a predictable, effective manner to attain specific learning objectives. (pp. 5–6)

The focus of the movement has been on the process and on the mode of learning one uses with the technology, rather than the technology itself. Saettler and his colleagues have little time for the highly practical Cuban definition of instructional technology and indeed the like-minded terms used by various education enquiries that have been constituted over the years to promote the widespread use of the technology.

Interestingly, an analysis of Saettler's writings provides little insight into why teachers have been so reluctant to embrace either the scientific view of teaching or the technology, only that the uptake of all the technologies had been very small.

Of note is that while the 'educational technology' movement continues to write papers and hold major conferences, it was difficult to identify in the interviews school settings where its thinking has had any real impact on the classroom use of the technology. One senses the educational technologists, with their desire to control the teaching and learning process, will have very real problems accounting for the 'chaotic learning' young people use with the digital technology in their homes.

CHAPTER **3**

THE IMPACT OF
THE TECHNOLOGY
CORPORATIONS AND
VESTED INTERESTS

THE DRIVING FORCE

The desire by the major technology corporations to make a significant profit has been the driving force behind the development, marketing, sale and, most importantly for this study, in the availability and use of appropriate instructional technology—from its inception until today.

None of the major technology has been developed by the public sector. All has been provided by private industry. The intensity of the drive for profits has been fuelled by the size, financial strength and standing of the major technology corporations behind each of the technologies. All the electric and electronic technologies have been marketed by companies that were, at the time, some of the most powerful in the world. All brought to the product launch immense financial backing, and the marketing and sales skills to take the technology through its inevitable capital-exhaustive start-up phase and into market acceptance and significant profits. They also inevitably brought a view on how the technology could best be used.

In reviewing the literature on the introduction of the instructional technologies and the reasons for the invariably limited use of each, there has been little mention of the role played by the companies or indeed the extent to which their marketing strategies shaped the adoption of the particular technology, the implementation of those technologies and the support given to teachers. It should come as no surprise that behind the introduction of each of the 'revolutionary' technologies were substantial corporations—often from the Fortune 500 list—with the research capability, finance, standing and international marketing, sales and lobbying expertise to persuade clients globally to use the new technology. Note the brands associated with each of the technologies.

- Film—Edison Lighthouse Company, Eastman Kodak, Victor Motorola, Pathe, and Bell + Howell, and the major film studios like Warner Brothers, 20th Century Fox
- Radio—Marconi, Radiola, AWA, Philips, Telefunken, Grundig, and the many commercial broadcasters
- Television—Admiral, Mitsubishi, Panasonic, Hitachi, Philips, NBC, CBC
- Photographic slides—Kodak Eastman, Fuji, Agfa, Ilford
- VCRs—Sony, JVC, Panasonic, Philips, Mitsubishi, Sharp
- Audio recorders—Sony, JVC, National Panasonic, Philips, Mitsubishi
- Computers—IBM, Apple, Microsoft, Intel, ARM, HP, Compaq, Acer, Fujitsu, Toshiba
- Printers—HP, Canon, Epsom, Lexmark, Brother
- Networks—Novell, IBM, Cisco, Microsoft
- Interactive whiteboards—SMART Technologies, Promethean, Hitachi, Panasonic, Steelcase/Polyvision, Rubbermaid/MIMIO

All of those corporations knew how to open the right doors, gain access to the key decision makers, shape the media and generate the hype invariably needed to bring a new product onto the market. The CEO of any of these companies could soon secure access to the head of an education authority or minister of education.

While not for a moment attributing Machiavellian motives to any of those companies, nor suggesting that any key government or educational leaders did not believe in the new technology, it is important nonetheless to remember that these were businesses first and foremost seeking to make a profit. They were powerful organisations that knew how to leverage the widespread acceptance of their product. If a new technology displaced an older technology, so be it.

While it is virtually impossible in a study like this to cite the strategies employed and approaches adopted by each of the major technology companies during the twentieth century, it is probably reasonable to surmise that the strategies were similar to those adopted by the major technology companies in the 2000s.

It might come as a surprise to some educators that the bottom line for the technology companies in 1930, 1960, 1990 and 2000 was significant profit and not so much whether the particular technology improved teaching or learning. Profit was the driving force. Without it, the companies ceased to exist. To achieve that profit and to convince potential clients to acquire their product, the corporations needed to play hard and to use all of the openings and strategies available to them. What will soon become apparent was how little support the vast majority of the aforementioned companies provided teachers. The exceptions stand out.

It is important to recognise, with but one exception, that all the major instructional technologies of the twentieth century projected to 'revolutionise' teaching were products designed from the outset for the wider consumer market. Schools, like the other 'training' sectors, were only secondary markets. (The one exception was the interactive white-board, which—as will be noted in Chapter 15—was designed initially for teachers.) It was a case of companies, perhaps even prompted by educators, seeking to widen their market base and to increase sales and profits. In addition to the major developers of the technology, there was with each technology a group of related companies also seeking to maximise their profits from the sale of the technology to schools, which helped market the new technology. All the instructional technology, for example, needed content or software, films to run on the projectors, programs for the radio and television broadcasts or software for the computers. It was in those companies' interest to help promote the new technology. Invariably there was also a host of companies providing the complementary products, the peripherals needed to get the most from the core technology. Whether it was trolleys to move projectors, blackout blinds, projector screens, PA systems, the makers of computer printers or indeed the technical support companies needed to maintain the technology, a large number of businesses were all working to increase the uptake of the new technology.

Collectively these companies, plus other vested interests mentioned below, worked to sell the new technology to schools. Their power was considerable and this needs to be borne in mind when considering:

- the choice of the new technology by education
- why significant sums of public money were spent on technology that was ultimately seldom used or wasted
- why there was such little use made of the particular technology by teachers, and
- how a particular technology was used, and why it did little to help achieve the desired educational outcomes.

THE VESTED INTERESTS

The technology corporations' aspirations have always been aided by interest groups within the schools sector keen to acquire the technology. Be it teachers, school leaders, tertiary educators, central office bureaucrats or governments, there have always been those who have foreseen—rightly or wrongly—the facility for all the new technology to be used in teaching and who have worked with industry on its introduction.

The reasons for the interest in the technology have varied but the reality is that no company, no matter how big or how many doors it can open, can sell its wares to schools unless there are decision makers prepared to buy the technology and teachers who are prepared to use the technology.

Early adopters

Throughout the history of instructional technology there has always been a group of early adopter teachers who have been prepared to trial the use of the new and overcome significant hurdles to use the tool to enrich their teaching. They have been a group that has been able to see past the various impediments and recognise how the use of the technology would benefit their students. Why they were prepared to do so is a moot point, but in most instances one would have to surmise it was mainly to improve the learning of their students. Often unwittingly, this preparedness to use the new has helped to advance the careers of the early adopters. Interestingly, virtually all the existing and former school leaders and tertiary educators interviewed had been early adopters of the technology able to recount the challenges they had to overcome to use the technology.

Within the early adopter group there has always been a subgroup imbued with the latest technology, a group we have called 'impetuous technophilia'. These teachers and school leaders have over the years been swept along by the hype of 'the latest and greatest' technology and who have been disinclined to question the educational appropriateness of the technology for use by all other teachers. For many years they have been a godsend to the technology companies and for the students they taught. Invariably, upon the release of a new technology, they are to the fore explaining how it could be used in teaching. In more recent times, with the advent of common-interest mailing lists, blogs and online newsletters, it has been that much easier for them to flourish. No sooner had Apple released its iPhone in 2007 with much hype than one noted on the lists the call to use them in teaching. *eSchool News* typified that approach when on 22 August 2007 it proclaimed:

Educators assess iPhones for instruction

As education-specific applications emerge, schools mull
whether to invest in the devices

(*eSchool News*, 2007)

This example also succinctly demonstrates how the hype generated by the major provider is amplified by the providers of the complementary technology to make it near impossible for the early adopters to resist acquiring the technology.

Tertiary education

In many countries key tertiary educators have had a significant impact over the years on the choice of the instructional technology adopted by schools. It transpired with radio, film, educational television and significantly with the various forms of computing education. Many with high profiles have used their standing—invariably on high-level advisory committees or through the media—to promote the use of a particular technology and indeed how it might best be implemented.

Granted, a few of those people might have vested interests; however, most, like the early adopting teachers, believed strongly in the potential of the technology to enrich teaching.

Bureaucrats

In the same way, so too have there been early adopters in the education authorities. They have foreseen the benefits in acquiring the technology, for both the students and their political masters, and have in turn approved the spending of considerable monies.

One should hasten to add that there have also always been bureaucrats who have used the latest technological bandwagon to advance their own careers. (The authors can well remember the internecine warfare between competing senior bureaucrats on which video format to adopt.)

Government

One of the realities of living in a democracy is that most in schools are reluctant to accept that the elected official—be it a minister of education or chair of an education board—needs to be able to demonstrate to their electorate that a good job is being done. The other reality is that one of the major tasks of senior bureaucrats is to ensure that the elected officials are provided with the required kudos. Anyone who has spent time in an education authority soon appreciates this need.

Over the years, the latest and most appealing of the new technology has invariably been a major part of that ammunition. Television sets, VCRs, computers and more recently interactive whiteboards provide compelling media coverage and photo shoots. Promising computers to schools was often seen as a way of winning voter support, and even revolutionising education.

One of the challenges for all bureaucrats is to package into the media releases the vital (but to many, the very mundane) infrastructure expenditure. The Clinton administration did it well in the US in the 1990s with its promise to connect every school to the information superhighway, but theirs was a skill not many governments have been able to replicate. Rather, one notes that most of the political releases simply focus on the core technology and provide none of the training, support, infrastructure or implementation that will facilitate its appropriate use.

While it is easy to criticise the political decision makers, one of the lessons schools need to learn is that in a democracy—and indeed we suspect any form of government—the importance of government support must be fully appreciated with all its implications. Schools should more openly acknowledge the contribution by the relevant government body. The irony is that schools globally are very up-front about acknowledging the contributions by sponsors as well as their own parent bodies, but invariably do not acknowledge their main source of funding—their government.

THE ECONOMICS OF THE SCHOOLS MARKET

The proportion of the total education budget available for spending on instructional technology has (as mentioned in Chapter 1) traditionally been very small. While reference has been made to the significant sums spent (and wasted) on instructional technology, that money represented but a small percentage of the annual education budget. As indicated, Anderson and Becker (1999, p. 5) have calculated that in 1998 the US spent 2.7 per cent of the education budget on instructional technology.

While one can debate the exact proportions at the different periods of history in the various developed nations, the reality is that the figure has always been very small. What is clear is that schools in comparison with the other information-rich industries have only ever had minuscule monies to spend on instructional technology.

Many technology companies in the last 50-plus years have learned that reality the hard way. They have lost considerable money chasing the elusive schools dollar. Increasingly, the technology companies took the approach that if the schools wanted to buy their technology, so be it, but few were prepared to invest in technology specifically for use in schools. (It is of note that Apple Computers and Microsoft are probably the only two major technology corporations that have maintained a strong involvement in the schools market for a reasonably lengthy period.)

If the pool of money available to the technology corporations increases significantly, history is already suggesting that their interest will grow and the investment in instructional technology will be made. This became apparent in the UK in the 2000s. The total investment in technology across education has risen from £102 million in 1998 to more than £860 million in 2007–08. Schools and local authorities (LAs) received funding for ICT through five major grants:

- Devolved Formula Capital
- School Development Grant
- Grant 121: National Digital Infrastructure for Schools
- Grant 122: Electronic Learning Credits (eLCs)
- Grants 125 and 210: Computers for Pupils.

The Electronic Learning Credits initiative, which provided funds for teachers to acquire both educational software, alone received an additional £50 million to add to the £200 million allocated in 2005 (Secretary for Education and Manpower, 2005).

With the Labour Government's decision to fund the placement of an interactive whiteboard in every classroom in the UK and to also fund the complementary hardware and software, the government stimulated the growth of an interactive multimedia educational software industry, not only in the UK but also across the world. Within a very short time one saw not only the emergence of a range of dynamic start-up companies like 2 Simple and Big Bus, but also sizeable investment in the technology by the book companies like Cambridge University Press and Heinemann, the television companies like Granada, Sky and the BBC, and the technology companies like RM and Hitachi. While UK-focused, these digital resources could readily be used by English-speaking schools across the world and, as RM found with its Easiteach in Mexico, the material could soon be converted to other major languages.

RECOGNISING THE IMPACT OF THE TECHNOLOGY CORPORATIONS AND THE VESTED INTERESTS

On reflection, throughout the biggest part of the twentieth century one sees schools and education authorities adopting the 'in' technology of the time, with little consideration being given to the appropriateness of that technology for everyday teaching. It happened with film and radio, and in particular with television, video, personal computers and interactive multimedia CD-ROMs. This is despite the fact that by the 1970s there was ample evidence in the scant use of 16-mm film, radio and television that something was fundamentally awry.

By the 1970s, and most assuredly by the 1980s, it should have been apparent to policy makers researching the scene that the emerging instructional technologies had experienced a common, unsuccessful life cycle. Cuban (1986) clearly identifies the common pattern of use with each of the main technologies. In interviews with two of the key policy makers associated with Australia's 'Computers in Schools' initiative of the early 1980s they full well understood the key human and technical variables requiring consideration.

However, it is not until the latter part of the 1990s and the UK's moves that one finds a concerted effort towards specifying what was required of the technology corporations. In brief, DfES (the national education department) or Becta (its communications and teaching authority) specified the standards expected of providers, and unless they satisfied those requirements they were denied access to government funding. This was amply demonstrated in the UK's approach to the choice of IWB providers.

Since then, other national educational authorities, such as those in Singapore, Mexico, France and New Zealand, have taken a similar responsibility for identifying the way forward, rather than simply relying on the market forces. That said, those pathfinders are still very much in a minority in 2008.

In addition to influencing the choice of a particular technology, the larger multinational technology corporations have, often unwittingly, strongly impacted on the use made of the technology. While the full extent and nature of that impact are a study in their own right, it is important to recognise the influence of the technology—particularly that technology not designed specifically for classroom use—on the teaching/learning process. As the school-wide use of digital technology grows, the likelihood of schools adopting practices alien to the desired educational outcomes will intensify. For example, schools and education authorities globally have adopted network security practices, with the associated constant changing of user passwords that were designed for office settings, often without asking if the arrangement was consonant with the desired educational outcomes. It is only when one encounters (as we did in our research) schools that question that approach that one begins to appreciate how much schools 'go with the flow' and fail to ask the hard questions.

The same situation is being evidenced in the design and choice of what are known as learning platforms or VLEs (see Chapter 14). Virtually all in use were heavily content-focused and placed considerable controls on the nature of student use. If their aim was to develop creative and lateral thinking and to have the students develop attributes like their networking and information literacy, few of the VLEs would assist.

While today the influence of the major technology corporations remains immense, the signs are that at last the more astute schools and education authorities are beginning to exercise the desired control over an ever-burgeoning suite of possible instructional technologies.

PART I

DISCRETE INSTRUCTIONAL TECHNOLOGIES

CHAPTER 4

TEACHING BOARDS

The teaching board—be it black, green or white—is synonymous with the classroom. It occupies a central position in virtually every classroom in the developed world and has been used integrally in everyday teaching since the 1800s.

Ironically, the boards have been so successful and so readily accepted that they barely rate a mention in the educational research literature. A Google search on blackboards will reveal only the barest details, while the same search will unearth a plethora of references to Blackboard, the online teaching software.

The teaching board has long been normalised in teaching. It has been completely de-mythologised as a piece of technology. That normalisation should have attracted far more consideration in that the long-term success and universal acceptance of this particular instructional technology provides valuable lessons for the total teacher acceptance and use of all other instructional technologies.

TEACHING BOARDS—A HISTORY

The first of the teaching boards—the blackboard, or as some like to call it, the chalkboard—emerged as a breakthrough instructional technology in the early 1800s. The year 1801 is mentioned as the date of sale of the first US blackboard, although mention is made of slate-based blackboards in Scotland in the late 1700s.

Andrew Coulson made the interesting observation that the last major development in instructional technology occurred in 1801.

> *Though computers have been introduced to many classrooms, their addition has been at best facilitative rather than transformative. In other words, the enormous potential of modern technology to revolutionize education*

remains largely untapped. A typical private school classroom today would be immediately recognizable by and intimately familiar to a student from the 1850s. The last dramatic instructional innovation occurred while Thomas Jefferson was president: the introduction of the chalkboard, around 1801.

(Coulson, 2006, p. 5)

While the exact origins are obscure, by the mid 1800s blackboards were commonplace in the classrooms of the developed nations. The substance used in the manufacture of the boards differed, with some being timber and others slate-based, but all teachers had a large, dark, smooth surface on which to write and draw, usually with chalk (Wikipedia, 2008a, 2008b). The uptake of the boards was helped in the mid 1800s with the development of the modern compressed chalk sticks, which were in fact usually made from gypsum.

The initial board surfaces continued in use until the 1900s when first steel and then rolled plastic tended to replace the wood and slate. The twentieth century also saw the emergence of the facility to use multiple blackboards via a pulley system, roll-ups or wings. The basic board technology remains today, although in the late 1950s and early 1960s there emerged a trend to use green rather than black paint on the surface. By the 2000s, the sale of blackboards had declined markedly but they were still on sale and being installed in new schools.

The next of the teaching boards to emerge was the display board, which often took the form of flannel or cork boards that complemented the blackboard and provided the facility to display student work. Both appeared initially in the later 1800s, particularly in the primary but also in specialist secondary classrooms. Although the technology used to create the display boards changed over time, in the 2000s the display boards were still serving the same purpose as when first introduced. An interview with one of Australia's major board providers revealed that in 2007 virtually every primary classroom in Australia included a display board or two, and indeed the design brief for each new state and territory primary classroom included the requirement to provide display boards. (Of note, the authors could not find any reference in the research to the use or effectiveness of class display boards.)

The chalk used with the blackboard was a problem for many teachers and students. Thus there was an ongoing quest to find a surface that would not cause allergies. The whiteboard technology—also known as the dry erase board—began appearing in schools in the 1960s and gradually over the next 40 years came to replace the blackboard as the main teaching board. Far cleaner and clearer than the blackboard, the porcelain surface of the whiteboard will work for decades without any significant maintenance.

TEACHER USAGE

As indicated at the outset, teaching boards are still being used in everyday teaching by teachers at all levels and within all areas of the curriculum across the developed world. In 2008, the teaching board—whatever its colour—remains the most used of all the instructional technologies.

So accepted is the teachers' use of this instructional technology that virtually no one has stopped to ask why, or indeed to contrast its universal acceptance with the minuscule teacher use made of much more vaunted electronic instructional technology.

In hindsight, the reasons for the success of the teaching board can be found in the following considerations:

- its ready facility to enhance the teaching of all, with no need for the teachers to vary their teaching style to use the technology
- ease of use by all teachers and students
- the facility for all teachers to readily create their own lessons in class using the board
- its facility to be used as an integral part of everyday teaching without any loss of teaching time
- the ready ability to use text and graphics to complement the teacher's voice
- the capacity to use the board with all manner of teaching styles, with all areas of the curriculum from K–12, and with any number of students, be it for instruction, communication, interaction or indeed classroom management
- its reliability, working every time regardless of electricity, batteries, networks or software
- ease of use with other teaching tools like the pen and paper
- its low cost and length of life; the boards have always been relatively inexpensive to acquire and maintain, and with a spare tin of paint will easily last for 50-plus years
- ease and safety of locating and making it available in every teaching room
- its use in helping to manage classes and handle the classroom administration.

The CEO of one of Australia's major teaching board manufacturers made the telling comment in his interview that one of the main reasons why teaching boards have not been surrounded with the hype apparent with the electronic instructional technology is that the boards are made by a cottage industry when compared with the punch of the multinational technology corporations. They simply do not have the marketing dollars to court the media. Moreover, teaching board manufacturers are selling a proven product used not only by all schools but also most government agencies and businesses, large and small. There are few board or seminar rooms without a whiteboard or two.

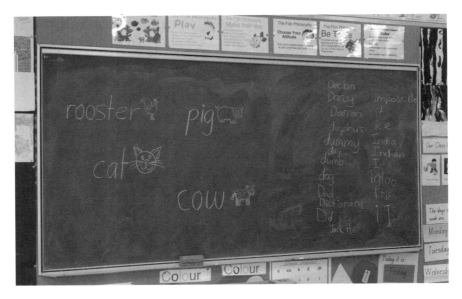

Figure 4.1 Chalkboard of today (Courtesy Greg Walker)

THE TRADITIONAL AND THE MODERN

Even with its many strengths the traditional teaching board had very significant shortcomings when compared with the new form of teaching board that began to emerge in the later 1990s—the interactive whiteboard.

Obviously, traditional teaching boards could not take advantage of the digital world. More importantly, they were highly inefficient. Considerable teacher time was required to prepare, remove and refresh the work on the board. Basically, teachers had to redo the work every time they wished to use the board. In contrast, interactive whiteboards (IWBs) could not only harness the opportunities of the digital world, but also replicate the workings of the traditional board. In brief, IWBs married the best of the teaching board heritage with that of the computer.

Despite this, the schools in the 2000s that had introduced IWBs throughout the campus invariably chose to also retain at least their traditional whiteboard. There were two very good reasons for this.

The first was that the traditional teaching board, and in particular the display board, provided teachers and students with the ready opportunity to 'permanently' display material—something not easily done with any electronic or digital technology. Whether for a brief notice, spelling lists, policy statements, classroom management, the display of student work, or simply to help create vital ambience and classroom distinctiveness, it was very handy to have a board or two with which to work. One only had to walk into a primary school classroom or an inspired science laboratory to appreciate the importance of the display facility in a classroom. The second and very basic reason was that most classrooms already had the boards, with years of life left in them, and that in many respects it was more expensive to remove them and remodel the room. One found schools either moved the existing central board to the side or dividing the existing board in two, affixing a new border and placing the two sections on each side of the IWB.

By 2008, however, it was clear that blackboards had passed their use-by date. In a classroom with extensive digital technology one most assuredly did not want teachers using blackboards with all the associated chalk dust— data projector maintenance was enough of a challenge without adding chalk dust. Schools were opting either to remove the boards or install an IWB over the top. (However, in so saying, we encountered a primary school where IWBs had been installed in the 32 new rooms of a new building with the principal intriguingly insisting on a blackboard being positioned beside each IWB!)

In hindsight one has to agree with Coulson's earlier assertion that the blackboard was the first dramatic innovation in instructional technology. One could, however, argue that at the start of the twentieth century the introduction of the interactive whiteboard was the second great innovation in instructional technology, 200 years after the introduction of the first.

The early experience would also suggest that these two genuinely revolutionary instructional technologies will continue to coexist for many years to come.

CHAPTER **5**

FILM—THE 'FIRST REVOLUTION'

The motion picture, and the vast industry behind it, was the first of the electric-driven instructional technologies that was projected to revolutionise teaching. In 1922, Thomas Edison observed:

> I believe that the motion picture is destined to revolutionize our education system and that in a few years it will supplant largely, if not entirely, the use of textbooks.
>
> ... The education of the future, as I see it, will be conducted through the medium of the motion picture ... where it should be possible to obtain one hundred percent efficiency.
>
> (Cuban, 1986, p. 9)

Undoubtedly, the motion picture offered teachers a new and exciting teaching aid. At last teaching had the opportunity to use the magic of the moving picture to add to the written word and the teacher's voice.

Throughout the period 1910–29, particularly in the US but also in Europe there emerged a vigorous, albeit silent educational film industry. In the US, companies that were to become synonymous with the motion picture industry produced an extensive range of silent educational films— companies like Bell and Howell, Victor Animatograph, Edison Film Library, the Pathescope Company, Kodak Eastman and Fox Films (Saettler, 1990).

Ironically, that output declined markedly in the late 1920s with the introduction of sound movies and the advent of the Great Depression. The silent film productions suddenly were not wanted, even if in the depressed economic conditions the schools had the money. Overnight, the clients expected films with sound (ibid.). However, while the strong educational film industry declined, the sound motion picture industry thrived and soon became an integral part of life and entertainment in the developed world.

The 1920s and 1930s saw the flowering of the documentary film industry and the production of films, which while not tied to the curriculum like the earlier offerings were of considerable educational worth. Robert Flaherty's *Nanook of the North* (1922) and *Man of Aran* (1934) were excellent examples of those offerings. This period also witnessed the emergence of national and large corporate film production units that were to add to the range of documentary film available to schools for the next 30 to 40 years.

In the 1930s, many education authorities in the developed world created audiovisual units to assist their schools' use of film. Some of the larger units produced films but most simply maintained film libraries, distribution networks and film consultants to serve their schools.

Figure 5.1 Early 16-mm projector (Courtesy Peter Dalwood)

With the advent of World War II, 'educational' film making grew significantly even though most of the productions could be more appropriately described as propaganda. By the later 1950s and 1960s, most schools had ready access to a wide variety of films, many of which were excellent.

MOTION PICTURE TECHNOLOGY

The projectors with which teachers had to work were a challenge. The vast majority were designed to handle 16-mm films, the lower-cost version of the 35-mm film used by the theatres. While the manufacturers of those projectors—companies like Bell and Howell, RCA Victor, Singer and Eiki—would have teachers believe otherwise, classroom use of the film was not easy. First off, one needed a darkened room in which to show the films. The 16-mm projectors were heavy and cumbersome; usually too heavy for many female teachers. They were relatively expensive and thus most schools had only one or two, even in the 1980s. The projectors were either set up in a special viewing room or transported from a secure storeroom to a room with blackout blinds.

The early versions of the 16-mm projectors, from the 1930s into the 1970s, were invariably manually threaded. As an electro-mechanical device, the operator had to thread the film by opening and closing a series of gates, ensuring the socket holes on the film were in the right place, and then attaching the film leader to a take-up reel. The facility to make a mistake was considerable, and thus it was no surprise in our interviews with education authority A/V unit directors to learn of the considerable damage to film stock. The challenge was often made more interesting by having the film arrive at the school not rewound, with a damaged film leader or a break in the film.

From the 1970s, self-loading projectors generally superseded the earlier manual loading models, but many of the aforementioned 'challenges' remained. Furthermore, teachers had to use the films provided, rely on the description in the catalogue and hope the selected resource would be appropriate. One could not pause a 16-mm film without burning a hole in the film itself—it was extremely difficult to show a part of the film.

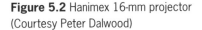

Figure 5.2 Hanimex 16-mm projector
(Courtesy Peter Dalwood)

In general terms, teachers could not use the movie film to create their own lessons. Movie films were expensive to produce and required considerable expertise in the making. While the tools to create 16-mm and 8-mm sound films have existed since the 1930s, the reality is that only the most enthusiastic of teachers travelled the film-making path. Teachers had to make do with the package provided.

As quality films were expensive to buy they were usually borrowed, and it therefore took considerable forward planning to obtain them at the desired time. With the inevitable short turnaround on the loans teachers simply had to use the film, even if it was not at an appropriate point in the topic development. (Memories still remain of filling triplicate carbon paper order forms six to nine months ahead and waiting anxiously for the courier or the train to arrive! A principal interviewed recalled standing on the station waiting for an overdue train as 200 students sat 'patiently' in the school hall of an outback town awaiting the film show.)

Furthermore, teachers generally had to use the film within the existing teaching periods and organisational constraints. If a teacher had a 40-minute period and a 137-minute *Henry V* film featuring Laurence Olivier to show, he or she hoped to fit it into the available lesson times before the film was due to be returned.

Another significant challenge for teachers using film—particularly up until the 1980s—was the perception held by many teachers, and in particular those with a strong academic bent, that films were entertainment. Serious teaching entailed bookwork.

Interestingly, it would appear that in the 1950s and 1960s many of the education authority A/V units made a concerted effort to not only get the appropriate films to teachers but also help them to use the films. For example, the units in New Zealand and Victoria, Australia provided the opportunity for teachers and pre-service trainees to acquire a licence to work a 16-mm projector, which could in turn be used when helping other staff. (All these challenges pale when compared with that facing one of the former principals interviewed who recounted the delights of using a battery-powered 16-mm projector in a rural school with no electricity and contending with the fumes emanating from the open car batteries used to power the projector!)

TEACHER USAGE

Not surprisingly, teacher use of film was usually limited to the early adopting teachers who were prepared to overcome all the aforementioned challenges. However, even the early adopters tended to use film as a supplementary aid, rarely as an integral part of the teaching. In contrast to the pen, paper and board, film obliged the teachers to markedly vary their style of teaching and use specialist rooms if they were to use the technology other than as an occasional supplementary aid.

In the interviews with a cross-section of experienced school leaders it became apparent film was used in many schools as an entertainment tool. Many rainy lunchtimes or a late Friday afternoon lesson were given over to watching a film. There was little doubt that the students in the 1960s loved watching a good film as much as they did in 2008. (The story was told by one of those interviewed of how the films destined for the school were also used by the local rural community and shown at the Mechanics Institute Hall.)

But despite the entertainment value of the medium, the actual classroom use was minuscule. Cuban noted of the use made of film in the US that:

> after almost forty years of experience with motion pictures in schools the evidence, flawed as it is, suggests most teachers used films infrequently in classrooms.
>
> (Cuban, 1986, p. 17)

The 16-mm projector with an anamorphic lens was the only way of showing cinemascope films inexpensively, until the late 1990s and the emergence of quality and relatively inexpensive data projectors. So while the general use of film was low, in time film found a niche market in the school and (as indicated in Chapter 18) was used extensively into the 1990s. That niche was within what became known as media studies or film studies.

The media studies niche also allowed a group of teachers and students to make excellent use of the Super 8-mm film creation facility, again until at least the late 1990s. While intended originally for the home market in the 1960s, the Super 8-mm format and the associated cameras, sound projectors and editing equipment allowed generations of students to learn inexpensively the basic principles of multimedia production well before the computer software opened the world to all.

In analysing the use of film in the classroom, the efforts made by the moving picture industry to 'provide' film for schools and the very considerable efforts made to assist all teachers, primary and secondary, it is very difficult to find any evidence of the educational leadership asking the hard questions about the motion picture as an instructional technology. Rather, what is apparent is a wholehearted embracing of the technology, a going with the market, concerted moves to support its widespread use by all those interested, and little consideration by the school or education leadership of the appropriateness and role to be played by film as the tool.

CHAPTER **6**

RADIO—THE 'SECOND REVOLUTION'

By the second half of the 1930s, radio had become an integral part of life in all developed countries, and together with the movie film provided much of the entertainment for those societies.

In the US, visionaries who had in fact seen the potential use of radio in teaching in the 1920s had made concerted moves to develop educational radio networks, but in the end lost in their efforts to secure the desired radio frequency, effectively being shut out by the commercial radio industry. Saettler makes the telling observation:

> *By the late 1930s, the growth period of radio education had already begun to decline. With the advent of World War II, professional activity in educational radio came to a standstill and has failed to appreciably revive.*

(Saettler, 1990, p. 197)

One thus finds the US efforts to use radio in schooling limited in nature, particularly when compared with those nations that provided extensive daytime school radio broadcasts. Where the US literature compliments commercial radio stations for providing five magnanimous hours of school-related radio programming a week in countries like the UK, Australia and New Zealand, Sweden, Finland and Denmark, it was not uncommon, particularly from the 1930s, for schools to have access to five or six hours of school broadcasts each day during the working week. Governments soon recognised the power of public radio to inform the populace, and it was not only the fascist leaders like Hitler and Mussolini who recognised the part it could play as an 'educational' tool. Radio, like film earlier, was considered to have the power to revolutionise teaching, and soon many European and British Commonwealth governments were spending considerable monies on the creation of education units within their public broadcasters and in equipping schools with radio receivers (Wikipedia, 2008c).

William Levenson wrote in 1945:

The time may come when a portable radio receiver will be as common in the classroom as the blackboard. Radio instruction will be integrated into school life as an accepted educational medium.

(Cuban, 1986, p. 19)

Radio had immense appeal with both the young and the old in the middle years of the twentieth century. It is important to remember that one is talking about a period when radio was king, and where all age groups within society tuned in for their regular programs, be they serials, plays, quizzes, sport or the news. It was therefore seen as logical to use the new medium to enrich teaching.

In Australia, for example, the new nationally funded broadcaster, the Australian Broadcasting Commission (ABC), was handed the brief of providing school broadcasts soon after its creation in 1932. A shortage of funding in the 1930s and World War II hindered the initial developments. Soon after the war, the ABC was able to work closely with each of the states to produce approximately six hours of programming, Monday to Friday. Preference was given to covering those areas that best suited the medium and where there were teacher shortfalls. Areas like reading, early childhood education, science and music received particular attention, with special texts and music books being provided to complement the radio program. Programs like 'Kindergarten of the Air' become part of Australian folklore. Many of the former primary teachers interviewed fondly remembered the book readings, the nature studies broadcasts and the quality of the music and singing programs (ABC, 1979).

The use of the school radio broadcasts grew in the 1950s and reached its peak in the 1960s before being superseded, at least budget-wise, by school television broadcasts. The ABC reported that during 1956–57, 88 per cent of schools regularly used educational programs, with 'most of the remaining 20 per cent outside the coverage area of transmitting stations' (ABC, 1979, p. 14). It reported further:

During the period 1965–75 regular usage of radio programs by schools became almost universal. By 1965, 94 per cent of schools used radio programs regularly, and by 1969 this figure had reached 97 per cent. (p. 19)

49

It is important to note that the ABC provided these figures and, as indicated in an interview with a former member of the ABC's national education advisory panel, at a time when the school radio broadcast unit was fighting for its continued existence against the threat of educational television. What was meant in the figures by 'used radio programs regularly' was that a teacher at the school had used the radio broadcasts regularly.

While an immense amount of thought, effort and expense went into producing quality radio programs and every effort was made to limit the broadcasts to the available lesson time, the uptake and use made of those programs were in general terms limited, like film beforehand.

USAGE AND CONSTRAINTS

There were different factors at play with the use of radio in comparison with film.

The use of school radio broadcasts in secondary schools and the larger primary schools was minimal. Use was primarily constrained by the organisational arrangements and the ready access to and control over the technology. But other factors did impact as well. While school radio broadcasts were invariably repeated, the chance of the lesson time coinciding with the program broadcast time was small. Initially there was no way of time shifting, but even with the advent of reel-to-reel tape recorders the challenge of lugging the likes of the early Byer or Rola recorders into class was only for the dedicated.

The other major constraint in the larger schools was what one of our interviewees aptly described as 'the bloody PA system'. In the larger primary and secondary schools the radio broadcasts were distributed across the school via the public address (PA) system. With that system the teacher had control of only the volume switch on the speaker in the classroom, and was dependent on the front office staff remembering to switch on both the PA and the radio—and the deputy principal not opting to use the override facility to make a 'serious announcement'. (Memories of having a class ready for a broadcast and having to sprint up to the front office still linger.)

The other reality was that teachers had little or no control over the lesson offered. They had to use the package in full.

It also needs to be remembered that even in the developed world many rural schools did not have electricity until as late as the 1960s, and a significant number had little or poor radio reception.

An interesting exception to the use of radio broadcasts was within the smaller rural primary schools where they were used extensively and integrally in the teaching for a significant period. One is talking about one- and two-teacher primary schools, where the teacher/s taught a cross-section of age and ability groups within one or two rooms. The teaching in those schools was of necessity far more individualised than the larger primary schools where the classes were invariably of a common age. In those small schools the teachers could schedule their teaching around the broadcasts. Most importantly, both the teacher and the students had direct control of the radio receiver. (One of the interviewees spoke of the senior students using the radio out on the school verandah or porch while the teacher taught the younger ones in the classroom.)

All the indicators point to significant use being made in the small primary schools of the music, nature and reading programs, particularly in the 1950s, 1960s and even early 1970s. Teachers had, for example, copies of the songs being broadcast and, conscious that many primary teachers were not strong on music, the radio supplemented their shortcomings well.

An important factor influencing the use of the radio in the rural schools in Australia was that the teachers could record in their lesson books for the inspector that they 'had done music' at 2.30 pm on Thursday afternoon.

Figure 6.1 Three-in-one hi-fi system with radio (Courtesy Peter Dalwood)

The contrast between the small and large school use of radio was well explained in an interview with a former principal who had responsibility for fourteen one-teacher schools. He made mention of the very extensive use made by the teachers in those schools of the radio broadcasts, particularly those covering music, nature studies and reading. He noted that each of the schools had its own radio receiver under the control of the teacher.

In time, the local education authority closed the fourteen schools and brought all the students together in one central K–10 school, with a new PA system that carried the radio broadcasts. Use of radio in the new situation declined markedly.

By the early 1970s, radio as the entertainment in the home had been supplanted by television. As with film, the same pattern was evidenced with the use of radio broadcasts in that the public monies were shifted to this new medium. As will become apparent in Chapter 8, the advent of television brought school broadcasts to an end, although television did not in general terms fill the void left behind.

NICHE USAGE

Ironically, as the provision of broadcast radio came to an end there emerged in many secondary schools—particularly within media studies—student-produced and distributed radio programs. It was not uncommon from the 1970s onwards for secondary schools to have their own student radio station, and indeed for a significant number of the newer schools to have purpose-built radio studios.

Where the general teaching population had been reluctant to use radio in their lessons, a selection of media and English teachers have used radio production as part of the student communications program from the 1970s onwards. Those moves were helped by the emergence of the ready availability of inexpensive, quality audio recording, editing and playback technology. By the mid 1970s (as noted in Chapter 9), schools could readily afford the audio recorders, mixing desks, amplifiers, turntables and microphones needed for student radio production.

The 1970s also saw the emergence of community-based radio stations, and with them the facility for the schools to merge their work with that of the community radio stations.

While one is talking only of a niche group, the interviews made regular mention of the use of student-produced radio well into the 2000s. The only real difference in 2008 was the use being made of digital rather than analogue technologies.

CHAPTER 7

VISUAL TOOLS—
THE EXCEPTIONS

Two visual instructional technologies were used integrally in classes by a small but significant number of teachers and, in so doing, provided an insight into why radio and film failed to revolutionise teaching. The two exceptions were the photographic slide and the overhead projector. Both were used by a group of teachers in everyday teaching for many years.

PHOTOGRAPHIC SLIDES

The use of the photographic slide as an instructional technology dates from almost the inception of photography in the mid 1800s and the use of magic lanterns, but it was not until the early 1950s that the technology became cheap and easy enough for the average classroom teacher to use on an everyday basis.

Figure 7.1 Magic lantern
(Courtesy Peter Dalwood)

Throughout the 1920s and 1930s a small group of expert users made very effective use of glass photographic slides, but the projectors were expensive for schools and the art of creating glass slides was tricky and something only the dedicated could readily master.

The photographic slide became a reality for all interested teachers after World War II with the release of Kodachrome colour film stock in 1954, and the advent of a brace of photographic creation and presentation technologies designed for the home market (Wikipedia, 2008d; Kodak, 2008). The facility to shoot slides on virtually all 35-mm cameras and, most importantly, the opportunity to have film readily and inexpensively processed allowed the interested teachers to finally use this powerful visual aid.

Figure 7.2 Slide projector with 35-mm filmstrip facility (Courtesy Peter Dalwood)

The usability of photographic slides was in turn aided by the availability in the 1950s and 1960s of relatively inexpensive projectors that were able to handle pre-assembled sets of slides. While different brand-based technologies sought to capture the market, Eastman Kodak's Carousel projector was the one that, in time, came to win the major market share. The first of the Carousel projectors was released in 1961. The Carousels were gradually refined over the years and the facility to use multiple projectors and synchronised sound was added. The last of Kodak's Carousels was produced in 2004, 50 years after introducing Kodachrome (Wikipedia, 2008d; Kodak, 2008).

A small but significant group of teachers soon began to use photographic slides integrally in their everyday teaching, while many other teachers made incidental use of the technology. In the sciences and subjects like geography and art, photographic slides were used extensively from the 1950s until well into the 1990s. It was not until data projectors reached a price point in the early 2000s when they could readily be acquired for classroom use that the life cycle of the photographic slide ended. Indeed one can argue that the ubiquitous PowerPoint and its use of 'slides' is in fact an extension of the photographic slide tradition.

The relative success of the photographic slide is to be found, at least in part, in the reasons for the failure of all the other electronic instructional technologies. First and foremost—in contrast to film, radio and television —teachers had control of the technology in the preparation, delivery and ongoing refinement of their lessons. Teachers could use the slide projector like the teaching board to assist their existing teaching—they did not need to significantly change their ways.

With the advent of daylight projection screens, teachers could use their normal teaching room. Any interested classroom teacher could readily use the slide technology to create their own lessons and share them with the class group. It was simple to shoot the slides, organise them and present them as and when desired. In contrast to the broadcast instructional technologies, the teachers had control of the pace and structure of the lesson. They could readily pause the presentation at any stage, enter into a discussion of the issue at hand and, if they wished, could easily add another slide during the presentation. Most importantly, teachers determined when they wanted to use the slides and for how long. They could thus readily use the instructional technology within the existing organisational structures and at appropriate points in a topic of study.

Teachers soon developed a pride in the slides and lessons they had prepared. The teachers interviewed spoke of the many slide sets they had prepared over the years and how they had been able to reorganise and use the slides over that time. (One can remember art and geography teachers coming to morning tea clutching their prized Carousel collections.)

Figure 7.3 Kodak Carousel projector (Courtesy Peter Dalwood)

In some countries teachers were able to claim the photographic technology they acquired—and indeed the international field trips they undertook shooting their slides—on their tax.

The advent of photographic slide cassettes and in particular the Kodak Carousel enabled teachers to assemble collections of slides on major topics and readily store them for future use. While the later model Kodak projectors allowed for high-impact, highly professional multi-projector presentations with synchronised sound, only the most proficient of teachers took regular advantage of the facility.

The facility to package slide sets inexpensively and to place them on Carousels came increasingly to be used by educational authorities, educational foundations and commercial houses selling content into schools. By the latter 1960s, the availability of quality A/V kits, invariably containing a selection of slides with accompanying teacher notes, had become commonplace. The local education authorities, national agencies and increasingly the educational publishing houses produced the kits. The quality of the slide kits produced by the likes of National Geographic and Encyclopaedia Britannica was well known. Increasingly teachers were able to complement their slide collections with the commercial and education authority offerings. Indeed it was of interest to learn in our interviews of the number of teachers who created slides out of the 35-mm filmstrips.

A number of education authorities around the world used photo-graphic slide collections as part of the student assessment moderation process. In New Zealand, for example, the interviews revealed that a cross-section of the previous year's student artwork was provided to all secondary art teachers across the country as a guide to the marking of student work.

By the 1970s the cost of the Carousel projectors had reached the price point where schools could acquire one for each of the specialists using them. When combined with the new daylight projection screens, the art, science and geography rooms could be set up permanently, enabling teachers to use the technology whenever appropriate.

Figure 7.4 A 35-mm camera kit, with single reflex camera, alternative lenses and filters, tripod and flash lighting (Courtesy Peter Dalwood)

Slides in the hands of a quality teacher could have an immense impact: with quality photographs and a well-shaped presentation, they could be a very powerful teaching aid.

In retrospect, the success of the photographic slide was also helped by the financial interest of the photographic industry keen to see its photographic stock and creative and presentation technology being used by teachers. Where the other electronic instructional technology industries were committed to marketing packaged content, the photographic industry focused on the creative process. Undoubtedly also driven by the wider home consumer market, all the major photographic companies like Kodak, Agfa, Ilford and Fuji provided extensive support for teachers wanting to produce quality slides. The authors can remember well how all—but in particular Kodak—provided extensive free advice for teachers. All, moreover, sought to improve the quality and impact of the slide projectors, moving from the early single slides to carousels, and synchronised multimedia technology.

However, even with all these positives, regular classroom use was restricted to a relatively small group of specialist secondary teachers and the occasional primary school teacher. The photographic slide was not a common tool of mainstream teachers.

THE OVERHEAD PROJECTOR

The second of the visual instructional technologies to be used by a significant number of teachers in their everyday teaching was the overhead projector, or what became commonly known as OHPs.

Overhead projectors, with their facility to project writing or an image onto a screen, emerged as an instructional technology during World War II. Designed primarily to assist in the training of the defence forces, the technology slowly became available for schools (Wikipedia, 2008e). In the early years—the 1950s and 1960s—the images were generated by the user, writing with a felt-tipped pen, directly onto an opaque transparency. Other image-creation facilities emerged such as the 3M overhead transparency maker (Figure 7.6—see page 59), but in time transparencies could be created with all photocopiers.

As with most new instructional technology, the initial versions were expensive and use was limited to the armed services and the corporate sector. By the 1960s, OHPs had reached a price point where most schools could afford one or two, and thus one notes their use being advocated by teacher training colleges and the education authority A/V units (Wikipedia, 2008e).

OHPs were simple to operate. All teachers could readily write on the transparencies, and most importantly—and in contrast to the traditional teaching boards—teachers could retain their notes and images for future use. That facility was aided by the emergence of acetate rolls that teachers could readily affix to the side of the OHP. The interviews consistently referred to maths teachers' use of OHP rolls.

Figure 7.5 Overhead projector (Courtesy of Peter Dalwood)

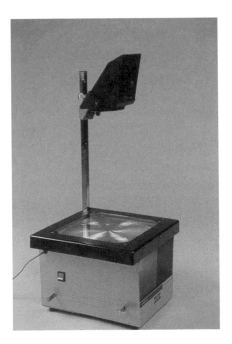

OHPs did, however, need a reasonably darkened room as the average projection lamps were not powerful. While most OHPs came with a spare projection bulb, the invariably constant movement of the OHPs between rooms did not help with the life of the bulbs, and many a teacher suffered the indignity of the blown bulb.

In essence, the OHP was another teaching board in that teachers prepared a visual image for the class to see on a large screen, be it text for the students to copy or an image or graphic to help reinforce the explanation of a concept.

Interestingly, in the latter 1980s, one saw the introduction of transparent computer monitors—or what were known as liquid crystal screens that were placed over an OHP and projected. The screens were in essence an early, albeit somewhat lacking, form of the interactive whiteboard.

Classroom use of OHPs was initially slow and spasmodic, gradually rising in time to a point in the latter 1980s and 1990s where they were used integrally in everyday teaching by a small but significant group of teachers. Maths teachers would appear to have been the main users, although extensive use was (and still is) being made by primary school teachers if they had/have an OHP in their room.

The slowness of the uptake can in part be attributed to the availability of the technology and the infamous propensity of schools to lock the instructional technology away in case it should be stolen. Those interested in using the technology invariably had to endure not only securing the key, but also trolleying or lugging the OHP to the classroom, darkening the room and returning the technology. In those situations one had to be keen. (One of the interviewees, who was the deputy director general of an education authority at the time, used an OHP at a school to extol the virtues of the technology. A year later he visited the same school to give a presentation and asked for the OHP to be made available. In turning to use the OHP he found on the transparency his writing from the year before. No one had used the technology in the past year.)

In the latter 1970s and the 1980s, OHPs reached a price point where, if there was the demand, schools could afford to position one in most classrooms, increasingly without fear of them being stolen. They were not the kind of item a thief could readily resell.

By the 1980s, the OHP had became the 'in' presentation technology. Anyone presenting at a conference or seminar was expected to use OHPs and, in fairness, some presenters could use OHPs to great effect.

Figure 7.6 A 3M overhead transparency maker (Courtesy Peter Dalwood)

However, even with all the refinements and the reduction in costs, most school principals were not deluged by requests from teachers to have their own OHP. The everyday use of OHPs was limited in the main to teachers who relied on an expository style of teaching, in subjects like secondary maths and science. Indeed, a wander around the average primary or secondary school in the 1990s would reveal a few still in use, but with many sitting at the back of the room, covered in dust.

By the 2000s, OHP use, even by the dedicated, had markedly declined.

CHAPTER 8

TELEVISION—
THE 'NEW SAVIOUR'

By the 1950s, television had reached the stage of technological development where it could be seen as having the capacity to revolutionise teaching. Here at last was a technology that embraced the best features of film and radio but could inexpensively be beamed into every living room and classroom.

The television industry and behaviourist educators promoted television —and in particular educational television—as the technology to bring teaching into the modern age. All that was needed was the production of a suite of programs to cover the school curriculum. Not only would those programs have more impact than any teacher, television would help overcome the teacher shortage created by the 'baby boomers' of the war years.

While it is easy in retrospect to dismiss the folly of that thinking, it is important to appreciate the immense impact the advent of television had on society as a whole. Look at the pictures of the crowds that sat outside the TV stores in the 1950s—invariably watching the wrestling—to appreciate the profound impact television had on people's lives and why both educators and governments should have been so taken with the potential of the medium.

In the US, in particular, there were many plans to use educational television to revolutionise teaching and to markedly enhance the productivity of schools. Television was seen in industry, government and tertiary education as being able to provide the desired expert instruction.

> *Television was hurled at teachers. The technology and its original applications were conceived, planned and adopted by non teachers, just as radio and film captured the imaginations of the earlier generation of reformers interested in improving instructional productivity.*
>
> (Cuban, 1986, p. 36)

The belief in the immense potential of educational television was fuelled by the USSR's launch of Sputnik in 1957 and the US perception that its school system was holding the country back. Sputnik opened the US coffers for education and released very considerable money for the vested interests. The US made its most notable use of educational television in American Samoa in the 1960s. When H. Rex Lee was appointed governor in 1961, he approached the US Congress for funds to provide most of Samoa's elementary school teaching via television.

> Twenty-six new elementary schools were constructed and four new high schools were built. A complete modern television facility was built with four production studios and ultimately ten broadcast-quality videotape recorders. The instructional television program was inaugurated in October 1964 and television lessons began to be transmitted over six VHF channels.

> Approximately thirty television teachers were brought from the U.S. mainland—along with producer-directors and complete production and engineering crews.

> (Saettler, 1990, pp. 369–70)

At its peak in the mid 1970s, 60 lessons a day were broadcast in Western Samoa. But by 1980 the experiment had all but come to end. Schramm, Nelson and Betham's classic in-depth study of the Samoan experiment, published as *Bold Experiment* in 1981, makes for a fascinating read and provides a valuable insight into why the immense investment and faith in this instructional technology failed.

While no other educational television initiative was of the same scale, there were nonetheless across the US in the 1950s, 1960s and 1970s a range of significant education-authority funded projects that made extensive use of educational television as a major medium of instruction. The likes of the St. Louis public schools, Pittsburgh, Chicago, and most notably Hagerstown, Maryland, made concerted use of educational television (Saettler, 1990; Cuban, 1986). The typical US educational television project was well funded and backed by a major industry group or foundation. Invariably the project engaged a group of 'experts' to design and produce the desired educational program and to measure how educational television improved student learning. The project usually also embraced a didactic, one-way broadcast model of instruction designed, often consciously, to minimise teacher input. It is estimated that the Ford Foundation alone invested over $US300 million in educational television projects (Saettler, 1990, pp. 372–74).

In the US the focus was very much on purpose-specific, invariably 'in-house' educational television, with the commercial networks—like radio beforehand—providing little educational content. While there were notable exceptions like *Sesame Street*, the US saw few educational programs on its commercial networks.

The path taken in the other developed nations was significantly different, and again more akin to the public radio model with national broadcasters being charged with producing educational television programs for showing during the school day. It was usually the same public broadcasters that had provided the radio broadcasts who now delivered the educational television broadcasts—the BBC in the UK, ABC in Australia, NZBC in New Zealand, ARD in Germany and YLE in Finland (Wikipedia, 2008c). All these public broadcasters were charged by government with producing television programs for the school curriculum, particularly in the 1970s and 1980s.

By the 1990s, the limited use made by schools of those programs was apparent and the number of programs produced was dropped.

Interestingly (as will be seen in Chapter 15), the same public broadcasters—and indeed the Public Broadcasting Service (PBS) in the US—used their media understanding to play a significant role in the production and provision of interactive multimedia teaching materials.

THE TECHNOLOGY

The early television sets were all black and white, and expensive, but the novelty and attractiveness of the medium dismissed those shortcomings. The cost, however, meant most schools could only afford one or two. Those precious items were in turn either locked away or placed in a special, darkened television room. Television reception was sometimes problematic, particularly outside the major urban centres. Invariably schools had only the one aerial and only a few outlets at the most.

However, a major problem particularly in the secondary schools was that in the early years of television there was not the ready facility to record broadcasts—to time shift—and thus teachers had to hope their lessons coincided with the broadcast schedule. Even when broadcast standard video recorders appeared in the 1960s they were well out of the price range of schools, and it was not until the release of the home VCRs that schools could consider video recorders.

Figure 8.1 TV in use with a class in the 1970s (Courtesy Peter Dalwood)

THE CONTENT

While considerable effort was made to broadcast programs that were tied specifically to the curriculum, the reality is that in the early years of television like schools made greater use of mainstream broadcasts. In this regard, little has changed with the passing of the years.

Interestingly, the one program all those interviewed could remember was the 1969 lunar landing.

TEACHING MATERIALS

Like others within society, quality teachers saw the potential of TV to enrich teaching, but in the main they were shut out of the creative use of the medium and, as with film and radio beforehand, had to make do with what was provided at the scheduled times. There was little chance of securing any ownership of the resource. Teachers once again had to work with the broadcast in its entity. Until the advent of video recorders, there was no ready way of teachers cutting and pasting the material broadcast and integrating it in their lessons.

The cost of producing quality television—even just to insert into a lesson—particularly in the 1950s, 1960s and early 1970s, was prohibitive for teachers, even if the teachers had the rare expertise needed to use the requisite tools.

Teacher training on the use of the medium in teaching was virtually non-existent, and was consistent with the attitude that those in control of the medium knew what was best for the students.

It ought to have been no surprise that this all-powerful medium should have been so little used by teachers when one reflects on the mindsets of those shaping the use of the medium and the logistical barriers that had to be overcome.

USAGE

All those interviewed reported on the non use—or, at best, scant use—of television before the advent of inexpensive video recorders. Larry Cuban, commenting on his own experience as a superintendent of schools in the US, noted:

> [about] ... 2% of teachers were using television when I entered the room.
>
> Instructional television occupies a tiny niche of the school day for teachers who use it.
>
> (Cuban, 1986, pp. 41 & 49)

The use was, at best, supplementary except in the aforementioned special projects.

The concerted class use of educational television obliged teachers to adopt a fundamentally different model of teaching—a model that most believed was inappropriate. In retrospect, school radio broadcasts were probably more widely used by teachers in most countries than television.

Niche use

Interestingly, like film, the use and study of television found a particular niche in the mass media and indeed English communications programs from the 1970s onwards where the major focus was on an analysis of its use and form.

While a sizeable number of secondary schools made use of small television studios for video production, few produced teaching materials. It should also not be a surprise when the research undertaken in conjunction with the aforementioned type of educational TV projects was unable to show that teaching with the new medium improved student performance.

Within a decade, virtually all the high-profile educational television projects had come to an end.

CHAPTER 9

VIDEO AND AUDIO RECORDING—REMOVING THE BARRIERS

The advent of relatively inexpensive audio and video cassette recorders in the 1970s once again opened the doors for what some at least envisaged would be a dramatic change in the nature of teaching. Here was the panacea that would overcome the logistical problems of broadcasts and enable all teachers to provide their students with quality audio and video materials when needed. Teachers finally had the facility not only to record and time shift, but also to readily edit, create and store their 'own' audio and video teaching materials. The impediments that had confronted teachers with the pre-packaged broadcast materials for the past 50 years were now overcome.

The release of the video cassette recorder (VCR) in particular seemingly represented a significant breakthrough. While the broadcasters and a few schools had had reel-to-reel video recorders for some time, they were expensive and cumbersome and required a degree of expertise to operate. The cassettes were a tool that all teachers could use. Teachers could at last store large quantities of quality sound and motion picture material, and then insert that material into their lessons when and where they wished. The new, portable technology could be used anywhere, in any classroom, and the teacher could readily pause both the audio and video presentations for class discussion.

The uptake of both the audio and video cassettes in schools in the 1970s was swift, but in both instances class use was limited and invariably supplementary in nature. Neither technology changed—let alone 'revolutionised'—the nature of teaching. However, while the video and audio playback and recording facilities only ever supplemented traditional teaching, they did become part of most teachers' toolkits for the next 25 to 30 years.

AUDIO CASSETTES

As previously mentioned, schools had had audio recorders prior to the 1970s but their cumbersome nature precluded their ready general use. Those drawbacks disappeared with the release of the Philips compact audio cassette and the associated availability of light, inexpensive cassette players. Every class could have one. Most importantly, teachers could secure copies of the school radio broadcasts and use them when convenient (Wikipedia, 2008f). Inexpensive pre-recorded audio cassettes created with the new Dolby sound facility were made available, particularly for use in English, with the teaching of foreign languages and the growing array of A/V kits being acquired by the school libraries. Students even in the early childhood classes could begin recording their own audiotapes.

With all these positives, the vast majority of teachers made little use of the technology, and even then they used mainly the playback facility.

With the advent of listening posts—a facility that allowed a group of five or six students to listen to the one cassette player—the hope was that more teachers would use the facility. It was generally not to be, although it is interesting to note that even in 2008 one still sees on the teacher mailing lists requests by teacher librarians for information on where to buy listening posts.

The one area where the facility is still well used is in the teaching of foreign languages and the teaching of students of non-English-speaking background. The digital audio playback had in 2008 still not reached a point where it could displace the audio cassette player.

On reflection, the cassette recorders used by most schools were cheap, with very average sound quality, and amplification was ill suited to a robust clientele. (An interesting observation by a very experienced primary school teacher was that with the listening post in operation one could not tell if the students were actually listening.) So while the audio cassette—and in particular the ubiquitous Walkman audio cassette player—was used extensively by all outside school, its use in the classroom was limited. The same situation prevailed even when the high-quality audio cassette recorder, and in time the digital variety, became available.

Figure 9.1 Sony Sports Walkman audio cassette player/recorder (Courtesy Greg Walker)

As with film, television and radio, the quality audio recording and playback technology found a niche in media studies, and to a lesser extent in language courses.

EARLY VIDEO

The use of video in teaching, like that with the audio, ramped up with the introduction of video cassette recorders (VCR). While again a few schools had dabbled with reel-to-reel video recorders, it was not until the release of VCRs that schools gave serious consideration to using this instructional technology widely.

Figure 9.2 Shibaden reel-to-reel black-and-white video recorder (Courtesy Peter Dalwood)

The solution lay initially in the ¾-inch U-matic video cassette recorder. Developed by Sony in the late 1960s–early 1970s as its initial home-market video recorder, these very robust and reliable recorders came with their own tuner, the facility to record and play back in stereo and to edit—in a fashion—existing material. These machines were bulky and the early tapes were regularly limited to a maximum length of one hour (Wikipedia, 2008g). The promotional literature referred to them as 'luggable'.

Despite the drawbacks, video recording offered so many advantages that most schools secured them. They suited classrooms and their operations. Teachers did not need to move desks, darken windows or alter timetables. Videos could be run when it suited and stopped at any time when discussion or other timetable constraints necessitated it.

The cost of the new equipment was initially relatively high, in keeping with all new technology. A U-matic VCR cost around $A1100 in 1975, even when on a government contract. Televisions to display the media were equally pricey, with a 26-inch Philips TV costing around $A740 at the same time. Despite this, there were plenty of schools willing to try the new media.

Figure 9.3 JVC U-matic video recorder
(Courtesy Peter Dalwood)

CAMERAS MAKE THE SCENE

Following the release of the U-matic recorder came the early video camera. Companies like Sony, Panasonic, JVC and Hitachi began making relatively inexpensive, quality colour video cameras. In some cases these were offered as part of the recorder package (for example, the Panasonic Porta-Pak) and promoted on the basis of producing one's own videos rather than breaching copyright.

Those who are sufficiently advanced in years to remember those times will recall the considerable misnomer of Panasonic's or Sony's 'porta-pak' nomenclature. Intended to be a portable camera station and recorder in one unit, the 'paks' were large and extremely heavy. Battery life was short and a couple of kilograms in weight. Spare batteries were a necessity and so the whole kit was a very substantial one, and not one that was readily carried on the school bushwalk.

However, the price was attainable, even for smaller schools, and the potential uses of the equipment were exciting. The immediacy of the play-back was a major factor in its use. Mistakes could be analysed and then removed, successes could be recalled again and again, especially at parent evenings.

The average school in the developed world could, if it wished, now acquire the technology to allow the students to produce their own media, and the teachers to compile their own video resources. Teachers now had a tool that they could readily use to create new material or record broadcasts. If they wished they could record their own television programs, either in totality or by 'cutting and pasting' broadcast and original material.

Figure 9.4 Panasonic black-and-white studio camera of the 1970s (Courtesy Peter Dalwood)

Pathfinding education authorities and schools across the western world recognised the educational potential of the ¾-inch VCR. As the decade progressed, bulk sales brought prices down and both the equipment and the 'software' became more affordable. Further, the success of the medium brought new development and video-on-demand became less of a dream and more of a reality.

By the later 1970s, there were a sizeable number of schools that built on the U-matic development, wired every classroom and provided the monitors that would enable every teacher to call up a program when they wished. Control equipment was still primitive, so many early systems employed a variation on the telephone technology so that classroom teachers could directly contact the A/V technician. In the Australian Capital Territory, for example, the new Year 11–12 secondary colleges opened in 1976 with a central video control room, a bank of U-matics and reticulated video throughout. One of the authors was fortunate enough to head up the media faculty in one of those schools. There was undoubted initial excitement shown by many of the staff, and from the outset the resource was well used in science, geography, humanities and media faculties. A highly supportive library staff and an enthusiastic A/V officer aided the use. In retrospect, however, a number of the subject faculties made little or no use of the facility, and the vast majority of the teachers simply used the programs provided in toto, with little teacher use being made of the college's then expensive video editing suite.

Figure 9.5 Common school U-matic recording set-up of the 1970s (Courtesy Peter Dalwood)

Some schools—such as Waverley College in Sydney and Wesley College in Melbourne, Australia—not only wired the school for video, but also created a significant production facility for the development of educational television lessons. Much hype and undoubted initial excitement accompanied these developments, but in time the enormous effort and expense entailed in producing quality lessons impacted and the use of the facilities waned.

These systems were limited to only the largest or wealthiest schools. For most, it remained a dream and if they were lucky their allotment might be a couple of VCRs, their attendant monitors and perhaps one camera and porta-pak for roving projects. While the sales hype was considerable, the bulk of the machinery, its cost and the relatively high skill levels that were associated with it made the technology a 'specialist' one. Most classrooms missed out.

THE ½-INCH VCR

In the later 1970s, Sony and JVC released the ½-inch VCR to capture the world home market. Sony launched the now legendary Beta format, and JVC and linked companies produced the VHS format. All came equipped with their own in-built timer so teachers or school libraries could record programs any time (Wikipedia, 2008h).

While seemingly inordinately expensive when compared with the price of a VHS/VCR today, these inexpensive, small and readily transportable video recorders ended the need to spend considerable monies wiring a school and maintaining a central control room. For a fraction of the cost schools could be provided with multiple portable VCRs and monitors that all teachers could control. Soon schools had the option of securing even cheaper VCRs that only had a playback function.

Early VHS tapes were of one hour duration (or shorter) and generally cost around $A30 each, but within two to three years mass market pressure saw three-hour tapes available for less than $10. For schools, the difference was significant. The lower cost of the machinery, its smaller size and the cheaper consumables brought video resources into more and more classrooms. School libraries could afford a bank of recorders to amass extensive VHS tape libraries.

The largest users were primary teachers and the humanities teachers in the secondary sector.

TEACHING PATTERNS

The pattern of video recording established in the early 1980s largely continued in use worldwide until the latter 2000s. One had only to note the daily requests on the teacher-librarians' mailing lists to appreciate how widespread the practice still was in 2008. While the digital video recorder (DVD) and hard-drive technology was slowly replacing the VCR in the home, most schools—with their very sizeable videotape collection, and the copyright 'challenge' of transferring programs from one medium to another—were slow to move to the new medium. (The memories of those we interviewed are that the vast majority of teachers and school leaders were, particularly in the early days, somewhat 'flexible' in their interpretation of the copyright laws if the material was being used simply for teaching. Any offering of the local video store was deemed a useful resource.) In time, the ethics of recording and the adoption of copyright laws that caught up with the technological reality undoubtedly changed the schools' approaches and respect for copyright.

In most schools the teacher-librarians—or what have been variously termed the library, media, resources and information services—have overseen the recording, storage and lending of videotapes, like so much of the 'software' used with the other instructional technology. They were ideally positioned to comment on the extent and nature of the teacher borrowing of videotapes. The comment made by all the experienced existing and former teacher-librarians interviewed was that:

- the video tapes were requested and used by only a small proportion of teachers
- a small proportion of teachers did make extensive use of the material
- the tapes were used as broadcast; there was little or no effort made to edit or use the 'cut and paste' facility to create new lessons
- the tapes were used as supplementary teaching materials; none had seen the tapes being used (as envisaged by the advocates of educational television) as central to everyday teaching.

The reality is that by the 1980s, VCRs, TVs and home entertainment centres were a normal part of most teachers' homes. While some teachers might have some reservations about programming their home VCR, the everyday use of the technology did not worry them. Why then should the VCR be used only as a supplementary teaching aid?

Those interviewed believed the answer lay in the broadcast communication nature of the medium. While teachers could control the time of use and the playing of the video, in many respects the video suffered the shortcomings of film, radio and television. It is a one-way, packaged communication, which the vast majority of teachers were unable or did not have the time to vary.

On reflection, the VCR has been a significant instructional technology for near on 30 years. While its use in teaching has been limited, and while the technology is nearing the end of its life cycle, it was a tool all teachers could readily use.

CHAPTER 10

COMPUTERS AS DISCRETE TEACHING TOOLS—THE 'GREAT REVOLUTION'

From the time of their first appearance in the 1970s a significant proportion of business, political leaders, educational administrators, tertiary educators, school leaders and teachers saw computers as the tool that would finally revolutionise teaching. While the earlier instructional technology had not had the desired impact, computers were perceived as having the power and potential to overcome the earlier shortcomings.

The considerable faith placed in the technology, from all its advocates from the outset was in the use of computers as discrete or stand-alone tools. Here finally was an instructional technology with the in-built capacity to replicate human thinking and shape the students' learning.

However, after 20-plus years of use, the considerable development of computers and the associated software, and a vast investment made by schools and education authorities worldwide, computers as discrete teaching tools experienced the same inauspicious life cycle as the previous technology and had minuscule impact on the nature of teaching and the development of the traditional academic skills. By the 1990s, and with the emergence of the World Wide Web (WWW), the reliance on computers as discrete teaching tools began to wane and over the next decade in the more astute educational settings they became increasingly an integral part of a suite of digital technologies.

In so saying, one could in 2008 still find many school situations where teaching revolved around the personal computer and relied on computer labs rather than the wider digital toolkit of the type described in Chapter 14.

It is thus important to examine the use of the personal computer as a discrete instructional technology and consider why, like the earlier technologies, it was not embraced by the vast majority of teachers for use in their classrooms.

THE TOOL OF THE REVOLUTION

By the 1960s, the educational potential of computers was being spoken of in awe. One of the authors well remembers his first school principal, Gil Hughson, commenting at a school speech night in 1968 on the role that computers were about to play in schooling.

> *The greatest change you will have to accept is the technology revolution which is leading us into the age of the computer.*

(Lyneham High Year Book, 1998)

While that comment was prescient and by no means common of school leaders at the time, it nonetheless reflects the potential envisaged.

The following observation by Seymour Papert in 1980 reflects the potential he had long seen and advocated:

> *The computer is the Proteus of machines. Its essence is its universality, its power to simulate. Because it can take on a thousand forms and can serve a thousand functions, it can appeal to a thousand tastes.*

(Papert, 1980)

Here at last was a technology that to many mirrored the thinking of the young and which, even in its early rudimentary form, could be used to help 'teach' the basic skills. Moreover, here was a tool that allowed the older students to develop their higher-order logical thinking and acquire the understanding that was needed in the future workplace. Most importantly, personal computers could be used every day by the students. Until this point only the teachers could use the instructional technology. At last the teachers and the students had the technology to create or present their work.

This fervent belief continued for many years, and even in the 1990s this kind of observation was common.

Recent developments in media and communication technologies are set to revolutionise the provision of education and training. With modern technology it will soon be possible to deliver lectures, assignments, tutorials, simulations, even the contents of the world's best libraries to anyone in possession of a modem and computer. Furthermore, amongst all these concrete benefits ... there is the shift towards a more student-centered approach. Learners are now freed from the barriers of time and space imposed by conventional classroom teaching, and encouraged to interact with the material in ways that could never be supported adequately by traditional teaching methods.

(Rose, 1996, p. 65)

BRIEF HISTORY OF USE

The initial general use of computers in teaching in schools began in the mid to later 1970s, invariably at the senior school level. Use was generally made of mainframe computers, owned by an outside institution, to teach programming in a new subject called computing studies. While at the time access to mainframes generated immense interest among the devotees, the reality was that those computers were primitive. Both the teachers and students had to work via mark sense cards and allow time for the cards to be processed, and thus ultimately use was limited to a very small group of early adopting teachers and keen students who were prepared to overcome the many hurdles confronting them. (Memories of teachers traipsing out to the local university well into the night remain with the authors.)

In the latter 1970s, the situation changed significantly with the introduction of personal computers, but in so saying it is important to remember the rudimentary nature of that early technology, its considerable cost and the lack of expertise in the use of computers with most teachers.

Apple released its groundbreaking Apple II in 1977, and in the same year Tandy released its TRS 80 and Commodore released its PET. Here at last were computers that could be bought by schools, even though initially at a very considerable price. (Bear in mind a TRS 80 retailed in 1977 for $US599, nearly as much as a colour TV.) While basic, these machines enabled the enthusiasts to finally undertake their work in the classroom (White, 2005).

White (ibid.) reminds us that the situation was further improved with the following releases in the early 1980s:

1981:

- IBM's personal computer 5150
- BBC's Acorn in the UK

1982:

- Commodore 64
- MS DOS
- Apple's Dot Matrix Printer, for US$700
- Compaq's Portable PC, which was compatible with the IBM PC

1983:

- the Apple IIe that was to remain in production as an educational mainstay until 1993

Of note, also in 1983, Atari signed an agreement with Nintendo for the worldwide licence of Donkey Kong and Donkey Kong Junior video games for Atari home computers.

Figure 10.1 Commodore 64 keyboard (Courtesy Greg Walker)

All of these early personal computers were aimed at the general consumer market, but the Apple and BBC Acorn were also pitched successfully at the school market. While all were limited and expensive, they were well received by a fascinated public. White (ibid.) notes that in 1982, for example:

- *sales of home computers in the United States were 2 million.*
- *shipments of personal computers worldwide during the year were 2.8 million, worth US$5 billion*
- *unit sales of home computers during the year: 2.2 million.*

A major shortcoming of all the early machines was the software. It was all text-based. While revered by the enthusiasts, it lacked the user-friendliness to be used more widely. That deficiency began to be addressed with Apple's release of its first Macintosh in 1984, and most importantly its graphical user interface (GUI) that, in time, was to become the norm with personal computers. While Microsoft introduced a PC with GUI in 1985 with its Windows 1.0, it was not until its Windows 3.0 release in 1990 that PC users began to enjoy the same ease of use as the Macs (Wikipedia, 2008i, 2008j).

By the mid 1980s, those of us leading schools were able to secure relatively cheap IBM PC compatibles, or what were commonly referred to as clones. 'Cheap' is probably the key term in that the majority of the clones were what is known in the IT industry as tier-three machines. In most developed nations there are usually three levels of computing:

- tier one, which are the quality machines produced by the major providers
- tier two, which are quality machines that invariably utilise the technology of the major providers
- tier three, which are inexpensive copies of the major providers.

The tier-three clones were significantly cheaper than a tier-one Apple unit, but at the same time were invariably of poorer build and unreliable, and came with limited warranty.

Schools keen to secure computers but lacking in cash tended to opt for the IBM clones. Indeed, mention was consistently made in the interviews that a significant number of education authorities that went out to tender also opted for both PC clones and the cheaper monitors. On the other hand, there were education authorities that insisted on the higher-quality machines, and thus one found a significant number of schools in the 1980s with Apple, BBC and IBM, HP or Compaq personal computers.

Figure 10.2 Apple II computer laboratory of the 1980s (Courtesy Peter Dalwood)

While the level of unreliability with the tier-three technology was very high, none of the tier-one machines of this era was particularly known for its reliability.

The latter part of the 1980s saw significant increases in the power and in particular the memory of all the personal computers, and in the use of the 1.2 MB floppy disks.

What soon became apparent to schools and education authorities was that the life of personal computers was limited by the rate of technological development, and that if schools wanted to stay approximately 'state-of-the-art' they needed to replace their personal computers every three or four years. As a consequence some schools opted to begin using some kind of rental or leasing model from the later 1980s onwards.

A significant impediment to the widespread teacher use of personal computers was the availability of a set of easy-to-use applications software that allowed the ready transfer of work between computers. Microsoft began redressing that shortcoming in 1989 with its release of Microsoft Office for Mac. It released its Windows version of Office in 1990, the same year it released its breakthrough Windows 3.0 (Wikipedia, 2008j). Finally most teachers were able to work with quality GUI interfaces, and most importantly teachers working with Macs or PCs could readily exchange files across computing platforms.

The advent and widespread industry acceptance of Microsoft Office led ultimately (as revealed in the interviews) to the demise of those computers like BBC's Acorn that Microsoft chose not to support. While the

Figure 10.3 Apple PowerPC of the 1990s (Courtesy Greg Walker)

Acorn with its RISC architecture and extensive educational multimedia software was in many respects well ahead of the opposition, it ultimately suffered because it was perceived as being unable to prepare young people for the workplace.

So rapid was the acceptance of Office, one could safely say that by the mid 1990s it had become the 'de facto' international standard for teachers. At the same time as the teachers were using Office and its associated operational conventions in preparing their teaching materials, so too were the young people using it in their homes. Office had become in essence the application tool of the young throughout the developed world, both in the home and at school.

In the early 1990s in Australia the move began to give all students in the school—or at least a significant proportion—their own laptop, or what in some circles were called notebook computers. The laptops chosen were usually Toshiba, Compaq, IBM or in some situations Apple.

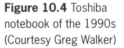

Figure 10.4 Toshiba notebook of the 1990s (Courtesy Greg Walker)

As usual, the initiative was launched with much hype, and significant marketing support was provided from the laptop providers, Microsoft, and the major resellers of the technology. Throughout the Australian media and the school conference circuit, school laptop programs were proclaimed as the way forward for all schools. In reality, the initiative was largely restricted by cost to the country's more affluent schools, even though in most instances the students actually paid for the machines (Shears, 1995).

An interesting point to note—particularly in light of the comments made in Chapter 11 on the technology of the home—is that when the

Australian Council for Educational Administration (ACEA) undertook its study of the Australian school laptop initiative in 1995, it found '46% of students have access to a personal computer at home' (Shears, 1995, p. 21). In keeping with other instructional technology initiatives the research was commissioned to 'prove' the advantages to students of laptops over traditional learning, and in this instance laptops over the use of desktops. What became evident was (again like earlier technology initiatives) that there was a group of very capable and committed early adopting teachers who impacted positively on the teaching of their students, but there was also a sizeable proportion of the teachers who either made little or no use of the technology or who used it mundanely. (One of the authors remembers vividly watching a history teacher working a class where all had laptops. The students were sitting at their desks, in perfect rows, copying the notes being handwritten in chalk on the board onto their laptops.)

In time, the number of schools using the model in Australia stabilised, with some schools dropping the approach and a few others coming on board. In the latter 1990s, the approach was 'discovered' by the US, particularly with the support of Microsoft, and once again became the way forward. Several of the leading figures associated with the Australian program were taken to the US by Microsoft to foster the program there.

The next major development in the use of personal computers as the instructional technology was the creation of the World Wide Web and the launch of the 'information superhighway'.

As becomes apparent in Chapter 13, virtually overnight the computer ceased being simply a discrete instructional tool and became a facility to access and work the online world. Quickly teachers, students and the more astute educational leaders started viewing computers as the portal for entry to the greatest teaching resource humanity had ever provided—the Internet.

The release of the Mosaic web browser in 1993, and in turn its transformation to Netscape in November 1994 (Friedman, 2006), opened a new world for teachers, students and prescient governments. With the ready, free availability of Netscape and the release of Microsoft's Internet Explorer in 1995, the use of personal computers as discrete instructional technologies began to wane.

In so saying, it took many schools another five to ten years or more to acquire the network access to allow that to happen, but in real terms by the start of the twenty-first century personal computers in most schools had become but one of a suite of digital instructional technologies.

IMPLEMENTATION

By the mid 1970s it was apparent to the wiser heads that if schools and education authorities were to get teachers using instructional technology wisely and extensively, the schools and the education authorities needed to adopt appropriate holistic implementation strategies. Plans were needed that ensured the teachers were provided with the requisite direction and ongoing support.

In retrospect, the strategies invariably used with computers left much to be desired and it should come as no surprise that computers as discrete instructional tools, with all their potential, should have been used so little in the classroom. There were undoubtedly initiatives around the world that did use well-reasoned implementation strategies, but in the main most of the rollouts left much to be desired.

Computer use in virtually all schools and education systems was initiated by a small group of enthusiastic teachers imbued with the potential of the computers. Many in that early group had a mathematics/science teaching background. While undoubtedly influenced by the pathfinding computer companies, there is also little doubt that those early adopting teachers believed in the educational potential of the technology and were thus prepared to move heaven and earth to get underway. The feedback from those interviewed points to this group of pioneering teachers putting in an effort unparalleled in the use of instructional technology. (Sadly, the same interviewees commented on the number of quality and committed teachers who became disenchanted with the lack of support from the school and education authority leadership, and who took their expertise outside teaching.)

In the 1970s one thus saw computing in schools being initiated by these devotees, often with the bemused blessing of their principals, but also usually lacking any coherent whole-school implementation strategy. In the first instance, most of the developments were in the secondary schools with the senior students and were focused on getting computing studies programs off the ground. The desire was to have the students learn the languages of computing—Fortran, COBOL and BASIC—and how to program.

By the early 1980s there was the chance to reflect on the efforts of the enthusiasts and begin integrating the use of computers across the curriculum in both the primary and secondary sectors, but with limited success. Computing remained largely a separate subject.

In the US, the advent of the personal computers opened the way to introduce into the classrooms what has been variously described as computer-assisted instruction (CAI), computer-aided learning (CAL) or mastery learning. While the devotees might argue about the subtle differences between each of the approaches, all built on the stimulus-response theories of the likes of Skinner and Watson to teach the basic literacies with highly structured, linear programs. Sacttler made the observation that in the US:

> by the mid 1980s a national pattern of computer use in the schools could be clearly discerned. The drill and practice mode had become dominant as well as teaching about computers.

> (Saettler, 1990, p. 458)

In Australia, the then federally funded Schools Commission took a very different approach and in 1982 launched a national Computers in Schools project, which—as those interviewed reinforced—built extensively on the constructivist school of learning and sought to provide Australia's young people with a general appreciation of the role computers could play in all areas of learning.

In hindsight, the team assembled to develop and steer the Schools Commission project was very capable and very reasoned in its expectations of the computer's use, and appreciated from the outset the importance in using a holistic implementation strategy that placed considerable store on providing appropriate ongoing teacher training and using teaching software that would engage the students. Unfortunately, as one of the team members observed, their thinking was years ahead of the technology available and needed in order to realise their vision.

This type of high-level, carefully reasoned and well-resourced holistic approach was the exception rather than the norm.

The approach followed by most schools and education authorities was to focus on buying the 'latest and greatest computers' and to assume that the mere provision of the technology would not only address all the implementation issues but also encourage teacher use and improve student learning. One has only to look at the school, education authority or computer company media releases of the period to appreciate the emphasis given to the technology and the scant attention given to teacher training, the provision of appropriate software or indeed the required technical support.

What became apparent in the interviews with former senior administrators was the importance placed on how many computers were being provided and how much was being spent. The lowering of the computer-to-student ratio was perceived as the all-important performance indicator.

Computer purchases for schools generated very good political capital. Many a government made great mileage out of announcing it was going to give all schools a computer. (It was revealed that one education authority took what it thought was a more reasoned approach and based its allocation of computers on the population of the school, and thus obliged three small rural schools to share the one computer!)

However, it was not only governments that sought to gain 'political' capital out of the acquisition of computers. Very early in the piece, schools and education authorities began using the availability of computers in their marketing. John Goodlad, in his famous study of US schooling in the early 1980s entitled *A Place Called School*, commented that 'purchasing microcomputers is becoming the "in" thing for school districts to do' (Goodlad, 1984, p. 340). (An interview with one of Australia's pathfinding computer educators brought back memories of the then major educational system integrator who was given an order for $10 000 worth of computers. When he inquired what was desired the school simply indicated that the principal had included in the marketing brochure that the school had computers worth that amount!)

A related development that was seen in various guises across the developed world was the creation, funding, branding, and often staffing of special lighthouse technology schools. Terms like 'schools of the future', 'technology schools' or 'computing schools' were used to describe them. Some—like Apple's ACOT schools—were subsidised by technology companies, while the local education authorities funded others. Schools like River Oaks Primary in Canada received international attention. In retrospect, those schools—like the 'television' schools that preceded them—had little impact on the use of instructional technology in teaching in general. Their 'special' nature set them apart from normal schools and the facility to transfer their work to the everyday teaching in other schools. While the schools generated great copy for the technology corporations and education authorities, their existence had little other than 'political' impact.

The laptop program launched in Australia in the early 1990s had a strong marketing imperative. While not suggesting the educational

Figure 10.5 Apple 'clamshell' laptops of the early 2000s (Courtesy Greg Walker)

rationale was not strong, most of the schools involved were private schools needing to succeed in a highly competitive market place. For a time in Australia it was very much the 'in' thing to use laptops school-wide (Shears, 1995). While the pathfinding teachers were prepared to take and make wise use of anything given, this kind of political rollout invariably led to great waste and boxes of computers were left literally unopened.

Implementation at the school and indeed education authority level was invariably determined and carried out by the computer coordinators, or what became in time the IT (information technology) or ICT (information and communications technology) coordinators. The focus was thus on the technical aspects of the implementation and ensuring that the equipment worked, and not how it might be used by all teachers.

Within the schools the computers were usually located in a computer laboratory or two, with a teacher or two given control of the operation. In time, in some situations technical staff were employed to assist in maintaining the labs, but the technical agenda prevailed. Issues like theft and ease of maintaining unreliable equipment held far greater sway than any educational rationale.

By locating the computers in labs, schools introduced organisational constraints that were to play a major part in limiting the use of not only computers, but in time all manner of digital instructional technology. While the issue is examined more fully below, in brief the lab placement left the general teaching rooms with only the old tools—the pen, paper and the board—and the majority of teachers to build most of their lessons around their use. The rest of the teaching staff, each with their own speciality, soon assumed 'computing' would be taught by the computing teachers. It is of note that as late as 2007 in the UK around half of the desktop computers in the primary schools were still located in computer labs (Becta, 2007, p. 7). In 1995, Gerstner et al. in *Reinventing Education* commented:

> *When schools do employ technology they treat it more often as an add-on or an extra. Computers are typically in separate labs, to which students are periodically sent. (p. 12)*

By the mid 1980s one began to see an increasing number of education authorities mandating the development and submittal of school computing plans, and then in time IT and ICT plans. They were 'stand-alone' plans that sat beside the many other discrete plans, like those on occupational health and safety (OHS), social inclusiveness, indigenous education, equal employment opportunities, and literacy, which schools were increasingly obliged to submit. Most were 'bolt on' plans that sat adrift from the school's main development plan. Invariably committees with a strong representation by the computing or ICT staff developed the plans. Principals were rarely involved. The work was left to the 'experts'. The focus was usually on the mechanics, although in time the question of computer integration in the curriculum became an issue.

Particularly in the 1980s and 1990s, the plans built on the notion of constancy that characterised much school strategic planning, and thus schools were obliged by their local authorities to submit three- and sometimes five-year ICT plans, even when it was becoming increasingly apparent that the ICT scene was changing at a pace and becoming increasingly uncertain. Of note is that many, and possibly most, education authorities were still obliging schools to submit their largely ineffectual 'stand-alone' ICT plans at the time of writing in 2008.

What separate ICT plans succeeded in doing was to reinforce the separation of the ICT from the everyday teaching. All of the schools featured in the case studies below did not use a separate ICT plan, but rather integrated the use of the technology into their overall school development planning.

It was unusual for the school or education authority leadership to play any major role in the introduction of personal computers, other than to promote the investment being made. Most school leaders had little understanding of computers and were happy to delegate their use to the experts. In a pattern akin to the initial use of computers in industry, responsibility was delegated—some might say abrogated—to middle managers, and as such the technical agenda assumed primacy over the educational.

Almost all the principals and educational administrators interviewed indicated that they left the deployment of and the best ways to use the computers—particularly in the 1980s—to the 'experts'. In the 1990s, the continuing lack of widespread use of the computers prompted the more astute school leaders to take a greater leadership role, but in retrospect there was little or no training provided to existing or prospective school leaders on how best to use the technology. The research and interviews unearthed very little literature or programs specifically designed to provide school and education authority leaders with the skills and understanding needed to make the best use of the computers.

By the early 1990s and with the drop in the relative price of computers, a growing number of primary schools opted to place the computers in the classroom, often in clusters in what became known as pods, but many well-intentioned deployments were frustrated by the dearth of teachers able to make use of the facilities.

The efforts to employ appropriate implementation strategies were made more challenging in many situations by the moves to school-based management (SBM) in the 1980s and the devolving of responsibility for computer deployment wholly to the school. In the larger schools there might be the requisite expertise on the staff, but not so in the medium-sized to smaller schools, where well-intentioned teachers or teacher-librarians were simply 'lumbered' with the task of making best use of the computers. In speaking with the cross-section of school leaders and pathfinding computer educators it became apparent that this devolution, without the requisite high-level direction setting and support, contributed to the use of ineffectual implementation strategies, and in turn to considerable waste of money and effort.

As the number of computers in schools grew and became more sophisticated, the facility to network those computers improved. And as the desire to use the computers across the curriculum intensified, so grew the importance of schools adopting wise, holistic implementation strategies and of central agencies providing the requisite advice and support.

In hindsight it is apparent there were a number of decisions relating to the use of computers, and in particular their networking, which would have been better handled at a regional or national level, rather than by teachers in the school.

In the latter 1990s, a significant number of national and regional governments such as those in the UK and New Zealand that appreciated this problem, while retaining significant school-based decision making, took responsibility for setting direction, determining procurement standards, establishing the networks, providing the requisite teacher and leadership training and commissioning the research.

However, in the mid 2000s there were still many situations in the developed world where this has not happened and schools were left to fend for themselves.

COMPUTER-TO-STUDENT RATIO

Special mention needs to be made of the computer-to-student ratio referred to above. It was a measure used with much abandon in the 1980s and 1990s, and indeed in government analyses and media releases, particularly in the US, in the 2000s. It communicates the desire for all students to have their own personal computer at school.

In the US, a survey undertaken by The Greaves Group and published as *America's Digital Schools 2006 Report* documents the continuing quest across the US to achieve what it terms 'ubiquitous computing'; that is, a 1:1 student–computer ratio. It is reported that in 2006, 24 per cent of US school districts 'were in the position of transitioning' to that point (The Greaves Group, 2006, p. 7). The same organisation was also lauding the use of student laptop programs, with the aforementioned survey reporting that 19 per cent 'of all student devices are mobile' (ibid.).

In 2007, the new national Labor Government in Australia announced a 'digital education revolution' by promising to provide a personal computer for every student in Australia in Years 9 to 12.

The student–computer ratio is a measure that should be viewed with considerable care. The mere existence of a technology matters little educationally if it is not being used, or used inappropriately.

While the quest to achieve a 1:1 ratio will enhance the profits of the computing companies and provide some political capital for the governments concerned, one needs to question the educational value of such a vast outlay of monies, ask why replicate technology already in the home and identify whether even the most affluent of nations can afford to sustain such a ratio, even if it was educationally desirable.

Chris Dede from Harvard University made the telling observation in 1998:

> I feel additional concern about attempts to supply every student with continuous access to high performance computing and communications because of the likely cost of this massive investment. Depending on the assumptions made about the technological capabilities involved, estimates of the financial resources needed for such an information infrastructure vary (Coley, Cradler, & Engel, 1997). Extrapolating the most detailed cost model (McKinsey & Company, 1995) to one multimedia-capable, Internet-connected computer for every two to three students yields a price tag of about ninety-four billion dollars of initial investment and twenty-eight billion dollars per year in ongoing costs, a financial commitment that would drain schools of all discretionary funding for at least a decade. For several reasons, this is an impractical approach for improving education.

(Dede, 1998, p. 2)

The more astute educational authorities in different parts of the world also began at a similar time to seriously question the educational worth of the ongoing improvement in the student–computer ratio. No significant studies were revealing any marked improvement in student learning resulting from the vast outlay on personal computers. These authorities believed schools needed some computers for teaching but that there were complementary digital instructional technologies that would be better used by teachers. They were increasingly conscious of the very short life of PCs, the cost of replacing them and the associated software every three or four years, and hence the questionable value-for-money they represented.

USAGE

The use made of computers as discrete instructional technologies by teachers and students in the classroom did grow in the 1980s and 1990s, but ultimately remained small. While in time most teachers came to use computers in their lesson preparation (Cuban, 2001; Balanskat, Blamire & Kefala, 2006), the vast majority did not use them in their teaching, nor in turn did they enable the students to use them in school, particularly in the period when computers were used discretely.

Despite very extensive and expensive national and education authority efforts, by the mid 1990s it was still rare to have more than 25 per cent of teachers using personal computers integrally in their everyday teaching. The level of teacher use in most schools and education authorities would have been far less.

Meredyth et al. in 1998 note:

> While many reports extol the potential benefits of computer use in classrooms international surveys suggest that around the world, the use of information technology in classrooms is the exception rather than the rule. (p. 13)

Larry Cuban in his aptly titled 2001 publication *Oversold and Underused* observed:

> Teachers at all levels have used the technology basically to continue what they have always done: communicate with parents and administrators, prepare syllabi and lectures, record grades and assign research papers. These unintended effects must have been disappointing to those who advocate more computers for schools. (p. 178)

Becker, in his analysis of Cuban's assertions, concludes:

> In response to Cuban's projection that computers are likely to continue to play a minor role in student learning of academic subjects in elementary and secondary schools, this article has presented an examination of related evidence. On the issue of whether computers are generally a central vehicle of instructional activities in classrooms, the data suggest that Cuban remains correct up to the present time. Although a substantial fraction of teachers are having students do word processing during class time, most in-class use of computers occurs as part of separate skills-based instruction about computers, in occupationally-oriented courses such as business and vocational education.
>
> (Becker, 2000)

In their interviews the authors seldom encountered schools where more than 25 per cent of teachers were using computers integrally in their teaching even in the 2000s, let alone in the 1990s when computers were basically stand-alone tools. A study of government school teachers in the state of South Australia in October 2003 noted that only 26 per cent of teachers believed they used ICT regularly in their classroom teaching (Measday, 2004).

Cuban makes the telling point:

Teachers tend to overestimate frequency of computer use. The discrepancy between self report and practice is common not only of teachers but also among other professionals.

(Cuban, 2001, p. 201)

It is appreciated that the use made of PCs varied across the curriculum, but the reality is that despite very considerable expense and effort to integrate computers into the curriculum teachers did not embrace the classroom use of personal computers. That was the case as much in the schools with laptops as with desktops.

In making this observation it is important to bear in mind that even by the mid 1990s in the more developed nations the computer–student ratio was in the region of 1:10–1:15, or in general terms two per class group (Coley, Cradler & Engel, 1997; Meredyth et al., 1998, p. 13).

With no ready facility to display the work done on the PC with others in the class, there was only so much that even the best of teachers could do. When one compares the school situation with that in the home (as we do in Chapter 11), it will be appreciated that schools were struggling.

One of the very real challenges in examining the use of any of the instructional technologies in schools—and personal computer use in particular—is that most of the data is compiled by government agencies, where the bureaucrats would appear inclined to paint the best possible picture for the governments concerned. Cuban noted this propensity throughout his 1986 study, *Teachers and Machines*. This inclination is particularly apparent in the recent OECD work. Scant mention, for example, is ever made of the age of the computers in use, even if half were so old as to be next to useless. Moreover, there is a marked inclination to use nomenclature and base observations on that data that portray a positive image, but which on closer inspection have little real meaning. For example, in its 2005 study *Are Students Ready for a Technology-rich World?*, the OECD makes the observation:

Access to a computer at home remains comparatively less common than access at school in most countries. (p. 21)

While that is true, a deeper analysis of the term 'access' reveals that all that is being said is if a school had only one computer and the students had access to it at some time in the year, they could be said to have had access. In reality, it is a largely meaningless observation that flies in the face of the data provided in Chapter 11.

The low level of teacher use of PCs in their classrooms impacted in turn on student use, although the organisational arrangements adopted by many schools also impacted. As indicated in Chapter 13, even in the mid to late 1990s when the Internet had added another dimension to PCs, students were fortunate to get over an hour's computer use a week. In the Australian study undertaken by Meredyth et al. in 1998 it was found that:

- 8 per cent of students had spent less than ten minutes using IT per week
- 9 per cent: 10–20 minutes
- 12 per cent: 20–30 minutes
- 15 per cent: 30–40 minutes
- 20 per cent: 40–60 minutes
- 34 per cent: more than an hour (p. 106)

Meredyth et al. reported that:

> The OTA's Teachers and Technology: Making the Connection report (1995, p. 20) found that in the United States schools computers were used about two hours per student per week, and that only 9% of secondary school students report using computers for English class and 3% for social studies class. (p. 13)

Pelgrum, writing as late as 2004, observed:

> In most EU (European Union) countries ICT is not used very frequently by a majority of students at school.

> (Balanskat, Blamire & Kefala, 2006, p. 11)

With the relative drop in price of all personal computers and the increasing availability of PC clones, the numbers did grow but (as indicated) use in the classroom remained low. Exactly why that is so has yet to be fully documented, but in our interviews the following variables have been mentioned.

1 Fundamental change in teaching style required

The personal nature of the computer, particularly in the 1980s and 1990s when there were limited opportunities to share the work with the total class, obliged teachers to adopt—virtually overnight—a fundamentally different mode of teaching, from working with the class to one that was individualised.

Rather than assisting the existing teaching, personal computers obliged the teachers to change their pedagogy to suit the technology. For some who were using a strongly discovery-based or personalised teaching approach the shift was easy, but for the vast majority of teachers the move away from a class-based approach would have been dramatic, and in the eyes of most unwarranted.

Figure 10.6 Primary classroom pod of iMacs of the 2000s (Courtesy Greg Walker)

2 Questionable educational value

Related was the teachers' questioning of the educational value of computers in improving student learning, and whether they were any more effective than books and teaching boards. In brief, teachers did not see first-hand dramatic improvements in student learning, particularly in the core teaching areas—either in their own classes or those of their colleagues. Moreover, there was no overpoweringly conclusive research countering this belief. Indeed, over time the research consistently revealed scant, if any, significance in student performance in the traditional teaching areas (Higgins & Mosely, 2002).

3 Structural and technological limitations

Personal computers, as the name communicates, were designed to be used by individuals and not with classes. Control rests with the user and not the teacher. Peter Sandery, the then principal of Angle Park Computing Centre in the state of South Australia, noted in a paper delivered in 1982 that:

the education market has not been big enough, experienced or united enough to exert pressure on the manufacturer to produce more suitable hardware. The concept of the personal computer simply does not fit in with the teacher-centred approach adopted in most classrooms. (p. 5)

Personal computers have never been renowned for their user-friendliness. In *Being Digital*, Nicholas Negroponte observed in 1996 that:

Personal computers are less able to sense human presence than are modern toilets or outdoor sensors ...

Your inexpensive auto-focus camera has more intelligence about what is in front of it than any terminal or computer system. (p. 127)

We think today solely from the perspective of what would make it easier for a person to use a computer. It may be time to ask what will make it easier to deal with humans. (p. 128)

He rightly bemoaned the continued reliance on the QWERTY keyboard:

For most people, typing is not an ideal interface. If we could speak to our computers, even the most confirmed Luddite would use them more enthusiastically. (p. 137)

As the authors underscored in their research on the acceptance of interactive whiteboards in Chapter 15, teachers need to feel comfortable using the technology. Personal computers, from their introduction onwards, have remained fickle and unreliable, particularly when used by a number of users. The reliability of the early computers, the generation of PC clones and the applications software was notoriously poor. Teachers needed to be mechanics as well as teachers.

While the reliability of both the hardware and software improved in the 1990s, all teachers worldwide undoubtedly experienced the displeasure of having well-prepared lessons ruined by computers that crashed.

4 Finance

The advent of personal computers and the desire to constantly improve the computer-to-student ratio brought to a head the funding of instructional technology in schools.

As mentioned, the traditional school funding model left only a small proportion of the school's recurrent funding for all operational expenses.

The demand for PCs for students—and often teachers—from K–12 was financed from that small proportion of the school budget: either monies raised by parents or supplementary government grants. Where personal computers placed a particular strain on authorities was their short life and the need to find monies for an ever-growing body of supplementary technology, infrastructure, software and bandwidth, as well as maintenance and support. The existing school funding model did not include the facility to find the monies for all of the above.

Although expressed a decade ago, the concerns mentioned earlier by the Wright Professor of Educational Technology at Harvard, Chris Dede, were still of major concern in 2008. The fulfilment of Dede's prediction is neatly encapsulated in the plight of the Central Okanagan school district in Canada that found that, not only could it not afford the desired one-to-one computing, but the vast majority of students already had computers at home. The following headline of 26 May 2008 in the *Vancouver Sun* succinctly described the scene:

District wakes up from laptop dream

Central Okanagan schools save more than $2 million by scaling back program to give each Grade 7-12 student a laptop

(*Vancouver Sun*, 2008)

5 Discrete use

The reliance on computers as discrete instructional tools, as the major instructional tool for all teachers K–12, and for all areas of the curriculum was simply too great an expectation of any piece of instructional technology. While the range and quality of the software available to teachers grew, and while the advent of the Internet finally provided a host of new teaching and learning opportunities, there was only so much teachers could do with PCs.

Chris Dede made another telling observation in 1998, which was still highly applicable in 2008:

> *Classroom computers that are acquired as panaceas end up as doorstops. As discussed later, information technology is a cost-effective investment only in the context of systemic reform. Unless other simultaneous innovations in pedagogy, curriculum, assessment, and school organization are coupled to the usage of instructional technology, the time and effort expended on*

implementing these devices produces few improvements in educational outcomes—and reinforces many educators' cynicism about fads based on magical machines. (p. 2)

6 School organisation

The traditional school organisational structure, and in particular that of the secondary school, also impacted upon and in turn limited the use of the personal computers in the classroom.

As mentioned, schools have invariably been organised around class groups. Teachers at all levels were allocated and expected to teach class groups, not individuals. Teachers thus need instructional technology that can readily be used with class groups.

While the personal computer can be readily used with individuals, it is much more difficult to use with the total class or even large subgroups, particularly without a data-projection facility. Laptop computers went part-way to overcoming this shortfall, but it was not really until the turn of the century that data projectors began to become affordable in large numbers for schools.

Another key variable was the classroom organisation. In the primary school, teachers traditionally teach the one group within the one room. It was thus relatively easy for primary schools to position computers in the teaching room and to create small pods of them as the technology became more affordable. In the secondary school where both the students and teachers move every 40 to 60 minutes, and where there was invariably no one teacher watching over a room, it became that much harder to locate the computers and provide some kind of protection.

Very early in the use of computers, secondary schools opted to create computer labs, initially with a few machines, then one between two users, and in time one per student in the class. In retrospect, it was probably the placement of personal computers in labs that unwittingly had the most to do with limiting the use of the PCs, and also in time limiting class use of the other digital tools.

The placement of virtually all of the computers in the labs had three major effects.

Firstly, and probably most importantly, it meant that the majority of teachers had to rely on the traditional teaching tools available in their classrooms. Even if they wished to use the computers as discrete instructional tools, or in time as a key part of a suite of digital technologies, they could not—except occasionally by taking their class to the lab. When one puts oneself in the position of the maths, language or English teacher preparing their lessons for the week, he or she is naturally going to build them around the tools in the classroom.

Secondly, if the teachers opted to use the computer labs they had to use a highly personalised teaching style. The layout and the size of computer labs with, for example, 30 PCs left little flexibility for other styles of teaching. Thus, teachers had to adopt what was for many a very different and unsatisfactory approach. Compounding the problem was that there were only so many teaching slots available in the lab and invariably (rightly or wrongly) first use was given to the computing classes.

That leads to the third point. The perception grew that computing would be handled by the specialist teachers, in their labs. Why change one's ways when the computing staff were handling the task? It is clear that many schools endeavoured to deploy computers to the classroom but after non use or vandalism they brought them back into the lab, never to deploy scarce resources that way again.

7 Security

Another variable impacting on the use of computers was security, and what some of those interviewed have described as the 'locked cupboard syndrome' of school administrators.

While this issue has impacted on the use of all instructional technology, it was not uncommon in the 1970s, 1980s and 1990s to either have the computers locked away in a barred room, or kept in a storeroom and rolled out and assembled when needed. Most teachers were not prepared to undergo the hassle of setting up and returning those machines.

8 Teacher training

Considerable mention was made of the lack of appropriate, ongoing training programs for teachers, on both the technical and pedagogical elements. In fact, most teachers in this period had received no pre-service computer training.

As mentioned earlier, little money was included in the computer rollouts for teacher training, or even time for teachers to become acquainted with the technology.

9   Leadership and support

The limited teacher training was invariably not helped by a school and education authority leadership lacking in computer know-how and, most importantly, an appreciation of the kind of high-level direction, support, recognition and time required if teachers were to use computers extensively in their classrooms.

In retrospect, school and system leaders probably should have 'listened' more to the reluctance of the vast majority of teachers to embrace computers in their teaching, and not so readily dismissed them, as had been done with earlier technology, as 'Luddites'.

In painting this somewhat bleak picture it is important to note that as with the earlier instructional technology there were undoubtedly thousands of young people inspired by the efforts of the pathfinding computing teachers.

The historical reality is that the mistakes made with the introduction of each of the earlier electronic instructional technologies were perpetuated, albeit in a grander and more expensive way, with the introduction of personal computers. The lessons that should have been learned from the earlier initiatives were not learned—and indeed may not have been learned at the time of writing.

PART II

INTEGRATED INSTRUCTIONAL TECHNOLOGIES

11

THE TECHNOLOGY OF THE HOME

On average, the technology available to the home has always exceeded that available in the classroom. The youth of the day have invariably had far greater access to the current entertainment technology—and its educative impact—at home than they have had at school.

In the last 20-plus years that access, or lack thereof, has had an increasingly profound impact on the education of young people. While the instructional technology and the nature of teaching in most classrooms did not change significantly in that time, there was a dramatic change both in the technology and nature of learning in most homes. From the 1980s onwards there was an ever widening divide between the use made of the digital technology in the classroom and the home that had profound implications for the education of young people in developed societies. By 2007, some governments were beginning to address that development, particularly with the disadvantaged, but the vast majority had still to address the dichotomy.

In considering the use and indeed the educational impact of the various instructional technologies, it is important to remember the point made earlier that all the electronic technologies were designed primarily for the home consumer market and that classroom use was a secondary consideration.

Over the course of the twentieth century the amount of entertainment technology in everyday use in the average home grew both in number and sophistication. By the latter 1990s, teachers and students had and were comfortably using in their homes and daily lives a vast array of entertainment, information and communications technology that invariably exceeded both the amount and quality of that in the classroom.

Gradually over the years teachers had not only acquired most of the 'instructional' technology but had also become comfortable in its use in their own homes.

The other significant development was that from the 1980s onwards the technology in the home gradually began to move from an analogue to a digital form. Where, with the analogue form, each piece of technology operated alone, with the shift to the digital form it became increasingly easy to converge technologies and readily merge and manipulate text, graphics, images, sound and video. The emphasis thus shifted from the single entity—the radio or TV—to a suite of interconnected or what became known as convergent technologies.

The same shift slowly began to happen in the classroom. Where for most of the twentieth century the focus was on the single piece of technology as the magic panacea, by the latter years of the twentieth and the opening years of the twenty-first century the focus in the more prescient situations shifted to the use of a suite of integrated digital technologies. Where initially the spotlight was on the use of the computer as a discrete tool, increasingly it was appreciated by astute teachers and leaders that the educative power of the computer could be markedly enhanced when integrated with other digital technologies.

HISTORY OF THE TECHNOLOGY OF THE HOME

Film was the first great entertainment technology of the twentieth century and while it was some time before the home had the ready facility to create its own films, from the 1910s onwards motion pictures have been a key part of family life across the developed world.

By the 1930s, the wealthy early adopters were beginning to capture home life on 8-mm film. With the advent of Super 8-mm colour film and the development of inexpensive, simple-to-use Super 8-mm cameras by the major camera and lens companies in the 1960s, the way was opened for the average home to capture family life in motion pictures (Wikipedia, 2008k). Granted, the capture was limited to three-minute grabs, but with a little splicing the grand family opus became possible. And while in time the home movie camera would be superseded by the video camera, the footage has nonetheless been able to live on.

Radio was the other great early technology to hit the home. By the 1930s, the mantel radio had come to play a central role in home entertainment.

Throughout the 1940s and 1950s radio was king, and although the advent of television in the 1950s removed its domination, radio in its various forms has continued to play a significant part in the life of the home, particularly in the provision of music, news and sport.

Any who experienced the introduction of television and its halcyon days would appreciate the immense impact that television—initially in black and white and then in colour—had on life in most homes. While the dominance of free-to-air television has waned slightly in recent years, the shift to digital technology and the introduction of various flat-screen technologies have ensured that the television—and, more likely, multiple televisions—retains a central place in home life.

At the same time as television was reshaping home life in the 1950s, the other significant addition to home entertainment was the hi-fi system that packaged the amplifier, stereo speaker system, radio, record player and audio recorder in the one unit. Variously described as radiograms, stereo or high-fidelity systems, those home entertainment units allowed homes to experience quality audio.

As with film and radio, these units have continued to be developed over the last 50 years, have added and dropped off features, spawned small and large versions and reduced markedly in price, and remain an integral part of most homes today.

The 1950s, 1960s and 1970s also witnessed a burgeoning of home photography, with virtually all homes by the 1960s having at least one 35-mm camera and many having 35-mm slide projectors.

In the latter part of the 1970s the home market embraced the ½-inch video cassette recorder. After the initial battle between the Beta and VHS formats, the VHS format emerged victorious and played a significant part in home entertainment well into the 2000s (Wikipedia, 2008h).

Paralleling the work on the home video recorder was the work undertaken in producing portable video recorders and colour video cameras. By the early 1980s, most of the major electronics companies had near broadcast-standard colour video cameras and recorders on the market. While relatively expensive in its early years—like most new technology—this technology soon killed Super 8-mm film and became the norm in most homes. Again, while moving through a series of technological iterations and shifting from analogue to digital mode, the video camera continues to be used in most homes.

The 1970s also saw most homes, particularly those with school-age children, buying electronic calculators. By the 1980s and with the significant drop in the price of the calculators, most members of the household had their own calculator, mostly arithmetic but many with more sophisticated scientific and graphic versions.

While personal computers appeared in the late 1970s and a significant number of households began to dabble with the likes of the Apple IIe, Tandy TRS 80 and the Commodore 64, it was not until well into the 1980s—and the growing sophistication of personal computers, the release of the Apple Mac and graphical interfaces, and the burgeoning of the computer games technology—that the sale of computers in the home became common. It is easy to forget the immense popularity of the early personal computers and the kind of take cited by White (2005) in Chapter 10.

Ironically, it was the rapidly expanding games market, particularly among the youth, that assisted the sales of computers in the home and indeed the specifications and power of many of the machines sold. In brief, young males wanted computers with the power, graphics and sound capability to play the burgeoning games on offer. Bear in mind Atari's very basic Pong was released in 1975, but it was not until 1985 that Nintendo's Entertainment System appeared, with Sony releasing its initial Play Station in the mid 1990s, and Microsoft launching its xBox in 2001 (Wikipedia, 2008l).

While the vast games industry did not impact directly on the school curriculum, there is little doubt that the technological skills and confidence gained by the young people in playing the various computer games on a range of technology made them highly adept with all manner of digital technology (Gee, 2007; Prensky, 2006).

The next big boost to home computer sales came with the development of the World Wide Web (WWW) in 1994, the hype surrounding the creation of the information superhighway, the release of free web browsers and the popularisation of email. At the same time the main applications software for the computers—be it for word processing, presentations, electronic communication or spreadsheets—became that much more user-friendly and reliable, and could readily be used by all members of the home.

By the mid 1990s, across the developed world about 35 per cent of homes had a personal computer, but in homes with school-age children that percentage rose to around the 50–60 per cent mark. Not surprisingly, the latter percentage was far greater in the more affluent homes (OECD, 2005, p. 18; Dutton, 2007, p. 70; ACMA, 2007). While the level of uptake varied between developed nations—a variation that in some respects might be a reflection of the different statistical gathering techniques and categories used—the point remains that in general terms every second family home had a PC. (Of note, that figure is increased if one opts to include the various types of computer game technologies.)

Remember, this is at a time (as indicated in Chapter 10) when schools in general terms averaged two computers per class or per 30 students. In reality, without a facility like a data projector or an interactive whiteboard, even the best of teachers could only do so much.

In the mid 1990s, home Internet use was largely limited to the early adopters, the better educated and more affluent. The figures universally were low, well under 10 per cent of all families.

By 1996, the average power of the personal computer in the home exceeded that in business for the first time, according to the confidential market research undertaken by the international consultancy group IDC— and (sighted by the author) helped no doubt by the need to cater for the latest computer games. Vitally, it became increasingly more apparent that parents believed having a computer in the home would improve their children's education. The aforementioned IDC market research sighted by the author corroborated this view, prompting the writing of an article for *The Practising Administrator* in 1996 on the educative power of the home technology (Lee, 1996).

In 2007, the study by the Australian Communications and Media Authority (ACMA) reconfirmed the parents' views on the importance of having the digital technology in the home:

Almost all parents see the Internet as beneficial to their children ... (p. 10)

Besides the developments with computers came a pronounced enhancement in telecommunications. Homes in the later 1990s were able to secure broadband access and benefit from a rapidly developing mobile phone industry. By the mid 1990s, most young people in the developed nations had not only ready access in their homes to all of the instructional technology that had over time been used to revolutionise teaching, but also access to the rapidly developing digital information and communications technology.

One is thus looking at what Don Tapscott (1998) has called the 'Net Generation' of young people who found it natural to use all manner of technology and who expected their schools to use the same kind of technology in their everyday teaching.

In 1999, a study of the use of ICT in Australia funded by the federal government, entitled *Real Time*, identified in the survey sample of teachers' homes the forms of technology listed in Table 11.1.

Table 11.1 Forms of technology in the home, 1999

Television	98%
Radio	97%
CD or cassette player	96%
Calculator	94%
Computer	82%
Video player	78%
Printer	75%
Mobile phone	53%
Modem	41%
Video camera	21%
SEGA or Nintendo game	21%
Fax	20%
Scanner	11%

Since that survey, the range of technology in the home has continued to expand, grow in sophistication and allow even greater integration of the digital technologies. In 2008, virtually all students not only had their own computer at home (increasingly with broadband access), they were also likely to have use of a flat screen TV, a CD and DVD recorder, a sound system, digital camera, an MP3 or MP4 digital player, a USB drive, multifunction phone (also with digital camera), digital games machine and a plethora of applications software. Most importantly, they were using that technology in much of their free time, be it listening to their iPod, texting their mates, using the chat facility, creating their own podcasts, inhabiting Second Life or preparing multimedia presentations for YouTube.

A comprehensive study by ACMA released in December 2007 found the average Australian family household had the following:

- *three mobile phones*
- *three televisions*
- *two computers*
- *two DVD players*

- *two portable MP3/MP4 players*
- *one VCR*
- *two games consoles.*

(ACMA, 2007, p. 49)

Those findings were comparable to the findings of the research commissioned by the US National School Boards Association on teens' use of the Internet. In releasing its research in August 2007, it reported:

… that 96 percent of students with online access use social networking technologies, such as chatting, text messaging, blogging, and visiting online communities such as Facebook, MySpace, and Webkinz. Further, students report that one of the most common topics of conversation on the social networking scene is education.

Nearly 60 percent of online students report discussing education-related topics such as college or college planning, learning outside of school, and careers. And 50 percent of online students say they talk specifically about schoolwork.

'There is no doubt that these online teen hangouts are having a huge influence on how kids today are creatively thinking and behaving,' said Anne L. Bryant, executive director of the National School Boards Association. 'The challenge for school boards and educators is that they have to keep pace with how students are using these tools in positive ways and consider how they might incorporate this technology into the school setting.'

Students report they are engaging in highly creative activities on social networking Internet sites including writing, art, and contributing to collaborative online projects whether or not these activities are related to schoolwork. Almost half of students (49 percent) say that they have uploaded pictures they have made or photos they have taken, and more than one in five students (22 percent) report that they have uploaded video they have created.

Today, students report that they are spending almost as much time using social networking services and Web sites as they spend watching television. Among teens who use social networking sites, that amounts to about 9 hours a week online, compared to 10 hours a week watching television.

(NSBA, 2007)

The technology included in the studies is that of mid 2007. By the time you are reading this observation, the range is likely to have expanded and indeed certain items become dated. When one considers that in 2005 few young people were using the likes of Facebook and yet in 2007 most were, one can begin to appreciate the rate of change.

In considering the level and nature of the digital technology in the home it is important to note the historic trend lines, the ever-upward and escalating rate of development and use, and what is likely to be the norm two or three years hence.

In addition to the aforementioned extensive array of hardware in the homes there is also the vast and ever-growing body of software that young people are using in their homes—a plethora of complex computer games, applications, music- and video-creation software and social networking facilities, to name but a few.

It is important to note that since the release of Netscape in 1995 free of any charge, there has been an expanding range of web-based facilities that are made available free of charge where the provider aims to make the money from advertising or is simply making available a public service. In addition to all the web browsers and search engines, virtually all the Web 2.0 applications available in 2008 could be used without cost.

A quick look at the 2007 OECD figures for home Internet use (OECD, 2008) reveals how dramatic the uptake of this facility has been across the developed world over the last five years. To give but a few examples, between 2003 and 2006 Korea's usage rose from 69 to 92 per cent, the Netherlands from 60 to 79 per cent, and Portugal from 20 to 35 per cent. By 2008, the vast majority of homes with school-age children in the developed world had reached the point where the children had their own computer and Internet account.

It is worth noting that while we have spoken of the technology being 'in the home', the reality is that by the mid 2000s much of it was mobile and could be used virtually everywhere. Increasingly young people had the technology to access the Web wherever they had network access, be it in their loungeroom, their bedroom, the train or indeed the school playground.

Of note is that a study by the telecommunications company AAPT conducted in Australia in early 2007 found eight out of ten Australians own a mobile phone. Significantly, 75 per cent have some type of Internet connection. Within the 16–34 age group, 80 per cent keep their mobile or cell phone on 24 hours a day and on average spend 2.4 hours each day on the Internet (AAPT, 2007). In New Zealand in 2006, 90.6 per cent of 15–24 year-olds had a mobile phone (Statistics New Zealand, 2007). Comparable or even higher rates of mobile phone use among the youth were to be found across the developed world.

In painting this picture of extensive and growing use of an array of digital technologies by young people it is important to note the proportion of households where they did not have access to the technology and where their learning was likely to have been disadvantaged. It is an important issue that, as will be seen below, is being addressed by some of the pathfinding national governments.

What the figures mentioned thus far do not identify are those cohorts within some nations that are making appreciably lower use of the technology than the rest of the population. This kind of situation was, for example, noted in New Zealand (Williamson, 2006) and Canada (Looker & Thiessen, 2003) with the indigenous cohorts.

To what extent one left the market forces or a social intervention policy to address the issue was a moot point. While the issue of a 'digital divide' within and between population cohorts warrants its own publication, Don Tapscott's discussion in *Growing Up Digital* (1998, ch. 12) is a very good start.

STUDENT LEARNING IN THE HOME

By the early 1990s, it was apparent to many that the young people's everyday use of technology in the home was having a significant impact on their learning and indeed their education. By the mid 1990s, it was clearly evident that the educative power of the digital technology within the home and the young people's embracement of it were having a pronounced influence on the nature of their learning and the competencies they were developing.

In 1998, Tapscott succinctly identified those developments (ibid.), and in turn put the challenge to educators to both recognise and take on board the education occurring within the home. Research vindicating those observations began to appear around the same time. Studies by Meredyth et al. (1998) and Prensky (2006) were but two that identified the impact of the technology on learning. The study undertaken by Meredyth and her team for the Australian federal government, for example, concluded that:

students tend to acquire their advanced information technology skills at home rather than at school. [In 1998] eighty-five per cent of students use computers outside schools ... There is a significant link between students' information technology skills, confidence and enjoyment, their use of computers outside school, the level of resources in their home and their personal ownership of resources ... Students who do not use a computer outside school had relatively poor attainment of information technology skills ...'

(ibid., p. xxviii)

These kinds of findings reinforced Tapscott's 1998 observation that for the first time in human history the young had an understanding of technology that surpassed that of most of their teachers. They were moreover acquiring and enhancing that knowledge and those skills in a very different manner to the way in which they were being taught in the schools. In 2000, Mal Lee wrote in an article entitled 'Chaotic learning: The learning style of the "Net Generation"' of the learning style favoured by young people, particularly in their homes, their preference for experiential or constructivist learning, emphasis on play, collegial support, multi-tasking and networking—often online. Young people, like most working online, were prepared to learn by jumping on and off task, opening a new door, checking out the new situation and returning to the original task. The approach was in marked contrast to the highly linear model favoured by most schools.

The young chart their own courses. Each sets his/her own goals. No teacher determines what they learn.

(Lee, 2000, p. 61)

That concept was elaborated on by Oblinger and Oblinger in their excellent 2006 online publication, *Educating the Net Generation*. Since then that approach to learning has continued to grow, clearly helped by the students' daily use of an ever-increasing range of digital and networked technology.

The reality is that most students in 2008 not only had better technology and online access in their homes, they also had many more hours to spend using that technology than they did in the classroom—the combination of home-based and mobile technology allows them to use it 24 hours a day, 365 days a year. In contrast, they can only use the digital technology in the school for, at most, 201 days a year—around six hours a day. While studies of student use of computers in schools were finding that students were lucky to use them two hours a week, at home they were spending two to three hours each day on their computers (ACMA, 2007; NSBA, 2007).

In 1996, Mal Lee wrote of the need for schools to appreciate the kind of learning happening outside the classroom and in the home.

> *Rather than seeking to replicate the resources of the home is it not time to consider developing models that marry the technological needs and resources of the home with those of the schools.*

> (Lee, 1996)

However, it has only been since the mid 2000s that a few schools and educational authorities are starting to recognise the networked, chaotic learning of the young, to rethink their education and to overcome the home–school dichotomy. In 2007, the UK and Singapore governments launched programs that recognised the educative power of the home and sought to ensure all the young, the rich and the poor had at least computer and Internet access in their homes. The UK, for example, in the 2007–08 financial year allocated £60 million for its Computers for Pupils and its Home Access Project programs.

The aims of the Computers for Pupils program was:

> *… at helping some of the most disadvantaged secondary school children improve their education and life skills by putting a computer into the home. It aims to:*

> * *give these pupils the same opportunities as their peers*
> * *provide the conditions that can contribute towards raising educational achievement, narrowing the attainment gap and supporting progress towards these pupils' targets*
> * *support the personalising of learning by providing access to ICT whenever or wherever is most appropriate for learning*
> * *encourage the development of ICT skills appropriate to the 21st century for the pupils and their families.*

> *Giving children access to computers at home has been shown to help their education—children that do not have access can be disadvantaged. Putting computers into the home can motivate pupils to learn, help develop key ICT and life skills and give them the same opportunities and experiences as their peers.*

> (UK Treasury Briefing Paper, 2007)

This approach—which was but an extension of the thinking in the UK's national department of education's guiding policy paper of 2005, *Harnessing Technology: Transforming learning and children's services*—is in marked contrast to the norm adopted by most schools and education authorities in the developed world. As discussed in Chapter 13, most (we suspect) still are of the view that the only 'real' learning occurs in the classroom and that all the other student activities are mere play.

A 2007 think-tank conducted by the Illinois Institute of Design (ID) on digital schools (which included such international luminaries as Charles Handy and Gary Hamel) concluded:

> *The learning experiences of kids outside school are increasingly more relevant to modern life than what is learned inside school ... Kids are increasingly motivated by what they learn in out of school programs and in their virtual online lives, and a mechanism for capturing and enabling them must be found.*

> (ID, 2007, p. 24)

The reality—as mentioned at the outset—is that homes have always had more and better technology than the schools, and that in the last ten to fifteen years young people have embraced the learning opportunities that the digital technology has offered and are using it to enhance their education, regardless of what is laid down by the schools.

What the UK and Singapore type of initiative reinforces is that any school or education authority wishing to make best educational use of the digital instructional technology available in the twenty-first century needs to adopt a holistic model that not only recognises the learning happening within the homes, but also marries that learning with what is happening in the school.

CHAPTER 12

THE ROLE OF THE SCHOOL LIBRARY

In many respects school libraries have been pivotal in the use of instructional technology in teaching and learning for the past 50 years. As repositories for much of the instructional technology, the hardware and the associated teaching resources, school libraries have played and continue to play a central and often leading role in the use of the technology.

That role has generally continued to expand both in scope, size and nature, but at times the centrality of the role and even the existence of the school library and school librarian has been challenged.

Allied to the custodial role has been the leadership shown by the school librarians or, as is the case in most developed nations, the teacher-librarians. Since the 1970s, and the move for school libraries to become what were variously described as media, resource or instructional learning centres—situations that managed the books and the various instructional technologies—one finds teacher-librarians playing a central role in promoting and supporting the school-wide teacher and student use of the instructional technology (Kennan, Willard & Wilson, 2006; Herring, 2007).

Indeed, it was apparent that teacher-librarians with their whole-school, macro perspective and everyday association with the latest hardware and 'software' were the part of the teaching profession most attuned to the educational possibilities and indeed shortcomings of the various instructional technologies. While there were a sizeable number of teacher-librarians that did not provide that leadership and preferred to stay with their books, it was the authors' experience, the experience of those interviewed and that of the case studies detailed in Chapter 17 that as a group the school librarians have played a central role in the use of the instructional technology in those schools that have achieved—and have been able to sustain—total teacher use of that technology.

Moreover, those teacher-librarians have been able to play that role largely because of their facility to adjust their role to cater for the changing circumstances. Larry Cuban (1993) speaks of constancy and change in classroom teaching over the last century. The leading teacher-librarians— probably more than any other group of teachers—have had the least constancy, having to vary their role significantly over the past 30 years, not only to meet the needs of their clients, but also to remain relevant and viable. They are the ones that had to move first from a predominantly book-based operation to one that is increasingly digital and networked. They had also to provide the lead in the development of school information services, often while contending with a school leadership largely unaware of the needs of a digital school.

Significantly, in those schools that had achieved total teacher use of instructional technology and had become digital schools, the role played by the teacher-librarian was even more central, but at the same time the entity called a 'library' was being diffused and its work undertaken by many in a wider information services operation.

What role teacher-librarians, or more pertinently the information professionals, will play in future years is uncertain. Suffice it to say that with the moves for schools to become increasingly digital, the need for them to support and manage an ever-growing body of information will intensify. One could hypothesise that an effective and appropriate 'school library'—or perhaps more correctly an effective and appropriate school information services and information management facility—will be crucial to the total teacher use of instructional technology.

PRE-1960s

Prior to the 1960s, few schools had libraries of any sort. Certainly the dedicated library space with resources organised on shelves and staff to help access those resources was up until that time confined to larger corporations and civic administrations. Even into the early 1960s, the concept of a dedicated library was not universal. Specific training for teacher-librarians and library technicians began in the late 1950s and only then was there anything like a concerted push to provide school libraries. Most schools were lucky to have a bookroom.

THE 1960s AND 1970s

That situation began to change dramatically in the late 1950s, the 1960s and in particular in the 1970s. New schools were built with libraries and many of the older schools had libraries added. In the US in particular there were growing calls—allied in part to the faith placed in technology to lift the nation—to make greater use of all types of instructional technology and to create libraries or media centres for that technology.

One thus saw significant changes in the nature of many of the school libraries and the role of the teacher-librarian in the latter 1960s and 1970s, with most taking on the responsibility for much of the school's instructional technology. That change saw the library begin to:

- take control of the instructional technology
- manage the lending of much of that technology
- maintain the hardware
- assume responsibility for the 'software'—the teaching resources, films, slides, audio tapes and the new audiovisual (A/V) kits—for their procurement, accessioning, storage and loan
- handle the recording and storage of the radio and television broadcasts
- manage the student use of the technology in the library, which in turn saw the creation of special viewing rooms and the introduction of powered carrels.

Most importantly, the library staff came to play a fuller role, particularly as schools engaged library A/V officers, in the professional development of teachers in the use of that technology and alerting teachers to the new teaching resources.

The 1970s saw the school libraries move increasingly to the centre of school operations, both metaphorically and literally. Many developed nations made concerted moves to ensure that all schools had a quality library with state-of-the-art technology. In Australia in the 1970s, the federal government's library grants initiative ensured that all schools—primary and secondary—had a quality library that met the national standards. In an interview with one of the federal architects of that program it was evident that the initiative not only cemented the central role of the library, it also provided the imprimatur and funding for school libraries to strengthen their role in the provision and use of instructional technology. A similar strengthening of the role of the school library was evidenced across the developed world, with some schools creating their own instructional design departments.

Allied to the development of the school library was the emergence of graduate and postgraduate teacher-librarian programs that impacted on the leadership and professionalism of the library staff. Those tertiary programs were in marked contrast with the short catalogue and book-covering training sessions run previously. One of our interviews was with a former teacher-librarian whose initial teacher training in the early 1970s was a two-week in-service on the Dewey system.

THE 1980s—GROWING TENSIONS

The role of the school library as the custodian of the instructional technology came under question, at least in part, in the 1980s—and indeed in many schools well into the 2000s.

The 1980s saw the first regular use of personal computers within schools. Within a short time school libraries were beginning to adapt this new technology to help with the labour-intensive tasks they faced every day. Cataloguing or lending packages were written, quite often by amateurs, to help in this work and the early, rather basic computers were put to work. There were schools whose libraries operated—quite effectively, too—on the power of Commodore 32s and Apple IIe computers. Printing was also offered from the library if there were students lucky enough to have a computer at home.

With personal computing came a new curriculum subject, variously called 'computing studies' or 'information technology' (IT). The new subject and its supporters—teachers that came from all areas of the wider curriculum—began to compete for the control of the use of at least some of the instructional technology, the computing hardware and software. The growing IT or computing 'empires' with their laboratories sought to control the acquisition of all the school's digital technology.

THE 1990s AND LIBRARY AUTOMATION

By the 1990s, often aided by education authority decisions, the control of 'computing' and computing purchases was invariably taken over by the computing faculty. Ironically, at much the same time, libraries became the first part of the school to be networked, largely due to the introduction of library automation systems. Overnight, library staff became instant experts in computer networking, backup, file sharing, basic maintenance and system issues—much to the consternation of the new 'computer' departments. Tension between these two areas was not uncommon well into the new millennium.

The automation of the school library systems stimulated another significant change in the role of the library and its staff; it took them into the digital world. Like so many other technologies in a school setting, this move was not initiated by schools but rather by commercial vendors. Despite the limited usefulness of the first designs, most school libraries quickly embraced automation. In the US where much of the software was developed, two companies offered automation as early as 1968. By 1980 there were thirteen significant companies involved, and by 1985 there were 35 (Breeding, 2007).

Take-up figures for the US lagged a little behind those for Australia where in 1993, 43.2 per cent of schools had automated libraries. By 1995, this figure was 69.7 per cent (Dillon, 1997, p. 6), while by 2000 few libraries of any significant size did not have an automated system. For comparison, in 1995, 38.5 per cent of New Zealand schools were automated (ibid., p. 32). In essence, automation grew 'like Topsy' following the early introduction of that technology at the start of the 1980s (ibid., p. 1). But its growth placed a heavy burden on the staffs of libraries across the nation. There were a host of new considerations for staff: What system? What platform? What support? How much? and so on. Many of these issues were being addressed in the library some time before they appeared as issues on the wider school scene.

While automation may be viewed as a library matter, and only a library matter, the change had far wider ramifications. The nature of automation requiring, as it did, a set of networked computers, common printer and significant daily support catapulted most library staff into a new technical environment. While their concerns in the 1990s focused on network support, computer access and the new Internet access issues, most classroom teachers were still relying heavily on existing blackboard/whiteboard technology and were only then beginning to see potentials for some computer access for their students. Also, there were skills being developed as a result of automation that would spread through each school and provide considerable support as teachers became more involved in technology themselves.

Most teacher-librarians soon became the network 'gurus'. They understood Novell! They could solve many of the problems that became more common as computers spread through classrooms or printers were joined to networks.

This new expertise catapulted a number of the senior library staff in the mid to latter 1990s into the role of whole-school information managers and directors of information services. They soon recognised the importance of schools adopting a holistic approach towards the use of the rapidly evolving digital technology and most importantly the use and management of the ever-burgeoning digital information that technology made available.

The 1990s thus saw school libraries having to manage the books, oversee the A/V holdings, attune their operations to the networked world, while having to work with ever-stronger computing or IT empires.

As mentioned earlier, tensions between the librarians (in the main female) and the IT staff (in the main male) were often strained. Those tensions were amplified when IT was given faculty status and another male executive position created. The strain between the two groups was probably greatest when it came to deciding who should provide the ever-growing school-wide ICT support.

Those tensions were not helped by 'ICT illiterate' school and education authority leaders, unable to conceptualise a holistic model that meshed all the ICT-related operations. Indeed, in the mid 1990s one saw calls and moves across the developed world to do away with school libraries, to dispense with teacher-librarians and to let the computer handle all the school's information services. With the global information village at the end of every computer, who needed dedicated information staff and a dedicated information location? Conferences across the globe saw considerable debate on whether an 'intermediary' was necessary or not. Where conference programs in 1995–96 saw papers advocating 'direct access', by 2000 'intermediaries' were again on the agenda. This shift is to be found, for example, in the agendas of the UK Online Information Meetings for 1996, 1999 and 2001 (Raitt & Jeapes, 1995; Raitt & Jeapes, 1996; Raitt, 1999). Active intermediaries provided the necessary catalyst for change, bringing new networking organisation and strong moves towards convergent instructional technologies.

With development of the Internet it was often the existing library 'networks' that were the first to connect to the outer world. For a time this new development was seen as a real threat to the morals and wellbeing of students. Again, it was almost a foregone conclusion that it was the librarian who was expected to know the legal issues surrounding the use of the Internet and who would be instrumental in formulating the Acceptable Use Policies (AUPs) that were such a feature of the first ten years or so of the Internet in schools.

It was also the librarian who invariably first perceived the need to teach the students how best to use the networked world in their learning. Information literacy programs emerged across the developed world. This development in turn led to library staff in the latter 1990s and 2000s playing a fuller teaching role and libraries being equipped with the latest digital instructional technology.

THE 2000s AND DIGITAL TAKE-OFF

In the 2000s, in those schools making extensive use of ICT and in particular those that had achieved total teacher use of ICT and digital take-off (see Chapter 17), the role of the school library and the library staff became increasingly more central and yet at the same time increasingly challenged in the use of instructional technology.

The continuing surge in the sophistication and use of ICT across the total school, in the administration, school communication and the educational program generated an ever-increasing demand on the school, and usually the library had to provide the requisite digital information services and, most importantly, also had to manage the information. The advent of school websites, intranets, learning platforms, student portals, high-speed Internet access, in-house and hosted databases, sophisticated digital administration and communications systems and digital integration—to name but a few—combined to generate a plethora of data in the school that had to be managed.

By the 2000s, virtually all school libraries housed an extensive array of digital technology for student and staff use.

The library staff was expected to provide the requisite leadership, support and information management. Moreover, the staff was expected to provide the expertise and the leadership in the growing number of legal and political issues associated with the use of digital information such as user acceptance policies, censorship or the increasingly complex world of digital copyright.

These demands were amplified in those schools that succeeded in getting all teachers to use the digital technology in their teaching.

As Lee and Boyle (2003) noted in their study of the impact of IWBs on Richardson Primary, suddenly every classroom became a 'state-of-the-art' library. In the likes of Richardson, classroom teachers in addition to the librarian took on the responsibility for developing the students'

Figure 12.1 Contemporary Australian primary school library with digital technologies (Courtesy Greg Walker)

information literacy. Teacher-librarians had thus to contend with the aforementioned demands as well as to operate in a learning environment where the students and the teachers did not have to come to a location called the library or resource centre, and where the classroom teachers were taking on board some of the roles traditionally played by only the library.

The emergence of Google as the ubiquitous search engine in the 2000s placed even greater pressure on the library and its offerings. Teachers and students in the classrooms with networked IWBs soon opted to use Google, rightly or wrongly, to search for information rather than using the place called a library or even the school's online library system. Why use a school or even education authority library system, with its inevitable constraints, when they could go directly to Google?

By the mid 2000s, Google and IWBs combined to seriously challenge the place of the school library

The irony was that the same IWBs and their facility to be used as the centrepiece of a digital teaching hub markedly increased the need for tailored information services and a high-quality information management. As Lee (2006) indicates in his article, 'Managing the school's digital teaching resources and assets', the school-wide use of IWBs—and their facility to readily create high-quality, interactive multimedia teaching materials and propensity to promote the collaborative development of digital teaching resources—obliged schools to markedly improve their procedures for the storage and retrieval of those increasingly large and multifaceted files.

It was no longer good enough to use the 'laissez faire' arrangements of the past where the materials were variously stored on C-drives, the system hard drives or the teacher's own thumb drive or CD-ROM. Schools needed a smart system for categorising, storing, retrieving, and in time culling the teaching materials.

The pressure on the school librarians to constantly attune their role to the ever changing circumstances was intense and, if anything, increasing.

What role the school library plays in the future use of instructional technology is debatable, but what was apparent in 2008 was that schools had to have both the personnel and the systems to ensure that the requisite information services and information management were provided.

It is noteworthy that all the case studies in Chapter 17 have the library and the teacher-librarian playing a key role in the school achieving and sustaining the total teacher usage of the digital instructional technology. It is appreciated that it is unwise to extrapolate from only five case studies, or indeed to add to that lot the eight international case studies undertaken by the authors in 2005 (Lee & Winzenried, 2005), but it would appear that if schools are to achieve and, most importantly, sustain the total teacher use of digital instructional technology, they will need an appropriately supportive 'school library' and library staff.

OUTCOMES

The net result of the changes in the 1990s and 2000s in particular was something of a revolution in library management, as well as in the ways libraries were used in schools. Rather than the repository for slightly out-of-date print materials, twenty-first century school libraries were viewed by their schools as gateways. Technology in the library meant that learners of all ages went there for a variety of materials, including all the 'older' style print ones, as a doorway rather than a stockpile.

One government comment here is worth noting:

> All Navigator schools [a Victorian initiative to 'modernise' schooling in the 1990s] have found that the role of the library has been refocused and become more important. The ability of the librarian to manage, organise and coordinate access to this information has become central to the core curriculum functions of the school and pivotal to the successful implementation of a technology plan.

(DoE, 1998, p. 11)

In many schools the library has reached out into the classroom, adapting intranet technology to offer their services in classrooms and even in students' homes. From being a defined physical entity, modern libraries have embraced the technology to offer more of the on-time-information aspects that our modern technology is so adept at providing.

Peake (1996, p. 4) refers to these changes as a 'quiet revolution'. From a beginning in the 1960s when the computer technology generally revolved around punched cards and their mechanical sorting machines and mainframe computers with less power than even the smallest PCs of today, libraries have embraced the technology. Quite significantly for schools, much of the quiet revolution occurred on the wild frontier of the library. More often than not it was the librarian who was first to say, 'What about trying...?' or 'Have you seen how ... works?'

Further, the trend towards convergence, which was gathering speed by 2008, is gradually settling the peace between the empires of library and IT. As learning technologies converge, the need for an intermediary remains, but that role is increasingly important at the 'coalface' right alongside the classroom teacher.

CHAPTER **13**

NETWORKED TEACHING AND THE INFORMATION SUPERHIGHWAY

The networked world has offered teachers and students immense and previously unimagined educational opportunities for over a decade. The metaphor, the 'information superhighway', neatly encapsulates the potential of the facility as an instructional technology.

Unfortunately, while its potential has been apparent to the prescient since the 1980s and to society as a whole since the creation of the Web in the 1990s, most classroom teachers did not have the wherewithal to begin using it in their classrooms until the mid 2000s.

The gap between the rhetoric and the reality in most schools was pronounced, and it took near on a decade of concerted effort and the convergence of a number of technological developments before most teachers could begin to embrace networked teaching. In 2008, even in the more developed nations there was a significant proportion of teaching rooms that did not have the facilities or opportunity to access that world. While the aforementioned proactive nations like the UK and Singapore have networked virtually all the teaching rooms, other developed nations were well behind.

It is now abundantly clear that unless teachers have the instructional technology in their classroom they will either not use it or will use it only occasionally. This has been equally true of the networked world.

The challenge of using that world was not merely constrained by the technologies. Probably an even greater challenge has been of a human nature—getting the school and education authority leaders to attune their thinking to allow teachers and students appropriate access to and use of the online world. In 2008, the signs in many parts of the developed world were that those in charge were imposing ever-more constraints on the students' and indeed teachers' use of the networked world at school. In 1995, Louis Gerstner, the then Chairman and CEO of IBM, suggested the reason why there was so little use made of technology in schools, in contrast to industry and the home:

> ... is that because schools are regulated bureaucracies, they are not organised in ways that lead them into the introduction of technologies. They are like eighteenth-century farms, not even ready to dream about the agricultural revolution that would sweep the world into the nineteenth and twentieth centuries.
>
> (Gerstner et al., 1995, p. 35)

At the time of writing there was ample testimony throughout the educational bureaucracies of the developed world that Gerstner may well be right, and not only are many of those bureaucracies unable to dream of a world of networked learning communities, they are unable to translate that dream into reality.

As Lee and Gaffney (2008), Balanskat, Blamire and Kefala (2006) and each of Becta's recent annual reviews (Becta, 2006, 2007) attest, the development of successful networked teaching and the harnessing of the online world require educational leaders to simultaneously articulate the desired vision as well as successfully addressing a suite of increasingly challenging human and technological variables.

After nearly a quarter of a century's experience with the networked world, there were in 2008 a substantial number of education authorities—maybe even the majority—that neither had a vision nor had provided the requisite leadership and infrastructure, and which were markedly constraining the efforts by teachers and students to use the networked world.

Gerstner's concern about the bureaucracy is also to be evidenced in even the more efficient and prescient school authorities. The development, financing and implementation of public policy take time—two years from conception to implementation is not that common for even the best of the authorities.

As will become apparent there has been, particularly since the mid 1990s, an escalating rate of development with the online world that few educational authorities have been able to accommodate, let alone get on top of. The phenomenon of social networks, for example, emerged from embryo to global acceptance within a two- to three-year period—a pace even the more efficient educational bureaucracies took time to accommodate, leaving the schools once again well behind the far more nimble-footed homes.

A related development, that both the schools and education authorities also found challenging, was the escalating integration of the various digital and networked technologies and the organisational implications of these developments, both within the schools and the education authorities.

While the authors have chosen to explore in brief the major networked teaching opportunities separately, the reality is that increasingly the opportunities are being integrated, with each providing ready access to a suite of other technologies and solutions. That type of integration would appear to be particularly challenging for the bureaucrats invariably operating in their discrete operational areas and many having limited appreciation of the ever-changing ways of the networked world.

While still early days, the authors in 2008 perceived, as mentioned, a growing divide between those governments and education authorities that had a vision for the networked world for some time and have sought to harness the online with well-reasoned programs, and those authorities lacking a vision and reacting to every development. The manifestation of that development begins to be seen from the early 1990s, but becomes particularly pronounced in the efforts made from the early 2000s onwards to take advantage of the networked teaching opportunities.

THE ORIGINS

The origins of networking in schools are to be found in the basic desire to link the newly acquired PCs to their peripherals and other computers within the school, and increasingly to assist the educational bureaucracies in the administration of their schools.

THE 1980s

Networked teaching for most teachers was simply an ideal of the more prescient at this stage. Sadly it was also a time of considerable waste and lost opportunities, not helped by the lack of leadership and vision within most education authorities. Invariably it was the school administrator and the educational bureaucrats who took advantage of the emerging facility to network computers, deciding it was more important to spend the scarce resources on administration and accounting systems than on improving teaching and learning. Throughout the 1980s one thus saw the 'front office' of the school invariably provided with the first networked computers.

In most schools and education authorities the administration systems in the 1980s, 1990s and even in the 2000s were physically separated from the educational or student networks, and it was not until the 2000s in many schools that the administration prepared to move to the one integrated system.

Educationally, the major moves in the 1980s were directed towards connecting the new computers to a range of peripherals. For cost reasons alone, it made sense to connect several computers to one printer. For the same reason, it was inevitable that the involved teacher would elect to provide the necessary cables and then make the connections themselves. The same early adopters who introduced the computers also took on the task of networking those machines. Coaxial cable became a common feature of some rooms—especially the library—and individual members of staff became the 'experts' in connecting the machines together.

From the first printer connections there soon developed connections to CD drives and the first multimedia teaching materials. Teachers could now 'share' Microsoft's digital multimedia encyclopaedia, *Encarta*, or other similar materials across a number of users.

By the latter 1980s networked CD towers began to appear in the more affluent schools. They offered students and teachers a choice of multimedia titles, but for the most part there were very real practical limitations in multiple user situations. The students could only choose a CD not in use and there were major limitations on how classes could use the new media.

As the number of users and the number of peripherals grew, so too did the need for intelligent networks. The need for simultaneous access to specific data, the need to provide backup during—not after—a user session, and similar needs saw the development of key international operational protocols. Among the earliest of these that received wide acceptance were Novell (1981), TCP/IP (1983) and Appletalk (1984) (Wikipedia, 2008m). The same needs were eventually to drive Microsoft into network and server versions of its interface software.

In retrospect, the 1980s also saw a significant amount of money largely wasted on the networking of schools by well-meaning teachers with a modicum of expertise. Many was the school that installed an amateur non-standard network 'on the cheap' with the aid of a well-intentioned parent or teacher—networks that invariably had to be replaced professionally in the 1990s.

This development (as indicated later in Chapter 19) was not helped by the lack of astute leadership, direction setting and support within most education authorities, and the move to school-based management (SBM). While under SBM the larger schools might have had the expertise and the funds to install the appropriate high-speed coaxial cable, many middle- and smaller-sized schools had to make do.

In 1982, in a paper that did receive some consideration at the national level in Australia, the then principal of Angle Park Computing Centre in South Australia, Peter Sandery, put forward the following challenge:

> Do we continue with educational computing on a 'cottage industry' basis or does Australia have the foresight to recognise the educational potential of the computer and to develop that potential in a planned manner nationally?

> (Sandery, 1982, p. 13)

Sandery then observed:

> The time is fast running out for a decision to be made in a time frame that will not involve the cost of overcoming the problems of increasing non-standardisation. (p. 13)

Sadly this kind of challenge was not taken up by most education authorities in the 1980s, and only a few even in the 1990s made concerted national moves of the type suggested by Sandery.

THE 1990s

The 1990s saw the building of the infrastructure and the laying of the foundations that schools and many classroom teachers were finally able to build upon in a regular way in the 2000s. In retrospect, many of the developments in this period were more about getting in place the infrastructure—rather affectionately known as the 'plumbing'—than on providing any new instructional technology.

From a teaching perspective, the first significant move involved the automation of the school library collections.

The second vital development was the creation of the World Wide Web (WWW) and the release of the Mosaic and Netscape web browsers that allowed everyone who wished to use the WWW.

For schools, the next major development was in telecommunications and the beginning of the work to provide high-speed bandwidth connectivity to each school's network, and in turn Internet access in each teaching room. Allied to that development was the little publicised backroom work done in deciding on the international standards and protocols that would allow all types of computer platforms to communicate with each other. The latter part of the 1990s saw most schools make the first moves to join the networked community, with virtually all schools, small and large, by the end of the century having their own web address, their URL, website, and in many instances an intranet that could also be accessed via the Web.

The 1990s also gradually saw most teachers acquire the skills and understanding needed to work online. Slowly at first, but increasingly at pace, the schools began acquiring the technologies, the hardware and the software needed for all the teachers and the students to operate within the networked and online world.

While at times those who foresaw the immense educational potential of this instructional technology might have wanted all teachers to take advantage of networked teaching earlier, when one reflects on the number of developments and changes that had to be made (as shown below), the tasks were undertaken remarkably swiftly.

Library automation and the growth of the school networks

As discussed in Chapter 12, the early 1990s saw an upsurge in the automation of school library systems, an associated networking of the computers in the library, moves to link the library network to the computer rooms, and most importantly the education of the library staff on the wherewithal of networking. By the emergence of the World Wide Web, most school libraries had in operation a networked library system, albeit invariably small and local.

Email

Electronic mail—or email as it soon became known—was the entry point to the networked world for most teachers. Many in the interviews could recall the pleasure and relief of successfully sending their first email. Email gradually evolved in form and sophistication from the mid 1960s onwards, but it was not until the release of the initial commercial packages like Eudora and Pegasus in the late 1980s that the facility began to be used widely.

Email was never used extensively as an instructional tool. It did, however, soon become an integral part of the teachers' toolkit and was used widely by teachers for communication, administration and professional development. Indeed, the mid 1990s saw the emergence across much of the developed world of a range of area-specific teacher mailing lists, many of which remained vital learning communities for many years thereafter. Suddenly teachers from seemingly the most distant and remote locations could instantly and at no cost communicate with teachers globally. (One of the authors can still vividly remember receiving in Australia an email from Newfoundland calling for advice, replying and then getting a note back mentioning he had received it the day before he sent the original email!) While a very basic technology, mailing lists provided teachers with a previously unrivalled opportunity to share ideas instantaneously, at no cost. Mailing lists like LM-Net, OZTL-Net and the various professional associations played a very important part in supporting teachers' use of the emerging technology.

Out of that facility online teacher conferences emerged in the latter half of the 1990s, where teachers globally could explore key issues and indeed the best use of the emerging technologies.

World Wide Web, Mosaic and Netscape

The development that fundamentally changed networked teaching—and indeed the world as a whole—was the launch in 1993 of the World Wide Web (WWW), the release of the first web browser and the opening of the Internet to use by everyone, not simply the 'geeks'.

> By the mid 1990s, the PC-Windows era had reached a plateau. It was wonderful that all people over the world could suddenly author their own content in digital form. But if we were really going to make the most of this breakthrough, we needed a breakthrough in connectivity—one that would allow each of us to take our digital content and send it anywhere at very little cost, so that others could work on it with us.
>
> (Friedman, 2006, p. 59)

That breakthrough came in part with the release of Mosaic, and probably more so with its release in its commercial form as Netscape in August 1995.

... the Netscape browser not only brought the Internet alive but also made the Internet accessible to everyone from five year-olds to ninety-five year-olds. The more alive the Internet became, the more different people wanted to do different things on the Web, so the more they demanded computers, software, and telecommunications networks that could easily digitise words, music, data and photos, and transport them on the Internet to anyone else's computer.

Today, we take this simplified browser technology for granted, but it was actually one of the most important inventions in modern history.

(ibid., pp. 62, 63)

Information superhighway and schools

In 1994, the then vice-president of the US, Al Gore, delivered the speech where he referred to the Internet as the 'information superhighway' and in so doing spelt out the use it needed to play in schooling.

It was in that spirit that then-Governor Clinton and I, campaigning for the White House in 1992, set as a vital national goal linking every classroom in every school in the United States to the National Information Infrastructure.

... It was in this same spirit that less than a month ago I pointed out that when it comes to telecommunications services, schools are the most impoverished institutions in society. And that has to change.

And so I have been pleased that so many companies participating in the communications revolution are now talking about voluntarily providing free access to the NII for every classroom in their service areas. And I would like to take the opportunity today to congratulate two companies, Bell Atlantic and TCI, for their joint announcement yesterday in which they both individually committed to do just that. That's leadership from the private sector.

Setting goals for ourselves is important. Setting the right goals is critical.

... So let me be clear here today in articulating what I believe is one of the most important goals for all of us to agree to at this meeting: That by January 11th of the year 2000, you will connect and provide access to the National Information Infrastructure for every classroom, every library, and every hospital and clinic in the entire United States of America.

(Gore, 1994)

The impact of that call on educational leaders across the developed world was immense. It flagged to the world that if it wanted to be abreast with the US it had to make some significant moves.

Connectivity and bandwidth

As Gore rightly observed, schools in the 1990s were 'the most impoverished institutions in society' when it came to telecommunications. The vast majority of classrooms did not have a telephone line, let alone a high-speed connection to the Internet. The task of remedying that situation was considerable and on many occasions governments opted for short-term political solutions, such as proclaiming that all schools were linked to the 'information highway' when a single, 56-K modem was provided to the schools.

Most schools, education authorities and indeed national governments embarked in some way in the second half of the 1990s on programs to provide high-speed Internet access. In the more prescient situations that linked the development of the information superhighway and classroom access to national productivity, highly ambitious, well-resourced programs were put in place. The US, for example, building on the Clinton–Gore initiative, set in motion the National Infrastructure Initiative (NII) and introduced its E-Rate scheme, Canada embarked on its Canadian School-Net program, Korea and Denmark set about with national broadband connectivity, while the UK began assembling its national grid for learning (NGfL) that would in time provide all UK government and Catholic classrooms broadband access (Meredyth et al., 1998).

That said, when one notes the level of classroom connectivity, even in the more advanced situations in the late 1990s, figures of around 20–25 per cent are common. The Alliance for Converging Technologies cited by Tapscott (1998, p. 261) suggests only 21 per cent of US teaching rooms in 1998 had Internet access. (One needs to be cautious with many of the government statistics that refer to X or Y per cent of schools being connected to the Internet in this period because many of those connections were low speed or simply to one or two parts of the school.)

The majority of schools in the developed world gradually grew their Internet access, invariably starting with the plain old telephone (POT) 56-K connection and a single modem, growing in time to 128-K ISDN or Frame Relay links, and eventually to broadband through either cable, satellite, wireless or a technology like ADSL.

In the 1990s some larger, wealthier schools moved into providing local area networks (LANs), wide area networks (WANs) and virtual private networks (VPNs). In their early stages the solutions were expensive and often based on proprietary software. Across the world, a variety of VPN promoters attempted to monopolise the school systems by using very limited application machinery or linkages. Systems often carried poor reputations simply because of the way current software was 'damaged' in order to carry out new functions. The undisputed issue though was that most schools saw considerable value in offering their communities a secure, virtual world in which teaching and learning could take place. VPNs, LANs and WANs offered safe, confined environments that allowed students to share files, use web pages for interactive tasks and email each other in safety.

While these arrangements proved popular with schools, in many instances the students themselves had reservations. For the most part they objected to using 'school' emails and having the school oversee their Internet use. However, it was not this issue that saw a rather quick demise to the early VPNs, rather it was the rapid progress in Internet technology itself. In the 1980s and 1990s, web construction was for the most part the role of paid specialists. In the later 1990s, Microsoft introduced its Vermeer-developed FrontPage web creation software (Wikipedia, 2008j). While other makers had similar software—some of it technically superior—for the first time there was a simple tool for building even complex web pages. Almost overnight, specialist web authors disappeared to be replaced by millions of self-taught web authors. Network solutions, once the realm of the VPN providers, suddenly became anyone's prerogative based on the faster and less expensive Internet technology. No longer was there a need for specialist servers and client downloads.

The general application of broadband technology over the next ten years would see this trend continue to grow exponentially.

School websites and intranets

In the latter part of the 1990s most schools in the developed world took their place in the online world, acquired their own URL (http://www ...), created their own website and many also developed their own intranet.

While many of the early school websites were little more than online school brochures, most recognised their vital importance in promoting the school and began to use both the website and the Web-enabled intranet as an instructional technology.

Networked and online instructional materials

Efforts—often substantial in nature—were made in the 1990s to capitalise on the rapidly emerging networks.

A number of interactive multimedia, mastery based instructional packages (such as Successmaker) that had been engineered to work on the new intelligent networks were heavily promoted, but few secured more than isolated acceptance.

There was also an increase in the availability of online instruction material. Computer-orientated teachers and a few similarly preoccupied publishers produced learning materials that could be networked and that provided sequential learning activities. For the most part, though, this development was limited by the belief that the materials could be 'ripped off' if placed on a network. Publishers tended to prefer packaging a single-user CD with a textbook rather than providing a network version. One of the major publishers who experimented with e-learning for a while was Macmillan. Despite some early interest in networked materials and online learning, they, like many of the other publishers, moved into the single-user format for the vast majority of their offerings.

By the later 1990s, significant moves had begun towards taking many of the older, reference-style publications online. Among the earliest developments was the arrival of online encyclopaedias. Issued first in CD-ROM format in the later 1980s, *Encarta*, *World Book*, *Encyclopaedia Britannica* and others quickly gained popularity in their electronic form. However, just as with the print-based materials, the time lag between the writing and the publication became increasingly critical. Students and their teachers became increasingly impatient as technology improved. Most soon had to adopt a subscription and constant update model.

Web search engines

A batch of ever-improving search engines also fuelled this change. While the early search engines were 'clunky' and gave indifferent results, this soon changed. The advent of Alta Vista, Lycos, Yahoo!, Excite, Metacrawler and others provided an increasingly effective means of locating resources. The more capable teachers and the school library staff were able to make good use of the search engines, but most felt the need to use several as none of the options available was particularly effective.

Early WANs/VLEs

The second half of the 1990s also saw the initial efforts to build upon the emerging wide area network (WAN) technology and create the first virtual learning environments (VLEs). The desire was to provide all within each school community—the students, teachers and parents—with ready and secure use of a web-based, centrally hosted, comprehensive teaching, learning and communications solution.

One of the pathfinding developments was Australia's myinternet that emerged in the mid 1990s, about the same time as the student laptop initiative mentioned earlier. The interview with one of its founding figures, Daniel Ingvarson, reflected the kind of issues that all those developing educational solutions for the networked encountered at this stage, in that:

- the development could be rapid and the update swift, but equally the life cycle of the solution could be very short and soon be superseded. myinternet was first deployed in 1997; by 2002 more than 50 per cent of Australia's schools had been signed up to use myinternet and yet by 2007 was under serious competition by a range of Web 2.0-based solutions.

- the developers opted to use an open source, Linux-based platform that provided the facility to save costs and to tap into the cutting-edge thinking from across the world, but which at the same time did not have the software to cater for all the developer's desires.

- it highlighted the vital importance in networked teaching of having a very fast, secure individual log-in that instantly provided secure individual user access to all their files. In 2008, that facility was taken for granted, but it was only around 2000 that an appropriate Linux solution was developed at the behest of myinternet.

- the successful deployment of myinternet highlighted the many other complementary human and technological issues that needed to be addressed before schools could make best educational use of VLEs. Issues like speed and cost of bandwidth, network reliability and support, classroom connectivity and teacher development were but a few of the matters that the rollout of this VLE to 50 per cent of Australia's schools raised.

Not surprisingly, the interview also revealed that only minuscule class use was made of the full capability of myinternet, despite the 50 per cent national coverage.

Network quality and effectiveness

While it is true that significant advances were made with the network infrastructure in schools in the 1990s and the early 2000s, all was not as rosy as the official figures would suggest. The importance of quality networking and the associated storage, backup and disaster proofing was not at all well understood by most educational leaders.

Sustained quality whole-school networking costs significant money. Network infrastructure is not a vote winner, unless handled skilfully by politicians of the calibres of Al Gore, Bill Clinton or Tony Blair. Many a school network manager during the 1990s had the immense challenge of convincing the educational leadership of the necessity to invest in quality, often unseen and expensive network infrastructure. Those efforts were often made that much more difficult by the lack of direction and support provided by many central offices.

As a consequence many schools had highly unreliable networks that were likely to be out of action for days. Many teachers suffered the horror of losing major pieces of work. Few schools had disaster plans.

For teachers, the important thing is usually the level of reliability, and not necessarily the latest software or largest computer. Despite this statement of the rather obvious, planning for technology, especially during the late 1990s, was marked by schools facing regular network crashes, loss of unprotected data and disenchanted students and staff. Success with technology came in the schools where planning was thorough, where those in charge were aware and knew the needs first-hand, and where management accommodated the need for sound infrastructure that could take the loads likely to be generated.

While by the mid 2000s the scene gradually changed, it has to be borne in mind that in 2008 there were still many schools whose internal network left much to be desired.

ICT support

In the early years the school networks were usually developed, and most assuredly were maintained, by the enthusiastic teachers or teacher-librarians.

Teachers historically have filled most of the staffing positions in schools, with only the occasional support staff. While over time the balance of teaching and 'support' staff has changed a little, teachers—invariably supported by their unions—have performed most of the jobs in schools, even if they were not qualified. This is what happened from the outset in the provision of network support and, as will be noted below, still happened in 2008.

Schools globally are staffed on a formula generated by the local education authority, a formula based in the main around the provision of teachers. The changing of the staffing formula was a major challenge. While it became increasingly apparent in the 1980s and 1990s that 'expensive' teachers should not be performing a technician's role, most authorities were unable to change that situation for some time, or at all. While that change was easier in the independent schools, it was particularly difficult in the larger systems where there was a strong education union.

It is of note that even in the UK, one of the largest users of digital instructional technology in schools in 2007, the postings to the likes of the Top Teachers and the ICT Research mailing lists showed teachers—and not specialist staff—still playing a major role in providing ICT and network support, particularly in primary schools. Most ICT support was provided by teachers, often only with a small face-to-face teaching relief allowance.

It is a major concern. While not in itself an instructional technology, what history has already shown is that teachers will not be able to rely on the networked world unless there is a quality network infrastructure that is maintained and supported by an expert staff.

THE 2000s

By the start of the twenty-first century most teachers and students had the skills and the basic tools to begin taking advantage of the networked world, but it would take the convergence of a number of key developments and some enlightened educational leadership before they could readily take advantage of networked teaching.

The technological developments that took place in the early 2000s, and the impact of their convergence, served not only to make the networked world available to all within the schools but at a level and of a form previously unimagined.

Sadly, while the technology was in place in many situations, there was not necessarily the educational leadership or the political acumen to take advantage of the ever-emerging opportunities, and thus one saw in the 2000s only those schools and education authorities with the astute leaders systematically addressing the many technological and human variables that were needed to begin harnessing the undoubted vast potential of the networks.

While it is appreciated that there will always be a time lag between the availability of the technology and the human capacity to take advantage of that technology, what was apparent by the mid 2000s, particularly within the more conservative schools and education authorities lacking the vision, was a blocking of the student and teacher use of many of the online offerings. The irony, as was evidenced in Chapter 11, was that while the young people in their homes were embracing and using all the 'instructional technology' of the networked world, the lack of leadership in many schools and education authorities was stymieing its educational use in classrooms and was widening the home–school divide.

Classroom access to the Web

Connectivity

In 2008, it was a challenge for the authors to accurately identify the percentage of teaching rooms with access to the Web, let alone the use made of that facility. The official statistics available were not only limited but, in keeping with the earlier observations about official statistics, they painted a somewhat rosier picture than was the likely reality. For example, the most commonly available figure was Internet connectivity to the school, and not surprisingly in virtually all developed nations all the schools were connected to the Internet. That connection could, however, be the most basic modem connection. What the statistics did not reveal— in contrast with the data on home Net connectivity—was the bandwidth. Nor did the data provide vital information on such variables as the cost of the connectivity and the ongoing use, the reliability of the connectivity or the percentage of teaching rooms connected.

An observation by Becta in its 2007 review *Harnessing the Technology* suggests that even the pathfinding nations would have some way to travel before they could say all teachers have access from their teaching room to the Internet. Conscious that the UK was very much to the fore internationally in connecting its classrooms, it is of note that the review observed that '... a third of all computers in primary schools are not connected to the internet' (Kitchen, Finch & Sinclair, 2007; Becta, 2007, p. 7).

Reference is then made to the increasing use being made of wireless networking, but the clear impression is that the UK still has some distance to travel. That said, by 2007 virtually every UK primary school had a 2-Mbps connection and secondary schools an 8-Mbps connection to the Internet (Becta, 2007, p. 8).

The US National Center for Educational Statistics (NCES) noted that in 1998, 54 per cent of US classrooms were connected to the Internet and that in 2005 that figure had risen to 94 per cent, but few details are provided on the exact nature of that connectivity and in particular its costs (NCES, 2008). Of note is that while the NCES has published data on classroom connectivity in the US for 1994–2002, the years of the Clinton administration, it has not published a similar study for the Bush administration.

In some developed nations, like Australia for example, the data on classroom connectivity has simply not been collected.

Cost of the connectivity and everyday use is a very important issue for schools, particularly when funded from a limited budget. While in theory the schools might have all rooms networked and with Web access, the cost of use could be a major constraint. The school's recurrent Internet budget usually needs to cover both the line hire and everyday traffic. The cost of the everyday traffic is invariably an unknown and, as any who have used a cell phone will know, can generate considerable monies for the telco. Schools have thus had to cut their cloth accordingly. In the interviews the authors encountered a fully networked primary school that was obliged to work within an $A11 000 annual Internet budget, and a K–12 school that spent over $350 000 on annual Internet use.

Another increasing concern, particularly in the pathfinding situations that have achieved significant teacher and student use of the digital technologies, is the load being placed on the network infrastructure and the ability of the network to handle the increasing use without major upgrading (Becta, 2007, p. 12).

Considerable work clearly needs to be done before one can speak with surety about the level and effectiveness of the classroom connectivity across the developed world.

As mentioned earlier, the physical access statistics did not in themselves communicate the degree of access enjoyed by the teachers and students. Many schools and education authorities imposed significant constraints.

Freedom of access

Exactly how extensive were the constraints, and whether the degree of constraint was trending upwards, is a matter for far more comprehensive international research, but the feedback from a sample of teachers around the English-speaking world points to a growing concern of many teachers that they are being denied access to learning opportunities freely available in the students' homes and the more proactive education authorities. The normal inclination of most teachers when online is to be delighted with the teaching and learning opportunities provided. The normal inclination of most educational bureaucrats and network managers—particularly when there is no overriding philosophy—is to identify potential problems for themselves and to use their position to institute a series of controls (constraints) over the use of the technology. (As former bureaucrats, the authors can well appreciate the importance of protecting their 'political masters' from possible complaints.)

That concern was soon evidenced after the emergence of the Web in the call for schools to introduce 'acceptable use policies' (AUPs) that precluded student access to 'nasty' sites. Rather than seeking to educate students on how best to work within a networked world, it would appear most education chose to ban access to the undesirable sites at school. Throughout the latter 1990s and 2000s one saw across the developed world the introduction of an array of web filtering solutions like N2H2, iPrism, Blox, Safesquid, Untangle and Net Alert, to name but a few.

While the filtering technologies became increasingly sophisticated, it was all premised on the belief that the students at school, K–12, needed to be protected. In contrast, despite all the media coverage, in the vast majority of homes the young have no such constraints or use filters readily bypassed by savvy young. While advocates like Nancy Willard (http://www.cyberbully.org/about/bio.php) tried tirelessly to have schools educate the students for life in an online world, with minimal constraints few schools in the 1990s or 2000s opted for that approach. Rather, one saw the introduction of 'black' or 'white' lists in conjunction with the web filters. In general terms, with the black list students and teachers could only access the approved websites, while with the white specific websites were blocked.

Invariably allied to the filtering was the protecting of the school's network from the very real challenge of computer viruses.

Network managers with their administrator status soon found themselves in control of network access. The comments gathered from the teacher interviews would suggest that in many situations it was the network manager deciding on access controls and not the leadership.

In the early years of web use (Web 1.0), when only the 'experts' could publish online, publishing was tightly controlled. However, when, as mentioned, 'automated' web authoring solutions became available and in particular the Web 2.0 technologies described below enabled everyone to publish to the Web, the scene changed dramatically and virtually —in historical terms—overnight. Suddenly schools and educational administrators had to contend with a very new world—a world a few understood and most did not.

As mentioned, the initial signs point to the schools and education authorities that have been on top of their game and understood the networked world, and had for some time adopted an underlying usage philosophy and were moving towards an increasingly networked mode of teaching and learning that sought to capitalise on the opportunities opened to them. In contrast, those schools and authorities, and in particular their network managers and responsible bureaucrats lacking a vision that gave direction to their work, opted to ban or at least markedly constrain student and teacher use of the emerging online facilities.

One could argue that the degree of control being exercised over student access to the Web was a very good indicator of the attitude adopted by the school or education authority to the wider use and acceptance of the networked world. While the pathfinders had opted for a highly positive view of the online world and placed minimal constraints on student use, the reactive schools and education authorities generally took a negative stance and placed seemingly ever-greater constraints with each new online development.

To secure a fuller appreciation of the situation, at least in Australia, Mal Lee and Pru Mitchell commenced research in 2008 on identifying the nature of student and teacher web access in Australia's 40-plus education authorities and its independent schools. They surveyed teachers in those situations and requested each of the authorities to provide their policy. The survey asked for feedback on the controls employed with the following facilities:

- WWW access—use of
- Email
- Website creation
- Podcasts—access to and facility to create and post

- Blogs—access to and facility to create
- Wikis—access to and facility to create
- Chat rooms—access to and facility to create
- VOIP—and Skype—access to
- Social networks—access to and facility to create
- Online games—access to and facility to create complex games. Is it an authority, school or individual teacher decision to permit access?
- YouTube—and the like—access to and facility to create
- Online music
- Multifunctional mobile phones—particularly those with web and email access. Are student mobile phones allowed?

While the research was not completed at the time of writing, what was already apparent was that:

- there was no national approach
- Australia in mid 2008 had just begun implementing a national strategy to use schooling to enhance national productivity, with few signs that it was prepared to mount a comprehensive national strategy of the type adopted by the pathfinders
- school and education authorities were operating at virtually all points along a liberal to strong control continuum; some church- and state-based authorities had virtually negated any use of the Web 2.0 facilities and multifaceted phones that would provide access at school to those facilities
- a small cadre of independent schools and education authorities that had embraced the use of the networked world for some time, had a shaping educational philosophy and provided ready classroom Internet access, were those with the least controls and are using all the surveyed facilities with their students and teachers
- the majority of Australia's schools—state, Catholic and independent— in 2008 had imposed significant controls over students' and teachers' use of the networked world, with few having any concerted vision to harness the opportunities of the networked and digital worlds. The replies from teachers across the nation expressed immense frustration with that lack of vision.

What the international situation is, only time and research will tell, but history would incline one to suggesting that the scene in Australia probably prevails across the developed world. Discussions on the international mailing lists, blogs and online forums point very strongly to the astute pathfinders, with their shaping philosophy employing minimal constraints and actively supporting their teachers' use of all the emerging opportunities. The UK, for example, has had a clear national strategy since the mid 1990s, initially expressed in the 1997–2002 plan, with its conscious broadbanding of the nation's schools with the national grid for learning (NGfL), the creation of Becta (the British Educational Communications Technology Authority) and most fully in the *Harnessing the Technology* policy statement of 2004 (DfES, 2005).

The effectiveness of the concerted moves by the UK to form a bridge between its schools and the home and embrace the opportunities offered by the online world is reflected in the following observation in the 2007 Becta Review, which noted:

Kitchen et al. (2007) found that 43 per cent of primary and 62 per cent of secondary school leaders felt that using technology to extend learning beyond the classroom was a high priority. This indicated a desire, among secondary schools in particular, to develop and realise the opportunities for independent learning afforded by technology.

The Becta Review 2006 described the range of ways in which schools use technology to improve access to learning beyond the school, including providing:

- *external, remote access to the school network, learning platforms and VLEs*
- *mobile devices such as laptops and PDAs, to use within and beyond the boundaries of the school, including in the home*
- *access to learning via the school website*
- *equipment loan schemes for pupils and staff*
- *access to lunchtime, after-school and breakfast clubs where ICT is available*
- *the provision of email accounts.*

A technology infrastructure to support personalised learning beyond the institution is at a relatively early stage, although developing rapidly in certain areas. (p. 57)

Not only has the UK sought to embrace the wise educational use of the networked world, but as is apparent in the last observation it also recognises that it has some way to travel before it succeeds.

New Zealand and Singapore have adopted similar national strategies that consciously aim to prepare the nation and schools for a digital future. Singapore's quest, like that of Britain's, began with the launch of a major national strategy in 1997 that saw the 'Thinking Schools, Learning Nation' aspirations of the government addressed in the Ministry of Education's *Masterplan for Information Technology in Education*. New Zealand's national strategy initiative was also launched in 1997 with its *1997–1999 Government Strategy and Education for the 21st Century*. That initiative was built upon in the 2000s with planning documents like the Ministry's 2006 *Enabling the 21st Century Learner: An e-Learning Action Plan for Schools 2006–2010*, and Secondary Futures' 2006 *Students First* vision for New Zealand's young. Importantly all that work was allied to the country's national Digital Strategy (http://www.digitalstrategy.govt.nz/).

Those situations are however in a minority. The perception of most teachers is that it is not worth the hassle of trying to overcome an insular bureaucracy, which has invariably not provided the requisite infrastructure, technology in the school or the desired support.

Google

One of the undoubted major developments in the opening years of the 2000s was the emergence of Google as the ubiquitous international search engine that changed the way society used the Internet.

While earlier search engines were available for teachers in the later 1990s, none dominated and thus teachers tended to use a range, recognising that none was sufficient in its own right. In September 1999, a beta version of Google, a search engine that worked on a completely different set of parameters to the earlier search engines, was made available to the knowing public (http://www.google.com/corporate/history.html).

Within a few years Google had become the dominant search engine.

At its peak in early 2004, Google handled upwards of 84.7 percent of all search requests on the World Wide Web through its website and through its partnerships with other Internet clients like Yahoo!, AOL, and CNN. In February 2004, Yahoo! dropped its partnership with Google, providing an independent search engine of its own. This cost Google some market share, yet Yahoo!'s move highlighted Google's own distinctiveness, and today the verb 'to google' has entered a number of languages (first as a slang verb and now as a standard word), meaning 'to perform a web search' (a possible indication of 'Google' becoming a genericized trademark).

(Wikipedia, 2008n)

In 2007, despite intense competition from all the major players, Google had 50.8 per cent of the Web search market while Yahoo! had just 23.6 per cent (ibid.) So ubiquitous was the use of Google in schools that by the mid 2000s teachers and students were often bypassing their own, often excellent, school library information services and going directly via Google to the Web. As any teachers who worked with Google soon appreciated, there was so much more than the search engine component that could be used in the digital toolkit. Google Earth transformed the way teachers viewed the world, while Google Maps and Google Docs added to that changing of the way things were done. Google's definition capability rewrote the use of hard print dictionaries, as did the facility to locate quotes make archaic the time-honoured quotation dictionaries. Alan Gold, vice-president of Airspace is quoted by Friedman as noting:

> *Google is like God. God is wireless. God is everywhere, and sees everything. Any question in the world, you ask Google.*

> (Friedman, 2006, p. 186)

Hosted solutions

The early 2000s saw a flowering of hosted, database-driven solutions able to be readily used, in part at least, as another instructional technology.

By hosted solutions—also known as ASP solutions—one is talking about a group of schools using, via the Internet, an educational service hosted anywhere in the networked world; for example, the use of professional databases like SQL, its Linux variant or Oracle. With Microsoft's release of increasingly sophisticated versions such as its .net development software in the early years of the 2000s, the possibilities grew significantly.

While many of the hosted solutions began life in the 1990s, most did not receive significant use in the schools until the advent of appropriate bandwidth at a reasonable price, networked classrooms and the availability of technology that facilitated ready access. The solutions on offer ranged from simple student portals, to extensive periodicals and newspaper subscription services, through to online lessons, the kind of services described below under 'Learning platforms', and indeed fully online schools.

Learning platforms

The mid 1990s and in particular the 2000s saw the development of another potentially significant contributor to networked teaching. It was what was variously called virtual learning environments (VLEs), managed learning environments (MLEs), course management systems (CMS)— or what Becta came to label as 'learning platforms' (Wikipedia, 2008o; Becta, 2008) These were comprehensive online teaching and learning facilities that were designed to provide all members of a school community with their own portal and online suite of teaching and learning materials.

Becta indicated in 2008:

A learning platform brings together hardware, software and supporting services to enable more effective ways of working within and outside the classroom. They can vary considerably, but every learning platform should provide a range of ICT-based functions:

- *Content management—enabling teaching staff to create, store and repurpose resources and coursework which can be accessed online*
- *Curriculum mapping and planning—providing tools and storage to support assessment for learning, personalisation, lesson planning, etc.*
- *Learner engagement and administration—enabling access to pupil information, attendance, timetabling, e-portfolios and management information*
- *Tools and services—providing communication tools such as email, messaging, discussion forums and blogs.*

A learning platform is therefore not a single 'off the shelf' product but a collection of tools that are designed to support teaching, learning, management and administration.

(Becta, 2008)

A problem was that the term meant very different things to different learning platform providers. Moreover, the educational philosophy underlying each of the offerings ranged across the continuum from highly controlled mastery or content-driven learning through to constructivist student-centred learning.

After the initial fanfare and hype, the more astute educators began to question the exact place of controlled learning platforms, particularly when they were integrated with student administration and management packages, and at a time when many of the Web 2.0 initiatives provided the opportunity for more creative and appropriate teaching.

The developments with learning platforms brought into sharp focus the vital but often forgotten importance of ensuring a consonance between the desired educational outcomes and the chosen instructional technology.

The rhetoric surrounding the potential of the learning platforms was on par with the introduction of most of the earlier instructional technology and indeed the price tag on many of the commercial offerings was considerable. By the mid 2000s, despite the rhetoric of the developers, the actual use by most teachers was minimal and once again was restricted to the devotees.

Becta, as late as its 2007 Review, concluded:

> Few practitioners, however, fully exploit the possibilities for learning and teaching offered by technology, especially learning platforms, and although 46 per cent of secondary schools report having one, only 24 per cent of teachers report using it. (p. 3)

The aspirations of many of the learning platform developers—be they the open source offerings like Moodle and Bodington or the commercial offerings like myinternet, ANGEL Learning and eCollege—were highly laudable but all in the mid 2000s had shortcomings.

As in the past, it is not enough for government to say teachers will use the technology. History has shown they will not. Wise implementation strategies and highly user-friendly software will be needed to gain acceptance by teachers.

Classroom teaching facilities

Teaching access to the networked world was until the early 2000s invariably via personal computers, an instructional technology that had pronounced limitations as a tool for teaching a total class (as indicated in Chapter 10).

Although the technologies like the data projectors and interactive whiteboards that could be used in the teaching of a class began their lives in the 1990s, it was not until the 2000s that they reached a price point and a level of sophistication and reliability where they could be readily acquired for general class use.

Online teaching resources

Of note is that the introduction of those large-screen class teaching tools in turn helped stimulate the development of a substantial body of interactive, multimedia teaching materials designed specifically for class groups and the large screen, and not thus far for the small personal computer and one or two users. Much of that material (discussed in depth in Chapter 14) was made available for downloading from the WWW.

While a significant proportion of the new resources was commercial, the 2000s also saw a pronounced production and placement online of excellent free multimedia teaching resources developed by teachers, education authorities, government agencies, universities, museums and foundations. Of note was the UK initiative of not only providing all teachers with £200 each year to buy software via a credits scheme, but also of creating a Curriculum Online site (http://www.curriculumonline. gov.uk/Default.htm) where they could readily acquire that software.

Web 2.0

The early to mid 2000s saw the emergence of a plethora of online tools that enabled interested web users to publish their ideas and work directly to the Web. That collection of online tools and the fundamental shift from when only the web authoring experts could publish to the Web to the position where anyone could, became to be known as Web.2.0.

Suddenly facilities like wikis, blogs, podcasts and chat rooms, and online facilities like Wikipedia, MySpace, YouTube, Facebook and Second Life enabled all those interested to publish to the networked world. As usual, the early adopters recognised the educational opportunities particularly with wikis, podcasts, blogs and the social networking facilities.

Wikis quickly provided the opportunity to use the online publishing and editing facility to assemble collective know-how online. The major expression of the facility was the emergence of the free online encyclopaedia Wikipedia in 2001, and its growth to challenge the traditional encyclopaedias by the mid 2000s. While there was the inevitable lag time in gaining acceptance and while many in schools rightly challenged unfettered reliance on the Wikipedia, within a very short time the world had an immense and ever-expanding, ever-updating source of information that fundamentally changed the encyclopaedia scene.

Podcasts—the facility for all interested to publish initially audio and in time multimedia files to the Web—was another facility that could be well used by the students. Developed initially by the technically savvy computer users, the facility was brought to the world market by Apple popularising its use with its iPods, the development of an international podcast directory within Apple's iTunes store, and Apple's provision within its iLife suite of a set of simple-to-use podcast creation facilities.

Blogs—which are simple and readily created, structured, web-based discussion groups to which anyone can contribute—opened another world for the students to both use and access. Within a few years a plethora of blogs had been created on any number of issues by many authors. Students, classes, schools and various student and teacher groups soon had their own blogs.

The development that impacted dramatically on the lives of the young people was (as indicated in Chapter 11) the rapid uptake of the various social networking facilities—that chance to use the online world to reach out and communicate with friends around the world. MySpace, for example, was in 2007 estimated to be the world's sixth most popular website in any language. So successful was MySpace that in 2005—only two years after its creation—it was acquired by News Limited for reportedly $US580 million. It is reported in 2008 that MySpace was averaging 230 000 new registrations a day (Wikipedia, 2008p). YouTube, which provided the facility for the young and creative to publish their multimedia video creations to a world audience, was similarly embraced by the young. Created only in 2005, its impact overnight was profound.

> *Few statistics are publicly available regarding the number of videos on YouTube. However, in July 2006, the company revealed that more than 100 million videos were being watched every day, and 2.5 billion videos were watched in June 2006. 50,000 videos were being added per day in May 2006, and this increased to 65,000 by July.[3] In January 2008 alone, nearly 79 million users had made over 3 billion video views.*
>
> (Wikipedia, 2008q)

The uptake of Facebook has been equally dramatic, particularly outside the US. Launched in February 2004, by 2008 the uptake was such that in May of that year 123.9 million people visited the site.

> *According to Alexa, the website's ranking among all websites increased from 60th to 7th in terms of traffic, from September 2006 to September 2007. [83] Quantcast ranks the website 16th in terms of traffic,[84] and Compete. com ranks it 20th.[85] The website is the most popular for uploading photos, with 14 million uploaded daily.[86] On November 3, 2007, there were seven thousand applications on Facebook, with another hundred created every day. [87]*
>
> (Wikipedia, 2008r)

Little wonder (as mentioned earlier) that more than 70 per cent of 14–17 year-olds in Australia had published online in 2007 (ACMA, 2007).

Web conferencing

Educators had for years striven to find instructional technology that would enable the ready teaching of students in remote and distant locations. No matter how wonderful they were for the teachers of young people in remote locations, the vast majority of those solutions were of no more than a passing interest to most teachers.

From the early 1990s with the emergence of broadband, concerted efforts were made across the world to harness its potential to better cater for the students in remote locations. Most of the solutions offered emanated from the business market and were invariably expensive and outside the price range of schools. In 2003, a facility that took advantage of the Internet for inexpensive telecommunications suddenly transformed the scene for schools. It was called Skype. Classes overnight could audio-conference free of charge with classes anywhere in the networked world, with at least 512-K broadband. Most importantly, the classes could conference across computer platforms. In 2006, Skype added a cross-platform video-conferencing facility. Classes with an IWB, a simple web camera and an appropriate digital sound facility suddenly had added to their digital toolkit the facility to conference with the world free of charge.

OVERVIEW

By the mid 2000s, it was apparent that schools had all the technology and many had the leadership that allowed them to begin to take advantage of the undoubted potential of the networked world in their teaching.

What was apparent was that the confluence of the variables that had taken place globally within nations was also taking place within schools.

> The convergence of the ten flatteners had created a whole new platform. It is a global, Web-enabled platform for multiple forms of collaboration. This platform enables individuals, groups, companies and universities anywhere in the world to collaborate—for purposes of innovation, production, education, research, entertainment, and, alas, war making—like no creative platform ever before. This platform now operates without regard to geography, distance, time, and, in the near future, even language.

(Friedman, 2006, p. 205)

The international think-tank organised under the auspices of the MacArthur Foundation in Illinois to identify the nature of Digital Schools in 2007, concluded:

> *Schools need to become network institutions, establishing themselves as the center of diverse, overlapping networks of learning, which reach out to the fullest possible range of institutions, sources of information, social groups and physical facilities. To solve this problem schools need to become nodes on a network instead of isolated factories.*

> (Illinois Institute of Design, 2007, p. 25)

It was evident that the sophistication and availability of the digital instructional technology available to support networked teaching was growing at pace. While the number of online teaching opportunities might appear immense, particularly when compared with those in the 1980s, the reality was that there are many opportunities and services in 2008 we have not mentioned, and that by the time you read this piece there will be many more.

In an increasing number of schools and education authorities across the world—and not just in the developed world—the use of networked teaching has become normalised, with the teachers and the leadership striving to derive the utmost educational benefit.

However, those users were still a minority in 2008. As indicated, the main limiting variables have been human, not technical. Unless there is the school or education authority vision and leadership to harness the technological change, teaching will continue to use the traditional technologies.

While in 2008 many educational leaders had still to open the use of the networked world for teaching, the 'Net Generation' were embracing the opportunities in their homes and teaching themselves.

CHAPTER 14

THE DIGITAL TOOLKIT

As mentioned in Chapter 10, the mid 1990s witnessed the start of a dramatic change in the use of instructional technology from a reliance on a discrete piece of technology to the use of a suite of digital technologies.

By the mid 1990s teachers, too, had the facility to converge the operations of an ever-growing suite of digital technologies. The implications for schools and teaching of digital convergence were profound, although it took time for the full impact to be appreciated. The more astute teachers, schools and education authorities quickly recognised the ability to move away from the traditional reliance on one tool and instead to use an ever-growing and increasingly sophisticated suite of integrated digital technologies. In brief, teachers now had a digital toolkit that they could draw upon.

Which of the tools they used depended on the particular teaching situation. Where in the past teachers used a film, a VCR or a computer, almost overnight they were able to readily integrate all types of media to generate a suite of tools. Allied to the emergence of the digital toolkit was a surge in the range of digital technologies that could be included in that kit. Seemingly every week a new piece of software, online offering or additional type of digital hardware was released.

Often unwittingly, this growth in the range of potential instructional technologies obliged the more astute educational leaders to evaluate the educational appropriateness of all that was on offer and introduce greater control over the selection of appropriate instructional technology. While the dreaded 'impetuous technophilia' continued largely unabated in many schools and authorities, one increasingly saw leaders beginning to apply greater rigour to the choice of instructional technology.

During the 1990s and in particular in the 2000s, it became that much easier for teachers to use the expanding digital toolkit but, as mentioned, it took several important developments to occur before the average classroom teacher or indeed the very young students were ready to draw upon the toolkit in the classroom. It is best in 2008 to consider the development of the teacher's digital toolkit in two phases:

1   1994–2003
2   2004–2008

The first phase from the advent of the Web was a formative one, where the wise began to acquire a fuller appreciation of the variables to be addressed in a digital future, and where the digital technology had the time needed to mature, drop in price and put in place the vital network infrastructure. In this first phase it was particularly important to research why the teachers' use of personal computers in their teaching was so limited and had such little impact on teaching and learning, and to identify appropriate alternative technologies. It is also important to remember that in the life cycle of all technology there is invariably a time lag between the release of a particular piece of hardware or software and its ready use in the classroom, usually stymied by price, funding, want of facilitating technology, and educational leadership.

The second phase commences around late 2003, early 2004, with the completion of the 'homework' done in phase 1 and the confluence of a suite of human and technological developments.

By 2003, the work done on the network connectivity had been largely completed in the pathfinding nations and education authorities, such as the UK, Singapore, the US and South Korea. Around the same time the interactive whiteboard and data projectors attained a maturity and price point where they could be acquired for every teaching room to integrate the other digital technologies. Up until this development it was near impossible for the average teacher to use a mode of teaching that readily integrated the various digital technologies in their everyday teaching with a class. Even if teachers had digital photos or scanned student work, they could not readily display the work with the class group. It could only be seen on the small PC screen or small CRT television screen.

At a similar stage:

* Apple and Microsoft made available a suite of free or inexpensive interactive multimedia software applications, like Photo Story, QuickTime and the iLife and iWork suites
* the IWB teaching software reached a sophistication, reliability and ease of use where it could be used by all teachers and students K–12
* Google had become the ubiquitous international search engine
* the first of the Web 2.0 applications began to appear, and

- as mentioned previously, the pathfinding education authorities made concerted moves to build upon the telecommunications and networking infrastructure they had put in place.

In brief, by 2003 a critical mass of teachers across the developed world could readily use an emerging suite of inexpensive, easy-to-integrate digital instructional technologies that assisted their existing teaching in their classrooms. The confluence of technologies was such that one could argue that the developments in the use of instructional technology between 2004 and 2008 exceeded those of the previous century.

THE DIGITAL TOOLS—A HISTORY OF THEIR DEVELOPMENT

Central to the digital toolkit was:
- the personal computer
- Internet access
- simple-to-use cross-platform multimedia software
- and, increasingly, a facility like an interactive whiteboard that provided teachers with a digital instructional technology that would enhance their existing teaching, while at the same time integrating the various digital technologies and enabling the work to be shown to the total class group.

The prime purpose of the various technologies in the toolkit varied like any other toolkit—some were basic applications, some were multi-purpose, others were primarily facilitating technologies, while others were used mainly as instructional technologies. But in the end all could be used in an integrated manner to enrich teaching.

The personal computer

The personal computer played a central part in the toolkit in that invariably it:
- was the driving console for much of the technology
- provided the access to the networked world
- powered the presentation tools
- carried the applications software
- facilitated the integration of digital technologies, and
- provided the working digital storage and enabled the storage and retrieval of digital materials.

However, what needs to be borne in mind was that many of the technologies included in the digital toolkit also had their own inbuilt computer, and while one speaks of digital cameras, DVD players and mobile phones, all these technologies made extensive use of their own internal computers.

In the latter part of the 1990s and the 2000s, the power and sophistication of the personal computers grew at pace. Where in 1997 the Pentium II with a cathode ray screen (CRT) and external 56-K modem was seen by most teachers as a very good work tool, by 2007 the average Windows personal computer was a multimedia unit with an LCD screen, with CD and DVD burner, wireless and Ethernet connectivity, and around 2 GB of memory. The personal computers—desktop and laptop—were increasingly designed to operate in conjunction with other digital technologies. For example, Apple Computer promoted its computers as the digital integration facility, while Microsoft and a range of the major Windows providers promoted the digital media centre facility.

While the personal computer in its laptop or desktop form was fundamental to that shift, the promotional literature focused on the opportunities made possible by the software.

Microsoft and Apple

Two software companies dominated the educational software applications scene from the mid 1990s into the 2000s and had an immense impact on the nature of education provided—Microsoft and Apple.

By the mid 1990s, rightly or wrongly, Microsoft Office had become the de facto application for teachers and students globally. Developed initially for the Mac and then the Windows environment, Office and in particular Microsoft Word and PowerPoint—and to a lesser extent Internet Explorer— became the tools most commonly used with computers (Wikipedia, 2008j).

While one can argue that Microsoft's dominance and its aggressive marketing and pricing killed off much of the more innovative educational software of the 1980s, the reality is that from the early 1990s the Microsoft software became the 'standard' that enabled schools globally to readily share material across computer platforms. The other reality is that much (and probably most) computer use with Microsoft Word was as a word processor and with PowerPoint as a presentation tool. Neither piece of software was used widely as an innovative educational tool.

Others will undoubtedly write in time of the profound impact of the spelling, grammatical and formatting 'conventions' of Microsoft on the writing of the world, and in particular the young, but suffice it to say that in both the home and the school that impact was considerable.

In the latter part of the 1990s and more so in the 2000s, both Microsoft and Apple—often in competition and often harmoniously—brought to teachers and students an increasingly user-friendly and sophisticated suite of software to facilitate the ready integration of the digital technologies. While Adobe, particularly with its PDF facility, did impact with its 'Macromedia' tools, it did not have the general impact of Microsoft or Apple.

In 1998, Microsoft released Windows 98 that controversially integrated Internet Explorer with its Windows operating system (Wikipedia, 2008j). In 1999, Apple released its Mac OS 9, or what it came to refer to as its Classic Mac, and iMovie which gave teachers a simple and yet very powerful facility to edit digital videos (Wikipedia, 2008i). In 2000, Microsoft released ME, which further enhanced the multimedia and Internet features, and introduced Windows Movie Maker (Wikipedia, 2008j). In 2001, Microsoft released Windows XP, which further extended the digital integration, and Apple released Mac OS 10.1—its UNIX-based operating system, and positioned teachers and students to readily create and integrate still and moving images, music, sound and graphics (Wikipedia, 2008i).

Seemingly each year thereafter both Apple and Microsoft provided more and more software to facilitate the integration of digital technology, and indeed the creation of interactive, multimedia teaching materials. Products like MS Media Player and Photo Story, Apple's iPhoto, iDVD and Garageband meant that all teachers and students had ready access to simple-to-use digital integration tools.

Apple's online iTunes store that was opened for US customers in April 2003 not only provided the music—and in time video—for its iPods, it also moved podcasting from the world of the 'nerds' to the general public (Wikipedia, 2008s).

Networks, the Internet and bandwidth

Another technology that played a major role in facilitating the digital integration was the networks within the school that provided classes with ready access to the Internet.

As indicated in Chapter 13, the Internet from the mid 1990s onwards transformed life and business worldwide. It was, however, some time before the Internet was readily available to teachers and able to transform their teaching. As mentioned, the vast majority of classrooms in the mid 1990s were—as Al Gore rightly observed—lacking in telecommunications; most classrooms in 1996 did not even have a basic telephone connection, let alone ready network access.

Over the next decade, most governments, education authorities and schools set about changing that situation and providing all classrooms with high-speed Internet access.

However, it should be noted that even in the more enlightened authorities, extensive classroom access to the Internet did not begin to appear until around 2003–04. In 2008 there were still a very sizeable proportion of classrooms across the developed world where the teachers could not use, as part of their digital kit, all the tools of the networked world. While not in itself an instructional technology, unless teachers had classroom access to the Internet, their use of many of the below-mentioned digital technologies was constrained.

A related element was the bandwidth available to the classroom. A significant number of school networks initially used low-speed cabling, and often only to the library and/or computer labs. It was only after the cabling was upgraded and an appropriate high-speed link secured to the Internet service provided that teachers could begin to use many of the tools. With the plain old 56-K telephone line, the transmission of text was the norm, but as the bandwidth grew and higher-speed broadband became the norm, so schools could look to increasingly use all manner of interactive multimedia technology.

THE TOOLKIT

The online world opened the way for the rapid development of the range of digital instructional technologies that could be used in digital toolkits. Each has been described in detail in Chapter 13, but in brief they included:

- email
- hosted solutions
- learning platforms
- Google
- Web 2.0
- web conferencing.

In addition to the many online facilities that could be used in the digital toolkit, there were in the major categories alone:

- digital cameras
- digital video cameras
- electronic calculators
- data projectors
- scanners
- surround sound systems
- digital 'video'—digital television, VCRs and DVDs
- interactive multimedia teaching resources
- mobile phone technologies
- portable digital storage, and
- computer games.

Digital cameras

By the mid 2000s, inexpensive digital cameras had become a significant part of the digital toolkit, and while their use was supplementary in nature they were being used extensively in a growing number of primary classrooms and teaching areas with IWBs.

The consumer digital camera market probably opens with Apple's release of its Quick Take in 1994, the first mass market product able to shoot in colour (Wikipedia, 2008t). In the latter part of the 1990s one saw virtually all of the traditional camera makers, photocopy manufacturers and many of the major electronics companies provide ever-more powerful, sophisticated and cheaper digital cameras. Brand names like Kodak, Canon, Ricoh, Sony, Fuji, Nikon, Panasonic and Hitachi dotted the offerings available. All the cameras could interface with both the Windows and Mac computers, initially in a rather cumbersome manner but very readily by the early 2000s.

As with most other digital technology the initial cameras were expensive, and most schools only acquired one or two for special purposes. However, by the mid 2000s with the dramatic reduction in price and increase in power and sophistication, the digital camera had all but replaced the traditional 35-mm camera in most schools. There were primary schools where there was a digital camera or two in every classroom as part of its digital kit. Use was limited simply by the teacher's mindset and not by its price. If schools wanted, digital cameras could be used from early childhood classes upwards. (Of note is that by 2008 a significant proportion of students, and in particular secondary age students, had phones with in-built digital cameras and were using that facility in their everyday lives, but seldom with permission in the classroom.)

In 2006, Apple built its iSight camera into all its computers, while many Windows providers did the same with their machines.

Digital video cameras

The situation with the teacher use of digital video cameras was much the same as with the still cameras in that the sophistication and power of the cameras grew at pace while the cost to schools plummeted. A series of camera and recording format enhancements, coupled with the release of Firewire and iMovie in the late 1990s, opened the way for the ready use of video in the digital toolkit. By the mid 2000s, every class could afford a digital video camera, with a special effects and an associated digital editing suite that far surpassed the professional video equipment of the 1980s. When coupled to an interactive whiteboard and a surround system the educational impact could be considerable.

While the pathfinding teachers made great use of the resource—like their colleagues 50 years earlier had done with Super 8-mm film—the overall number of teachers using the facility was limited. Although use of the tools, like 40 to 50 years earlier, was supplementary in nature, the ease of use made it in turn that much easier for all teachers and students to use when they wished. That said, the level of use of this technology, particularly in the primary school and in classrooms using IWBs, was undoubtedly up on film and analogue video, but overall it was still only used by a minority of teachers.

Electronic calculators

An often forgotten component of the digital toolkit is the various types of electronic calculators. Indeed in many schools and education authorities, electronic calculators—arithmetic, scientific or graphic—have been used integrally in everyday teaching since at least the 1980s. However, their use has largely been restricted to the computational parts of the curriculum, and in the secondary school to subjects like maths and physics.

Electronic calculators began to appear in schools in the early 1970s. They were initially expensive and basic; however, within a relatively short time the costs dropped rapidly and their power and level of sophistication grew at pace (Wikipedia, 2008u). By the early 1980s, every student could afford an arithmetic calculator.

However, the widespread uptake and everyday use of this technology was stymied by heated debates between the 'traditionalists' who believed (and still in 2008 believe) that the technology hinders the development of computational skills, and those who sought to use calculators to assist the learning process. That debate has seen (as the interviews revealed) across the developed world some education authorities and student assessment bodies actively supporting the everyday use of the various types of electronic calculators, and others—even in 2008—preventing their use.

In the education authorities that have supported the calculators one has seen the use—and sophistication of the use—ramp up over the past 25 years, and the technology being used integrally in everyday teaching in both the primary and secondary school. From the 1990s, the use of graphical calculators have been woven into the curriculum and factored into the external examinations.

The refinements to the graphical and algebraic calculators in the 2000s allowed many to be interfaced with both personal computers and interactive whiteboards. Indeed, it has to be said that by the mid 2000s it was very hard to differentiate between the high-end graphical calculators of companies like Casio and TI with the hand-held computers.

Data projectors

Digital data, or what are also known as video projectors, began to appear in the early 1990s, particularly for use in corporate boardrooms and conferences (Wikipedia, 2008v). As was the norm with the other digital technology, they were very expensive, cumbersome and low on lumen power. For example, InFocus units were selling in the $A15 000–20 000 range in the mid 1990s.

Initially data projectors were generally used as computer presentation tools. In the latter part of the 1990s they came to be used in home theatre systems, and with this shift of focus to the general consumer market the competition grew, the lumen power increased and the prices began to fall. However, it was not until the early to mid 2000s that the projectors dropped to a price where schools could afford them for general class use.

The widespread adoption of data projectors by teachers was further stimulated by their use with front-projection interactive whiteboards. They were a fundamental part of the board's set-up. In brief, the data projector provided IWBs with their touch-screen capability.

Figure 14.1 Toshiba data projector of the mid 2000s (Courtesy Greg Walker)

There were those particularly inspired by the virtues of the personal computers and with a strong teacher-centric approach to teaching who believed all that was needed was a computer and a data projector.

Scanners

Scanners that could readily convert text and images into a digital form began appearing in numbers and at an affordable price in schools in the early 2000s. Most in the early years were acquired for teacher lesson preparation and in-school publishing. However, with the introduction of interactive whiteboards and the ready facility in particular with the optical character recognition (OCR) software for teachers to use the scanners to simply and swiftly convert printed text, handwriting and images into a digital form on the large screen, they took on a new lease of life and became a fundamental part of the digital toolkit.

Some of those interviewed referred to the humble $A80 scanner as being a 'revolutionary' tool when used with IWBs, in that it provided that vital nexus between the old instructional technology and the new. Teachers were suddenly able to convert a student's handwriting into a digital form, project it onto the IWB and, if desired, have the students edit with their fingers the digital text on the board. They could then convert the handwriting to text with the board's character recognition software.

Similarly, teachers were finally able take exercises from a textbook, digitise the material and have the students complete the exercise on the screen for all to watch and join in. Suddenly old word and number games took on a new life when made available on a large touch screen enabling whole-class interaction.

While in time the digital conversion could also be handled by digital cameras, the low cost and convenience of flat-bed scanners saw them used extensively as facilitating tools in classrooms with IWBs.

Surround sound systems

The introduction of interactive whiteboards with a digital sound recording and playback facility, and their ability to be used as monitors for digital television and surround sound DVDs, prompted the installation of 5.1 surround sound systems in classrooms with boards. While initially teachers made do with cheap computer speakers, they soon appreciated the fundamental importance of quality sound in teaching and thus took advantage of the increasingly inexpensive systems available for the home in the mid 2000s and installed them with IWBs.

'Digital' video—digital television, VCRs and DVDs

An increasingly important part of the digital toolkit in the latter 1990s and particularly in the 2000s was the facility to use packaged digital video in the teaching—either in full or edited. Classroom teachers now had the capacity with digital video to work it as they wished, within the bounds of copyright. They were able to draw digital broadcasts from the air or cable, from the Internet or from DVDs, readily edit that material and project the revised material on the IWBs or simply via a data projector in a 4:3 or 16:9 format.

Virtually all of the technical and indeed organisational impediments that had stymied the widespread use of film, television and video had been removed. The material could be recorded with digital video recorders or directly onto the hard drive, and then edited accordingly.

The only real block now was the preparedness of teachers to use the material. The pattern of teacher use of digital in the mid 2000s was akin to that with analogue video in that the teachers generally used the total package, and not edited versions, as a supplement to their teaching. There were, however, the early signs in schools with IWBs using Apple's Garageband and podcasting facilities that pre-packaged video was increasingly being edited by the students to create their own work.

While most schools began taking advantage of the digital video, they also continued to use their own extensive analogue video collections. Not only had many schools created large and valuable video collections, they also had to contend with the illegality of transferring much of that content to video.

Interactive multimedia teaching resources

Another significant part of the digital kit was the facility for teachers to draw upon a burgeoning body of interactive multimedia teaching material. Teachers were able to secure that material initially on CD-ROMs, then on DVD, and increasingly off the Web.

Teachers, education authorities, government agencies, foundations and commercial houses—small and large—produced the material. Much of the material was free to schools, although the 2000s also saw a significant growth in the availability of commercial interactive multimedia teaching resources.

A significant proportion of the commercial material emanated from the UK and was designed for use with IWBs, and significantly for class groups. The UK government not only made a very significant investment in digital technologies in the second part of the 1990s onwards and in particular interactive whiteboards for its schools, they did it in a way that stimulated the growth of the British educational multimedia industry, globally. The traditional school publishers like Heinemann, Pearson and Cambridge University Press as well as the traditional television producers— Granada Television, Channel 4 and the BBC—began producing interactive teaching resources. At the same time, the investment saw the emergence of a series of start-up companies and soon the likes of 2 Simple and Big Bus were producing quality materials for the global English-speaking market.

The UK developments in turn impacted on the US and one saw by the mid 2000s a series of collaborations between the major US educational software producers like River Deep and the UK IWB and multimedia software providers. The UK took the unusual but in retrospect inspired step of providing its teachers with individual, annual software acquisition allowances. That money helped stimulate not only the wider industry but also the use of the software in the classrooms.

Another major resource that could be used in the toolkit that emerged at the same time—helped undoubtedly by the expansion of the bandwidth— was the growth of hosted educational databases. In brief, schools could opt to subscribe to an online magazine or newspaper service rather than purchase the traditional hard copies.

By the mid 2000s, the volume of digital teaching resources available to teachers was such that most had very real difficulty keeping abreast.

Intriguingly, while the digital technology facilitated integration in the mid 2000s, teachers, education authorities and governments were still all producing their own variant of key resources. There was considerable overlap of the offerings. There was little collaboration even when the curriculum footprint was almost identical. It was as if every education authority had to produce its own maths and science courses, even when the content was near identical.

Mobile digital technologies

Another promising but, in 2008, little used part of the teachers' toolkit was the plethora of mobile, web-based communications and organisational devices such as PDAs, Blackberrys, the various multifaceted telephones and the MP3 digital music players in the hands of the students.

By the mid 2000s, a number of schools and education authorities had experimented with the use of the emerging PDAs in particular in the teaching/learning process, often as a low-cost substitute for laptops. However, in most instances the subsequent wider use in classrooms did not occur or was limited, hampered in many respects by technological limitations.

What was apparent (as mentioned in Chapter 11), however, was that a very significant proportion of teenage school students were making very extensive use of MP3 players and the multimedia facilities available on their phones, and were in a position to bring those facilities into the teacher's digital toolkit. Far greater mention was made on the teacher mailing lists of these technologies being banned by school authorities than of their use in the educative process.

While virtually all of the world's major electronics companies, and companies like Microsoft and Creative, produced excellent MP3 players, the 2000s were dominated by Apple's iPod and then in turn by the iPhone. Launched in 2001 as an audio player, the iPod soon became the 'in' item of both the young and the not-so-young. In 2005, Apple introduced its video version (Wikipedia, 2008s). The year 2007 saw the sale of the hundredth million iPod, making it the biggest-selling digital audio player in history (ibid.).

While a walk around any secondary school in the mid 2000s would reveal the students wearing the distinctive white iPod headphones, the potential of the technology as part of the digital kit was seldom realised.

On 1 June 2007, Apple released what was in essence an extension of its work in simplifying the everyday use of digital interactive multimedia technologies—its iPhone. The iPhone left behind the world of button controls and provided users with touch-screen control over all manner of digital technologies (Wikipedia, 2008w). The first-generation iPhone epitomised the quantum leaps being made in the latter 2000s with the digital technology and the ever-expanding opportunities for both the students and teachers that emerged in the period.

With the release in June 2008 of an even lighter, more functional and less expensive second-generation iPhone, Apple provided what Marc Andressen, the figure behind Netscape and the social networking facility Ning, and Matt Murphy contended:

> is the first real, fully formed computer that you can put in your hand.
>
> Matt Murphy—a venture capitalist at Kleiner Perkins Caulfield and Byers who oversees the $100 million iFund to seed startups that build great iPhone apps—goes even further. He claims the iPhone will 'absolutely be the driver of the post PC world'.

(Quittner, 2008, p. 42)

If one follows the developmental trend line apparent throughout this history and notes the ever-greater digital convergence and miniaturisation of the technology, the signs are that schools in June 2008 finally had access to an instructional technology that, used wisely, could have the profound impact foreshadowed by Andressen and Murphy. The challenge in 2008, as indicated elsewhere, will be to have the school and education authority leaders recognise and open the way for the harnessing of this potential.

Portable digital storage

The functionality of the digital toolkit was markedly enhanced in the 2000s by the emergence of a range of inexpensive, portable digital storage facilities that enabled both teachers and students to transport the increasingly large files. While very much a facilitating and not an instructional technology, the portable storage—like the expanding networks—made it much easier to carry around one's work.

The latter 1990s and early 2000s saw the demise of the traditional 1.2 MB floppy disk, and the emergence—and often rapid demise—of a range of portable storage facilities. The one that made the greatest impact in the classroom in the period was the USB, or what was also called the thumb or flash drive. Smaller than a matchbox, this facility that slotted into a USB port on the desktop or laptop was of a price and size that allowed every student to back up the digital files they were working on and take them between home and school. For around $A15–20 students in 2008 could have a 1-gigabyte USB drive.

Computer games

By 2008, the computer games industry was reputed to be comparable in size and worth to the movie industry.

It was becoming increasingly evident through the work of people like Gee (2007), Prensky (2006, 2007) and Johnson (2006) that complex computer games were having a significant positive impact on the learning of the young outside the classroom. As David O'Brien indicated in his chapter in *Leading a Digital School* (Lee & Gaffney, 2008), there were important lessons schools should be learning from the computer games developers.

Chris Dede in 1998 highlighted the very real contribution the increasingly sophisticated computer games technology could play as part of the teacher's digital toolkit.

> What if these devices—ubiquitous in rich and poor homes, urban and rural— were also utilised for educational reasons, even though not acquired for that purpose?

> (Dede, 1998, p. 4)

However, despite all this—and the games technology being in vogue as long the personal computer—computer games and consoles have barely been used in schools.

OVERVIEW

By the early 2000s, the digital instructional technology had reached the stage where there were few, if any, technological or indeed financial constraints curtailing the use of digital technology by every teacher. Most of the technology was used every day in both the students' and teachers' homes. Even the youngest of school students could readily use most of the technologies, if only in a simple way.

Gone were the very considerable technological and financial hurdles that had frustrated teachers well into the 1980s. But in most classrooms in 2007, minimal—albeit excellent—use was being made of the ever-expanding digital kit. The limiting variable was human, and found in the main within the school and education authorities.

15

INTERACTIVE WHITEBOARDS

At the beginning of the twenty-first century a new technology began to appear in schools in significant numbers: the interactive whiteboard or IWB. The interactive whiteboard brought together in the one convenient unit the best features of the teaching board, the capability of the computer, the motion picture, television and audio recorders, video conferencing, access to the networked world, and the ready facility to integrate all manner of digital teaching tools. It could be used as a traditional whiteboard, a large digital convergence facility or a highly sophisticated digital teaching hub, depending on the expertise of the user. In reflecting on the use of the other instructional technologies over a 50-year period, Emeritus Professor Phillip Hughes, noted that the interactive whiteboard brought together in the one teacher-friendly unit all the main instructional technologies of the last half century.

Developed initially in the early 1990s, by the mid 2000s pathfinding schools around the world had 100 per cent of their teaching staff using IWBs integrally in their everyday teaching. This happened in primary and secondary schools, from kindergarten through to Year 12, and within every area of the curriculum, with both the slow learners and the gifted.

While the photographic slide and the OHP were significant exceptions to the normal pattern of use of instructional technology, and were used in everyday teaching, they were only ever used by small groups of teachers. Here at last was an instructional technology that every teacher was prepared to use and embrace.

What became evident in the interviews with Nancy Knowlton, the CEO of SMART Technologies, and Peter Lambert, Director of Product Marketing for Promethean, was that both companies designed their boards from the outset primarily for teachers.

This instructional technology had the facility to assist teachers with their teaching, and in time enhance that teaching and help move it from its traditional paper-resource base to one that was predominantly digital. Professor Hughes noted in the interview that by the mid 2000s the introduction of the interactive whiteboard was already shaping as one of the defining moments in the history of teaching, on par with the introduction of the book, the blackboard and free and secular schooling. In Professor Hughes's mind teaching had not fundamentally changed in the past 50 years, and yet virtually overnight total teaching staffs were embracing the use not only of IWBs but also the expanding and developing complementary digital technology.

THE TECHNOLOGY

Interactive whiteboards are in essence large, touch-screen computer monitors that are able to accommodate virtually all manner of digital signal.

The history of the interactive whiteboard differs in several significant ways from all the earlier instructional technology. Most importantly, IWBs were to be used by teachers and not the general consumer market. Secondly, not only did the main companies adopt different technologies in the creation of their 'interactive whiteboards', there was no concerted effort to adopt an international industry standard.

In the early years, three main types of technology emerged:

- Resistive membrane technology, which became known as the 'soft' boards. Pioneered by SMART Technologies, a Canadian-based company, this technology was also used by companies like Egan Teamboard, Polyvision and Panasonic.
- Magnetic pickup boards, the so-called 'hard boards'. This technology was developed by companies like Numonics in the US and Promethean in the UK.
- Ultrasonic tracking technology developed by Virtual Ink, a Boston-based dot.com, and marketed as the mimio board.

The key is that all of the technologies worked well, providing teachers with a simple-to-use, highly reliable and an immensely powerful technology. And most importantly, while the operating systems were not compatible, all the boards were able to run the existing mainstream software applications and the main web applications. In time, all the bigger-selling IWBs also catered for both the Windows and Mac platforms.

Figure 15.1 Promethean interactive whiteboard of the mid 2000s (Courtesy Greg Walker)

Over time other IWB technologies—some variants of the afore-mentioned and some completely new—came onto the market, but again with the ready facility to handle all existing software. One was soon able to secure rear-projection IWBs and, over time, plasma and LCD screen-based variants as well as 'boards' based on emerging technology. Of note is that the ultrasonic tracking technology could be used on a wall without the need for even a whiteboard.

The vast majority of the IWBs used in schools have been what are known as front-projection boards. In time, that situation could change as the cost of alternatives diminishes. In brief, with an IWB there is the need for a board, a data projector projecting onto the board, a computer, and a carefully calibrated relationship between the data projector and the board. With that calibration, students and teachers are able to work the board, using the finger or a stylus, as they would a mouse on a computer monitor.

The boards varied in size, but within the few years of use the trend was towards larger boards, with 72-inch being regarded as basic by the mid 2000s. The computer that drove the board also served as the control for access to all the other digital facilities, be it the network, the Internet, digital television, sound systems or the many other facilities within the digital toolkit.

The key variable, however, was not so much the board itself but rather the teaching software that was provided, and the key differentiator between boards was the quality of that software.

In the early 1990s, as revealed in the interviews, the leadership of SMART Technologies, David Martin, and his partner Nancy Knowlton recognised the immense education potential of the IWBs and began developing applications software specifically for use by teachers. Throughout the mid 1990s they gradually refined that software and in 1998 released the first of the SMART Notebook series, a very sophisticated and yet simple set of digital teaching applications (SMART Technologies, 2008). That software, which came free of cost with the purchase of the board, provided teachers with a comprehensive suite of:

- digital templates from which they could readily create lessons
- interactive presentation tools
- multimedia recording and playback facilities, and
- tools that allowed teachers to use on their boards a plethora of mainstream software applications, be it MS Office, web browsers or Flash.

In the UK, Promethean (a company within the TDS group) also recognised in the mid 1990s the immense educational value of IWBs. Building on the technology being jointly developed by another TDS company, Numonics, Promethean developed its Activboard and its own teaching software, Activstudio. It soon came to vie with SMART Notes as the major IWB teaching software.

Virtual Ink, the developer of the mimio board, emerged initially as a dot.com company with a wonderful piece of smart technology developed by a team at M.I.T. In interview it was revealed the company believed it had a product that all boardrooms would want, and opted for a low-priced, WalMart-style of marketing. The approach failed, the company all but collapsed, and the team within also recognised that the way forward was the schools market and so reshaped its software accordingly.

The teaching software developed by all these companies was of high quality and very reliable, and provided all manner of teachers with a comprehensive set of digital facilities to enrich their teaching, save time and generally work more productively. Average classroom teachers could in a few seconds 'cut and paste' a collection of text, images, video and sound files to create their own interactive multimedia lesson, and then with a few clicks store that presentation in the school's information management system for future use. (One of the principals interviewed commented on a teacher who had gone into Google at 8 am for material on 'The Hare and the Tortoise', had found a Flash presentation online and had edited the original work for use in a 9 am class.)

The software upgrades provided by all the IWB providers were free, in marked contrast to the traditional approach where schools were obliged to purchase the software upgrade.

It is of note that while the SMART and Promethean boards were designed from the outset primarily for teacher use, there was a range of boards—produced in the main by the large technology corporations—that were designed primarily for use in corporate seminar and boardrooms. Those companies chose not to develop their own comprehensive teaching software but rather to take advantage of the generic teaching software produced by RM, called Easiteach.

Interactive whiteboards could be used (and came increasingly to be used) in classrooms as a digital integrator and to give additional life and functionality to other digital tools. Mal Lee, writing in early 2004 for the IWBNet website http://www.iwb.net.au, referred to the facility as creating 'digital teaching hubs' in each classroom, with the IWB being the hub for a suite of complementary technologies, such as scanners, DVD players, digital still and video cameras, digital TV and video conferencing (IWBNet, 2004). As indicated in Chapter 14, IWBs added another dimension to many of those often underused digital technologies.

Teachers finally had an instructional technology designed specifically for teachers. Until the introduction of IWBs, teachers had had to make do with technologies designed for the home or office markets. Most importantly, teachers had a group of international technology companies in whose interest it was to listen to and better cater for the needs of teachers. Throughout the 2000s, major upgrades to the teaching software were made every few years, and not only did the quality, range of offerings and sophistication grow, so also did the facility to take advantage of emerging digital hardware and software.

THE EDUCATION AUTHORITIES 'TAKE CONTROL'

As flagged earlier, in the latter 1990s one notes an emerging propensity for at least some national educational authorities to take greater control of the instructional technology being used in their classrooms. The UK was one of the first national governments to ask the hard questions about the appropriateness of certain instructional technologies for general classroom use, and to use its national buying power to set standards for the technology companies wanting to sell to the schools it funded.

In the 2000s, a growing number of national and regional authorities followed the UK lead. Nations as diverse as Mexico, China, Hong Kong, South Africa and France began making widespread use of IWBs. Most were particularly concerned with the wisdom of continuing with a personal computer-based ICT and education strategy. Study after study was showing that the very considerable investment in personal computing was having little impact on the nature of teaching or student learning. Most importantly, teacher classroom use of that technology remained low.

In the early 2000s, the British government decided to switch to a strategy based heavily on the use of interactive whiteboards. The intention was to use a phased approach that would in time see an IWB in every government-funded classroom. Becta was charged with facilitating the wise acquisition and use of the boards, the associated teacher and leadership training and the conduct of appropriate research. Building on the vision set by government and the very considerable monies allocated to realise that vision, Becta was able to leverage off that investment and establish a set of purchasing standards that all IWB providers who wanted to sell in the UK had to follow. That benchmarking, and the associated practical ongoing advice provided to teachers, has been built upon around the world.

The UK investment in the boards and e-learning also helped spawn a British interactive teaching materials industry. By the mid 2000s, not only was that industry growing rapidly in the UK, its product was being sold globally. The British government recognised early the need to provide teachers with digital templates they could use. Rather than develop and market those templates itself, it outsourced the operation. RM won the contract, for example, for the creation of a suite of generic digital teaching templates and used that funding to develop Easiteach. Easiteach was able to run on all boards. It was gradually taken up by many of the 'second tier' IWBs. When Mexico decided to adopt a national IWB-based strategy in the mid 2000s, RM was able to build on the investment in Easiteach and produce a Spanish variant that could in turn be sold internationally.

IMPLEMENTATION

In examining the introduction of interactive whiteboards across the developed world in the 2000s one notes a growing appreciation of the importance of an integrated whole-school strategy, but at the same time a perpetuation of the follies of the 'impetuous technophilia' and the historic propensity to focus on the technical rollout and give little consideration to the many human variables.

Each of the case studies in Chapter 17 provides an insight into the kind of reasoned, whole-school implementation strategy required to secure the sustained total teacher use of IWBs, but unfortunately for all those kinds of reasoned situations there were in the 2000s far more schools and education authorities that did not exercise the same astute leadership.

The implementation of IWBs in the 2000s is probably summed up by a situation observed by Mal Lee at a conference in 2007. One of the principals featured in Chapter 17 had completed an excellent overview of the implementation approach used by his school community. A group of teachers from a range of schools approached him at the end and mentioned how they had had principals and business managers acquire four to five IWBs and simply hand them to the teachers to use. Afterwards the principal asked, 'How can school leaders do that kind of thing?' He then inquired of Mal, 'Does that happen often?' Sadly, in 2007 that occurred all too frequently.

The UK in the 2000s showed very considerable acumen in its national implementation of IWBs and development of the associated interactive multimedia teaching materials. But in interviewing a cross-section of school leaders, consultants and IWB providers, even with all its acumen there was still a propensity to focus on the technical rollout rather than the wise, whole-school use of that technology. Nonetheless, by setting clear national goals, funding the wherewithal to realise those goals, creating and supporting Becta, setting up a national broadband network for schools, commissioning genuine research, funding ongoing professional development and the City Learning Centres, and providing £200 to every teacher each year for them to buy software, the UK was placed well ahead of most other educational authorities.

What the UK's IWB experience reveals is the enormity—and increasing challenge—of orchestrating a successful national digital instructional technology implementation. When one contrasts the UK lead with those authorities that made great noises about providing one or two IWBs for each school, and who did not provide any training, ICT support or research, the approach taken by the UK deserves very considerable recognition.

At the school level, the 2000s saw astute pathfinding schools across the developed world successfully addressing the many variables required to achieve and sustain the total teacher use of IWBs and the related digital technology. However, like the UK, they were very much in the minority.

Of note is that aside from work undertaken be Her Majesty's Inspectorate of Education in Scotland (HMIE, 2005) and the study undertaken by Lee and Winzenried in 2005, little was written on the school or education authority IWB implementation arrangements.

TEACHER DEVELOPMENT

The variability of the approaches taken with school and authority implementation strategies was reflected in the approaches taken with the training and ongoing professional development provided to the teachers.

However, even with this variability there was a clear appreciation by educational leaders of the vital importance of professional development, even though many chose not to fund it. The more astute schools and education authorities appreciated the fundamental importance of quality, ongoing teacher and leadership development. Those schools and authorities attached high priority to this aspect and provided extensive ongoing funding. The UK, for example, not only provided significant funding for a multi-pronged national teacher and leadership training, but also invested in in-depth research and even mandated that the sale of boards had to include the provision of training.

At the other end of the scale there was much of the aforementioned 'dumping' of the technology on the teachers and education authorities, making great noises about installing an IWB in each school and providing no real training.

TEACHER USAGE

As indicated earlier, by the mid 2000s there was a significant number of pathfinding schools across the developed world where all teachers were using IWBs and complementary digital tools integrally in their everyday teaching. The major IWB providers report successful whole-school use in such diverse situations as Hong Kong, China, France, South Africa, New Zealand, Ireland, the US, Mexico and obviously the UK. The kind of case studies described in Chapter 17 could readily be found in every Australian state and territory in 2008. There were, moreover, a growing number of national and regional educational authorities that had embarked on programs to place IWBs in every classroom in their jurisdiction.

The UK led the way and by 2008 had IWBs in over 60 per cent of its classrooms, with planning underway to begin a second wave of purchases to replace those IWBs more than ten years old (Futuresource Consulting, 2008). Of note is that while a sizeable number of education authorities across the US, and in particular those in the higher socio-economic areas, had also opted to fully equip their schools with IWBs, the second-largest rollout of IWBs had occurred in Mexico with over 40 per cent of classrooms having IWBs by 2008, with sales exceeding those in the US (ibid.). One can gain an appreciation of the uptake of IWBs by noting globally the total sales of IWBs:

- In 2002, 70 956 boards were sold.
- In 2006, 410 457 boards were sold.
- In 2008, the projected growth is 44 per cent, with sales reaching 603 881. (ibid.)

While it is appreciated that the availability of an instructional technology does not mean it is being used by the teachers, of note is the similarity between the reported percentage of sales of IWBs in the UK and the note from the Becta research below indicating that 64 per cent of teachers in the UK were using IWBs.

The Becta Review of 2007, *Harnessing Technology*, notes that in the period 2002–05 the instructional technology most used by both primary and secondary teachers in the UK was, by a significant margin, the interactive whiteboard (Becta, 2007, figure 4.3). Of note was the observation that:

> *Interactive whiteboards were used most frequently in lessons in secondary schools by maths teachers, three-fifths (60 per cent) of whom said that interactive whiteboards were used in at least half of maths lessons. Interactive whiteboards were least likely to be used frequently by music teachers, with 27 per cent saying they were used in at least half of lessons. (p. 43)*

In the 2007 Review, Becta charts the rapid teacher acceptance of IWBs in the UK, with only 5 per cent of teachers using the boards in 2002 and 64 per cent by 2006 (ibid., table 3.9).

In making this observation it should be stressed that, although not specifically stated in Becta's Reviews, there undoubtedly were in many parts of the UK, and indeed across the world, schools where—like the instructional technology beforehand—the boards sat unused. Several who were interviewed, including both consultants and senior IWB executives, noted situations where the boards were not being used or were markedly underused.

REASONS FOR ACCEPTANCE

The big question is why did teachers embrace the whole-school use of IWBs when they did not accept earlier technologies? The answer is obviously complex, but by the mid 2000s a number of the factors were becoming apparent and, not surprisingly, most were evidenced in the failings of the earlier technology and indeed in the long-term acceptance and use of the traditional teaching boards.

In 2006, the authors undertook a small study of the reasons why teachers in schools with boards throughout were universally prepared to use IWBs in their everyday teaching. The study was an extension of:

- a 2003 analysis of the impact of IWBs on Richardson Primary School (Lee & Boyle, 2003)
- a 2004 research project on the attitude of the teachers at Richardson Primary to the whole-school introduction of IWBs (Lee, B. & Boyle, 2004)
- a 2005 examination of the nature of the implementation processes used in a cross-section of schools in the UK, US and Australia that had succeeded in introducing IWB s throughout the schools (Lee & Winzenried, 2005).

The telling point in the ten school teaching staffs surveyed was that there was a 100 per cent teacher acceptance of the technology. Moreover, although the gender, years of teaching experience and ICT expertise of the teachers were ascertained, none of those variables was a factor influencing the preparedness to use IWBs.

The experiences of the five case studies in Chapter 17 reinforce those findings.

Educational benefit of the technology

In identifying the reasons why all the teachers surveyed were prepared to use the boards, the three main reasons given were educational and had to do with the teachers' belief that use of this technology would enhance their teaching and student learning. The three main reasons given were:

- 'Potential to enrich my teaching'
- 'Impact on student learning'
- 'Appreciation of educational potential'.

The gatekeepers to the use of the technology clearly believed that use of the technology would benefit their students.

Comfort of use

The survey asked how long it was before they felt comfortable using the board in their teaching. Of note, the schools involved in the survey were using different types of boards, and both Windows and Mac variants.

The vast majority of the teachers felt comfortable using their IWB within two to four months. One young teacher noted that she was comfortable using the board after five minutes. It is important to stress that the feedback we received from those interviewed indicated that many teachers using IWBs felt comfortable and at ease with the technology when they could use their Microsoft Office or Apple iLife software with the boards, rather than necessarily the teaching software provided with the board.

When one watches five-year-olds comfortably using the boards—hard and soft—one can appreciate how simple they are to use, at least in their basic mode. Helping in the comfort of use was the simplicity of the operating systems and their reliability.

Building on the known

Interactive whiteboards are first and foremost teaching boards. The skills and confidence that teachers had built up in using blackboards, whiteboards and/or overhead projectors could be used with IWBs. (As indicated, IWBs can be used as a whiteboard [sometimes inadvisably], as an interactive whiteboard or as a large-screen digital convergence facility. The manner of use depends on the teacher's intentions and expertise.)

While the capability of IWBs is markedly enhanced when linked by broadband to the Internet, they can nonetheless be very powerful in their 'stand alone' mode, as was often the case in the pathfinding schools.

Assisting existing teaching

In brief, teachers finally had in the interactive whiteboard an immensely powerful digital instructional technology that could assist their existing teaching. Vitally, it could assist that teaching without them having to change their pedagogy. The contrast with the personal computer was pronounced. If in time when they were comfortably using the technology they perceived the need to vary their teaching style, they could.

Graduated uptake

All IWBs can be used at various levels, from the very basic through to the very sophisticated. As mentioned above, teachers become very comfortable with the technology in a very short time. However, as they made greater use of the technology, as they watched other colleagues and the students using the boards, their expectations rose and so too did their desire to use increasingly sophisticated facilities.

Teachers controlled that uptake and thus did not need to plunge into the deep end and fundamentally change their teaching overnight as occurred with computers, and in particular computer labs. With the growing confidence and expertise the teachers could in their own time gradually attune their teaching to get the most from the technology.

Ready fit with existing teaching

It was very easy and relatively secure to position IWBs permanently in every teaching room for the teachers to use whenever they wanted. Teachers had instant access—if at 2.45 pm on a Friday afternoon they wanted to access the Net, they could do so in a few clicks. They did not have to waste time going to special rooms or taking equipment out of storerooms. Moreover, every teacher had the technology in their room and could factor its use into their everyday teaching. The IWBs allowed teachers to readily work within the givens of teaching mentioned earlier.

Importantly, in contrast to personal computers, IWBs could be used to teach a total class or sections of the class or to facilitate small-group or individual work. Like the traditional board, IWBs could moreover be used to help manage classes. It was interesting in the interviews to hear teachers opting to use those IWBs that needed a stylus, arguing that the teacher's control of the stylus helped in classroom management.

A major difference between the traditional boards and the IWBs was that teachers could use the boards in classroom administration and communication. The boards could be used in the marking of rolls, the sending of digital work by email directly to the parents or sister schools and in the management of the teacher's and students' materials when there was a learning platform with which to interface.

Digital convergence facility

IWBs make excellent, simple-to-use and immensely powerful digital convergence facilities. As large touch-screen monitors they can readily connect with, and in many instances add significant capability to, all of the digital tools described in Chapter 14. Instructional technologies like digital cameras, scanners, the World Wide Web, surround sound systems, graphic calculators and digital microscopes—all of which had been available before the widespread acceptance of IWBs—take on an added dimension when used in conjunction with the boards.

Of note is that all five of the schools featured in Chapter 17 have provided scanners, digital cameras and sound systems with their IWBs in each classroom.

Creation of digital teaching hubs

The digital convergence facility allows every classroom to become a digital teaching hub. Each of those hubs can in turn be linked to like hubs across the school, the education authority or the networked world. As the centrepiece and indeed control panel, the boards can be used as 'state-of-the-art' libraries, as video and audio production and presentation facilities, as digital television monitors or video-conferencing centres. In the item that Mal Lee wrote in 2004 for the IWBNet website http://www.iwb.net.au/advice/digital-hubs/1-intro.htm flagging the concept of the digital hub (IWBNet, 2004) he noted that the main inhibitor to what can be included in the digital hub was the teacher's mindset and not so much the technology.

Facility to create own lessons

Allied to the comfort in using the boards was the ready facility for teachers to create their own, highly professional interactive, multimedia lessons.

Reduced workload

It was apparent very early in their use that IWBs had the facility to significantly reduce the teacher lesson preparation time and enhance teacher efficiency. It is easy to forget how much time was consumed in traditional paper-based teaching with the mundane clerical work, photocopying assignments, literally cutting and pasting teaching aids, and as mentioned earlier simply copying lesson materials onto the teaching board. The digital technology had the capacity to reduce teachers' clerical tasks, and to allow them to load their lessons onto the IWB from home. In the Richardson Primary School studies (Lee & Boyle, 2003; Lee, B. & Boyle, 2004) it soon became apparent that after an initial acclimatisation the teachers could make their lesson preparation ever-more efficient and reduce their workload. (Of note is that the Richardson initiative was strongly supported by the local teachers' union, conscious of the facility to enhance teaching while reducing the load on teachers.)

Those findings were reinforced in Becta's analysis of IWB use in the UK. It noted in its 2007 Review that:

> More than half of primary teachers who used online resources and interactive whiteboards felt that they saved time using these resources. Interactive whiteboards were felt to save time by 55 per cent of primary teachers, with 16 per cent reporting saving more than two hours; however, 13 per cent felt they lost time.
>
> Secondary teachers were less likely than primary teachers to report time savings. Forty-four per cent of secondary teachers felt they saved time by using interactive whiteboards, with 16 per cent saying they saved more than two hours, while 17 per cent felt that they lost time by using interactive whiteboards (Kitchen et al., 2007). The majority of primary teachers in the Harnessing Technology Schools Survey (Kitchen et al., 2007) expected to save time by using online resources and interactive whiteboards in the next twelve months.
>
> Secondary teachers were less likely to expect to save time in this way. Evidence from the ICT Test Bed project indicates that improvements in the detail and efficiency of learner assessments occurred. (p. 48)

Timing

On reflection, the introduction of interactive whiteboards came at an opportune time. A host of variables that could and would impact on the use of the boards in everyday teaching came into play at the same time in the early 2000s.

The use of digital technology in society in general and in the home in particular was extensive, and growing. The world as noted by Thomas Friedman had become flat (Friedman, 2006). The students, from the very young, were not only comfortable with the digital technology but had come to regard its use as the norm. Most teachers were making general use of a variety of digital technologies in their everyday lives, and the vast majority, as noted by Cuban (2001), were using personal computers at home and in their lesson preparation.

Digital convergence was becoming the norm with an ever-growing suite of sophisticated digital technologies. The mainstream computer applications had grown in sophistication and made the creation of multimedia teaching materials that much easier and faster. By the mid 2000s, most schools in the developed world were networked, with at least reasonable access to the Internet. In many situations all the classrooms had high-speed Net access.

This development, and the associated ongoing increase in the bandwidth available to schools, was particularly important because although the IWBs could operate as stand-alone tools, their potential was markedly amplified when they had high-speed access to the Net and World Wide Web. At the same time the online educational offerings on the Net that could be used by teachers grew at pace and with sophistication. Google had transformed the search for online materials.

Society's expectation of what could be done with the digital technology had grown at pace, and those expectations impacted on government and school leaders. As indicated earlier, the UK's injection of sizeable monies into both interactive whiteboards and software served, if not to spawn, to markedly stimulate the development of an international interactive multimedia industry that through the 2000s produced many high-quality commercial and free teaching materials for use with IWBs.

Support provided by IWB technology providers

The teaching software provided by the major IWB providers was very much designed to make it very easy for teachers to readily create high-quality, interactive multimedia lessons. Here was a technology that was not only designed for teachers, but which worked with the teachers to both enhance the teaching options in the software and allow teachers to create the lessons more efficiently.

Peter Lambert, Director of Product Marketing for Promethean, provided the authors with this telling recollection of the attributes that Promethean bore in mind when designing its Activstudio software:

> When we first started to design the product set we were clear from the outset that we had to model the tools that teachers were familiar with in non digital environments. We were also clear that those tools were to be accessed on a large surface using a pen and thus the standard windows menu system would be awkward to access the top of the board to choose File—Edit—View etc.
>
> Thus, we designed the tool palette to be 'floating' with the menu items popping up from a menu button. Thus the toolbox could be moved to any

position on the screen to suit the user. This conscious decision to move away from the 'comfort' of a standard Windows interface was purely from a usability perspective.

So what about the tools on the toolbox? We were always mindful of the shift from a traditional dry wipe marker board to a digital board and the first tools we placed on the palette were digital versions of the old tools—obviously a pen and an eraser. We deliberately chose to have a single pen with a colour choice rather than 4 pens with pre-defined colours. Because we were now in a digital environment we allowed pen width choice as well. Because we could we added a highlighter pen as well.

Once these digital annotations were on screen they could be manipulated so we added a select tool and allowed object selection and manipulation such as drag, resize, rotate and re-shape. These 4 tools have stood the test of time and are still the first 4 tools in the Activstudio 3 toolbox.

Our next thought was about saving teacher time and really pushing the advantages of the digital environment. The flipchart concept involved simply turning to a new page once the first page had been filled—no need to clean the board and lose all your annotations, simply move forward and a new page was created. Move back and your first page could be re-displayed. Saving the flipchart and printing the pages were then added to the menu.

Our next step was groundbreaking; we designed a library of annotations which were pre-drawn shapes, objects, apparatus, maps etc. etc. that teachers would usually have to draw every time they used a chalkboard or dry wipe board. We pre-defined many of these from our teaching experience but soon started to receive requests from our early adopters. We were very flexible at the time, being a small team, and could adapt the software extremely quickly. A curriculum-based library of annotations was rapidly established. Once we had the library established we then added a curriculum-based page background pack. In the early days we got gasps of delight when we showed graph paper, music manuscript or maps.

Other tools were added to the toolbox, which enhanced the 'presentation' effect, spotlight, reveal and magnify. We were always conscious that some tools would be used in some curriculum areas that wouldn't be used in others and so our toolbox was always customisable.

We also developed the 'profile' concept, which had basic, intermediate and advanced user configurations.

Over the years more sophisticated tools have been added, mainly due to user requests, but the customisable toolbox has always been a constant. Maths teachers would want the ruler, protractor and compasses on their toolbox whilst a history teacher may not.

(P. Lambert, personal communication with authors, 21 September, 2007)

While this example is from Promethean, the same kind of regard for teachers has been evidenced with all of the IWB providers that have designed their product for use in schools. At the time of writing one of the authors was called upon to assist an international school in Papua New Guinea. The school's boards were clearly experiencing the challenge much technology encounters in the tropics. Within a very short time both the board manufacturer and the Australian reseller had flown in a team to address and alleviate the school's concerns. While it is appreciated good technology companies have always done this, particularly with large clients, this kind of swift, high-level support for a school in a remote setting is rare.

At the same time as the board providers were enhancing their offerings, a growing group—some government, some commercial, and some simply altruistic teachers—was providing an array of interactive teaching resources for use with IWBs. While a small portion of the offerings was packaged, most allowed teachers to readily cut and paste the material to create their own lessons.

Facility to cater for the sophisticated user

By the mid 2000s, the major boards—through the medium of their own and third party software and their facility to work with virtually all of the emerging digital technologies—allowed the highly sophisticated users to work text, graphics, images, sound and video at a level never previously possible in the classroom. Indeed, in many respects at that stage the capability of the facilities available exceeded the thinking of most teachers.

In the pathfinding schools many teachers had used their board, in conjunction with a suite of other digital technologies, to transform their classrooms into what have been termed digital teaching hubs. In those situations the IWB served as the axis or hub for any number of digital inputs and outputs, be it for the networked computers in the room, use of digital television, creation of digital music, video conferencing, basic email communication, Net access or simply to convert each classroom into a 'state-of-the-art' library.

Knowing school leaders

As indicated earlier with the comments on whole-school and whole-education authority implementation strategies, there was an emerging group of school leaders who appreciated the vital role of the school principal in achieving total teacher use of instructional technology. That importance came through in all the aforementioned research and was underscored in each of the case studies.

Despite the many variables in favour of IWBs as an instructional technology, none are as important as a knowing school principal.

Affordability

It was also evident by the mid 2000s that virtually every school in the developed countries could, if the school leadership so decided, introduce IWBs throughout the school and also provide Net access, a surround sound system, a scanner, a digital camera, a card reader and a bank of PCs in each classroom.

An interesting point to emerge from the study undertaken by the authors was that three of the schools were of low socio-economic standing, but the leadership had managed to resource the whole-school introduction of IWBs themselves.

The initial reaction of teachers, school principals and the school 'ICT experts' is to say how expensive the IWBs are, and yet the cost of setting up each teaching room in 2008 was largely a one-off figure of around $A5000 or the cost of four or five personal computers. What the comments do not take into consideration is the total cost of ownership of the technology, and in particular personal computers. IWBs will outlast at least three generations of PCs, the software upgrades are free, there is no annual licence fee per machine and the maintenance and support are appreciably lower.

CONCLUSION

In the space of fifteen years the interactive whiteboard had moved from its expensive prototype form to being used by total school staffs in pathfinding situations around the world. Market research at the beginning of 2008 noted some 30 countries were at the tender stage in the acquisition of IWBs (Futuresource Consulting, 2008). While it was estimated that in 2005 around 500 000 interactive whiteboards had been installed in schools, the projection in 2008 was that by 2012 one in six classrooms across the developed world would have an IWB, with annual sales approaching 1.5 million (ibid.).

The historic impact of interactive whiteboards is probably best evidenced by the following telling observation made by Becta in 2007 in its overview of the extensive battery of research that had been conducted on the use of ICT in the UK over the previous decade. It concluded:

> This sharp rise in use of ICT resources in the curriculum has been driven to a large extent by the adoption of interactive whiteboards (IWBs) and related technologies. Interactive whiteboards are a popular technology, in heavy demand by schools and practitioners. They offer transparent benefits to learning and teaching. That is, it is easy for institutions and teachers to recognise how IWBs enrich and enhance learning and teaching—something which may not always be so immediately transparent to practitioners in the case of other technologies.
>
> (Becta, 2007, p. 66)

16

DIGITAL
TAKE-OFF—
THE HISTORICAL
SIGNIFICANCE

In the early 2000s, the authors noted a historic change occurring in a group of pathfinding schools across the developed world. After nearly a century of abortive efforts, seemingly overnight these schools had succeeded in getting all the teachers in the school to use the digital technology in their everyday teaching. The breakthroughs started being made around the same time as Friedman found his 'flatteners' impacting across the networked world.

The obvious questions were:

- Was this so?
- What was its exact nature?
- Why was it happening in only some schools?
- What were the implications of this development for future schooling?

The questions prompted the authors to delve further and undertake the aforementioned series of consultations and research projects with the successful schools in Australia, New Zealand, the UK and the US. What became increasingly apparent was that the world was seeing a historic and in many respects a revolutionary shift occurring, with teaching and schooling beginning the move from its traditional, paper-based form to one that was predominantly digitally based. Schools were beginning to operate within a digital paradigm, and to contend with the many implications of that shift.

The first—and probably still the most important—sign of the shift was evidenced in the total teacher use of the digital instructional technology in their everyday teaching.

TOTAL TEACHER ICT USAGE

The authors first encountered this total teacher uptake at Richardson Primary School, a small and (as indicated in the case study in Chapter 17) disadvantaged school in Canberra, Australia. The study of that school by Lee and Boyle found:

> *Richardson is the first school in the ACT, and probably Australia, where the total school community, the students, staff and parents, has embraced a new approach to the use of ICT, which enhances the holistic education of the students.*
>
> *It is also the first school to build its strategy around interactive whiteboards rather than the conventional desktop or laptop computer.*
>
> *It has achieved this outcome in less than two years.*
>
> (Lee & Boyle, 2003, p. 2)

Of note is the situation the authors encountered when they next visited Richardson Primary in early 2004. Because of a crossing of wires both the school principal and his deputy were away from the school at the time of the visit. We were told to simply wander through. The interactive whiteboards and the associated digital tools were being used integrally in every classroom. In some situations the students were using the boards while the teachers provided individual support, in other rooms the board was being used to facilitate small-group work, while in another room extensive use was being made of the scanner and the board in a discussion of the students' writings. The use of the instructional technology had become normalised.

In 2005, the authors undertook a research project with a group of eight schools in the UK, US and Australia that had installed IWBs throughout. The desire was to examine the implementation strategies used in each and identify if there were any commonalities. What we found were commonalities but, more significantly, what we also unearthed was that all teachers within the eight schools had embraced the everyday use of the interactive whiteboard and the complementary digital technologies (Lee & Winzenried, 2005).

Since publishing that study the authors have either visited or spoken at length with a cross-section of schools—wealthy and disadvantaged, primary and secondary, government and independent, in situations as diverse as the UK, Ireland, Hong Kong, South Africa, the US, New Zealand and Australia—that are using interactive whiteboards and complementary digital instructional technology throughout. What is important to note is that:

- all were normal schools, receiving in the main their normal recurrent funding
- there were a significant number of schools from lower socio-economic circumstances, where it was found that the school leaders opted for an IWB-based strategy to help 'level the playing field'
- all had opted to build their teacher usage strategy around IWBs, an instructional technology that could be readily used in teaching in every room
- a significant number of schools had IWBs in every room but most teachers still did not use them. (In one fascinating situation the authors found the principal had mandated that the students were not to touch the IWB, but rather to use the electronic slates provided, for fear of teachers being unable to manage the classes.)

SPEED OF TEACHER ACCEPTANCE

The speed of total teacher acceptance in all of the aforementioned situations had been remarkably fast. In the early 2000s, when the pathfinders were moving through completely uncharted waters, total teacher acceptance was still being achieved within two years. One of the secondary schools studied, with 750 students, achieved total teacher acceptance within eighteen months. In more recent years where the work of the pathfinders has helped chart the way, the total acceptance has been even faster. One of the schools in the case study achieved total usage of the technology within three months.

While a range of variables impacted on the speed of the acceptance—factors like finance, school size, leadership and implementation strategies—the point remained that in contrast to the earlier instructional technologies schools that have successfully introduced interactive whiteboards throughout experienced a veritable surge in the use of digital instructional technology.

DIGITAL TAKE-OFF

That surge, that shift from a minority of teachers using the digital instructional technology to a position where all or virtually all teachers were using the technology integrally in their everyday teaching, we have termed a 'digital take-off'.

However, it was not simply the dramatic surge in use, but its catalytic impact on the schools' total operations. By the early 2000s, the vast majority of schools—primary and secondary—were using digital administration, communication and information systems, and many were using some kind of digital learning platform.

The one large non-digital component was the paper-based teaching. When the schools achieved digital take-off, it quickly changed their whole modus operandi and often within months they were not only using the digital technology in most operations, but were also beginning to question the traditional paper-based way of approaching tasks.

RISING EXPECTATIONS

In the schools that had achieved digital take-off and had the teachers taking advantage of the ever-emerging digitally based opportunities, the authors found that the teachers' expectations of what was possible continued to rise at pace. Interactive multimedia lessons, which they had produced with such pride in the first few months of IWB use, had become passé six months later.

When the total teaching staff—not just a few keen early adopters—and the students began to identify the educational opportunities of working within a digital environment, the impact on the total school operations was dramatic. The total teaching staff was not prepared to put up with the many shortcomings that the few early adopters had had to endure. For example, teachers now expected the school's network to be operational 100 per cent of teaching time. Any downtime was simply not acceptable.

DIGITAL OPERATIONAL PARADIGM

Often unwittingly, the schools that had achieved digital take-off soon found themselves working within a digital operational paradigm and no longer the traditional paper-based one that teachers had only ever known.

Almost overnight teachers and school leaders began questioning many of the ways of the past that had been shaped in the main by paper-based operations.

In the paper-based paradigm, schools had for example been characterised, among other things, by their:

- 'Industrial Age' organisational structures
- operation as discrete, largely stand-alone entities
- segmented organisational structure, with a widespread division of labour
- discrete and constant instructional technologies in paper, the pen and the teaching board
- individual lesson preparation
- reliance on mass media
- staffing hierarchy, with fixed roles
- well-defined and long-lasting jobs
- slow segmented paper-based internal communication and information management
- long-established operational parameters.

The potential of the paper technology had long been maximised.

Within the digital paradigm it is already apparent one will be working towards fostering the following attributes:

- 'Information Age' organisational model
- networked, incorporating the total school community and its homes
- integrated synergistic operations
- suite of changing, increasingly sophisticated, converging and networked digital instructional technologies
- increasing collaborative lesson development
- interactive multimedia
- changing, flexible team-oriented staff roles
- uncertainty, untapped potential, rising expectations and frequent job changes
- instant communication and management of digital information across the organisation
- few established operational parameters.

The schools that had moved into this phase where its teaching materials and its administration, communications and learning systems were digital, we termed 'digital schools'.

IMPLICATIONS

Schools soon began to experience the profound implications of this paradigm shift in a host of different daily occurrences, particularly as they endeavoured to take advantage of the educational opportunities that were opening before them. To take maximum advantage of the ever-emerging digital instructional technology, a range of significant changes would have to be made, many of which impacted on the total school.

One of the most profound was the shift—particularly in most secondary schools—from a largely segmented, faculty-based operation to an integrated operation where digital integration was central. The desire was to have the one network, preferably with a common database able to run virtually all of the school's educational and administrative operations. Many of the schools with their strong faculty base and a clear delineation between the school's educational and business operations, and also their ICT and information services, needed to rethink their staffing organisation and indeed their staffing mix.

The ICT infrastructure, even in the smaller schools, assumed a heightened importance, as did the need for an appropriate ICT support operation. A quality information services and information management operation became vital. Digital storage and appropriate backup quickly became major issues when both the teachers and the students began generating sizeable multimedia files. More than ever the schools needed to put in place an ongoing professional development and curriculum support system. School leaders were placed under increasing pressure to find the monies to fund all these developments.

These are but a few of the implications that began to emerge in the mid 2000s, and that were apparent in each of the case studies considered in the next chapter.

Suffice it say that the schools soon appreciated that if they wanted to take full advantage of the opportunities offered by the digital instructional technology over a sustained period, significant and often fundamental changes needed to be made. Indeed what might have been appropriate three or four years earlier had to be re-thought.

It is also apparent that the challenge of addressing those implications could in many situations be considerable. Lee and Gaffney's work on *Leading a Digital School* (2008) explores all the implications in greater depth.

While, as mentioned, there were in 2008 national governments and education authorities attuning their education to the twenty-first century, there are many more that had little understanding of what was transpiring, and that made sustained development very difficult.

ACHIEVING DIGITAL TAKE-OFF

All the schools achieving digital take-off addressed the nine variables briefly mentioned in Chapter 1 and amplified in Chapter 19.

In 2008, it was the pathfinders who were charting the way forward, but it was already apparent that there was a plethora of schools, education authorities and indeed national governments across the world also wanting to achieve digital take-off and harness the educational benefits of the digital instructional technology.

CHAPTER 17

TOTAL TEACHER USE—CASE STUDIES

Each of the case studies provides a further insight into what is entailed in achieving total teacher usage of instructional technology and how virtually all schools in the developed world can achieve that kind of use. A selection has been made of five schools. All are in Australia, and all achieved total teacher usage of digital instructional technology in the period 2002–07. The authors could have drawn them from any part of the developed world. They could, moreover, have drawn upon many more in Australia but, in so saying, in 2007 these kinds of situations were still limited in number.

The examples are drawn from across the socio-economic spectrum, from the government and independent school sectors and from different education authorities. All of the selected schools have opted to place interactive whiteboards as well as complementary digital tools in every classroom. All have succeeded in getting all their teachers to embrace the use of the digital instructional technology in their everyday teaching. They fully appreciate there is variability in the nature and the effectiveness of the use of the digital instructional technology by the various teachers, but in all schools the use of the digital has become normalised.

Each of the schools has, however, opted to use a combination of traditional and contemporary instructional technologies, with all opting to retain their traditional whiteboards and display boards.

The school principal has played a leading role in the moves by all schools to achieve total teacher use of the instructional technology, invariably with the support of a senior staff member who has coordinated the day-to-day, whole-school implementation plan. Several, however, have reached the stage of development where they have opted to spread the mentoring and staff support across a group of teachers, both to ensure the school sustains the change it has made and to enable the 'mentors' to provide particular expertise.

In each school the school library and the teacher-librarian have played a central role in supporting the whole-school use of the instructional technology, with the teacher-librarians having to significantly adjust their role to continue to provide the required support.

In each it was the individual school that took the initiative to achieve total teacher use of the digital media, without any specific support from an education authority. Indeed, several had the going made that much harder by the local education authority and, as will be seen, one had its efforts undermined by the actions of the education authority.

This is not to say that a supportive education authority might not have made the school's efforts that much easier. If we had opted to draw a case study from England, Hong Kong or Forsythe County in the state of Georgia in the US, that would have been so.

All of the chosen situations approached the total teacher use of instructional technology as part of a whole-school quest to enhance the quality of teaching, opted to integrate that quest into the school's overall development strategy and did not use a separate ICT strategy.

The scene described in each of the case studies was as existed in mid 2007.

RICHARDSON PRIMARY SCHOOL, CANBERRA, AUSTRALIAN CAPITAL TERRITORY

Richardson Primary School (K–6) led the way in Australia—and in many respects, internationally—in achieving the total teacher use and indeed the total school community's embracement of interactive whiteboards.

Richardson is located in one of the lower socio-economic areas of Canberra, Australia's capital. It has around 220 students, including a number of special education units. It was, in 2002, the kind of school that no teachers applied to join. Teachers were simply sent there and aimed to get out as soon as possible. It was a school with considerable challenges.

In 2002, the then principal identified the potential of interactive whiteboards to transform the nature of teaching and learning at Richardson. She was conscious of the magnitude of the task, but set in motion an initiative that Lee and Boyle were subsequently to describe as the 'Richardson Revolution' (Lee & Boyle, 2004). While that principal moved on at the end of 2002, her initiative was built upon by the new principal, Robin Geier, and his deputy, Peter Kent.

Within three years Richardson Primary succeeded not only in getting every teacher to use the interactive whiteboards and have the total school community—the teachers, the students and the parents—embrace the use of the boards, but also in taking out one of Australia's national quality teaching awards for the improvements it had made with the students' literacy and numeracy results.

Much of that success can be attributed to the quiet and humane leadership of the principal, and the drive, enthusiasm and general program coordination of the deputy principal. Their focus was very much on enhancing the quality and appropriateness of the teaching and learning, the holistic development of all aspects of the school's operations and the use of the technology to facilitate those developments. The deputy, Peter Kent, wrote and spoke extensively of what he termed 'e-teaching'. Of note was how Richardson integrated the use of its boards into the school's socialisation and behaviour management programs, its instructional program and its everyday student administration.

A very astute teacher-librarian, although new to school teaching, soon appreciated that the library had to provide a new type of digital resource support for teachers and ensure that all the classroom teachers taught information literacy.

The rapid teacher, student and parent acceptance of the IWBs into everyday teaching in the latter part of 2002 and 2003 prompted the school to engage Mal Lee and Dr Maureen Boyle to evaluate the school's use of the boards. That study was released in October 2003 (Lee & Boyle, 2003). In brief, it was highly complimentary of the work undertaken by the school. It transpired that both Mal Lee and Maureen Boyle had at one time been the director of schools responsible for the region that included Richardson Primary, were aware of the 'challenges' that had beset the school and were thus struck by the dramatic change that had occurred in the learning environment and culture of the school. Virtually overnight teachers wanted to remain at the school and did not want to teach without an IWB, and the students had become more caring. (Copies of the report, entitled *The educational effects and implications of the interactive whiteboard strategy of Richardson Primary School: A brief review* [2003] can be secured from http://www.richardsonps.act.edu.au/interactive_whiteboard_initiative.)

The dramatic educational change at Richardson occasioned Lee and Boyle to prepare a monograph entitled *The Richardson Revolution* for the Australian Council for Educational Administration (Lee & Boyle, 2004).

(Note that in retrospect—and conscious of the way in which virtually all the instructional technologies of the twenty-first century have been labelled 'revolutionary' and found wanting—the authors stand by the choice of the title with Richardson. It was in fact a precursor to the changes that subsequently transpired in many other schools in different parts of the world using IWBs throughout.)

There are several aspects of the Richardson situation that bear particular mention.

Richardson, although located in a lower socio-economic community and thus unable to draw upon the level of parent fees or contributions of many other schools, was able to fund the acquisition of IWBs for all teaching rooms from its normal recurrent funding. No special government funding or support was provided, although it should be noted that the parent community raised $A10 000 in 2003 specifically to buy extra IWBs.

The level of technology in the school when Richardson embarked on its quest was basic. The boards were run using tier-two, low-end, two- to three-year-old Windows PCs. There were no broadband services in the suburb and thus the school had to make do with a 56K dial-up connection for several years.

In time the school came to appreciate the role that the IWBs could play as a digital convergence facility and in providing an added dimension to other digital technologies. The Richardson teachers found the humble, low-cost scanner to be a revelation when used with an IWB, in that it allowed the ready conversion of handwriting into digital text and the whole-class consideration and editing of the text. By 2004, in addition to front-projection IWBs, all classrooms had a scanner, DVD player, sound system and digital camera.

Richardson, like many other pathfinder situations, had no one to turn to for teacher training; it had to handle it in-house. However, in so saying, the school appreciated the fundamental importance of ongoing professional development and thus it accorded it priority, found the time for the teachers to 'play in the sandpit' and set aside every second week's staff meeting to the simple sharing of ideas of what could be done with the technology. It was soon appreciated—as is so with every primary school—that all teachers had their own particular areas of expertise and interest, and as such that knowledge, when applied to IWBs, could help other colleagues.

In general terms, the ICT expertise of the Richardson teachers was low when it began using IWBs. Indeed, there were excellent classroom teachers at the school who had declared that they would never use a computer before they retired. Within eighteen months all the teachers, including the latter group, were happily using the IWBs in their everyday teaching and soon could not contemplate teaching without an IWB. Their story is documented in a research paper prepared by Beth Lee and Maureen Boyle entitled *The teachers tell their story* (Lee, B. & Boyle, 2004).

> *The technology allows teachers to manage the digital convergence spontaneously in real time enabling teachers to add dimensions of interactivity into their existing pedagogy. The mix of IWBs and the concept of e-teaching have allowed teachers at Richardson Primary School to use ICTs to enrich and enhance their existing and proven teaching methods.*
>
> (ibid.)

That study today still provides an invaluable insight into how a group of everyday teachers responded to the wise, whole-school implementation of digital instructional technology.

The collective effort of the teachers was reflected in significant improvement in the school's education authority mandated literacy and numeracy scores, achieving above the authority mean in literacy for the very first time. While the school was wary about attributing that success solely to the introduction of IWBs, the boards were the only major new variable added to the school's operations. The parents had little doubt that the boards were responsible for that improvement. Fuller details can be found at http://www.iwb.net.au/advice/casestudies/richardson/1-intro. htm (IWBNet, 2008).

Of note is that Ingle Farm Primary School, which is also featured in these case studies and is also a low socio-economic school, experienced the same kind of improvement. Experience with a cross-section of schools using IWBs throughout the world would suggest that while it is common to find this improvement in low socio-economic settings, it is not so readily found in higher socio-economic schools where the students are already performing in the top quartile.

The impact of the introduction of the IWBs on the students was also to be seen in a pronounced drop in the level of absenteeism and a reduction in the amount of vandalism during the school holiday breaks.

The Richardson case study unfortunately does not have the happy ending of the other schools in this chapter. The local government education authority in its wisdom had a policy that every teacher and school leader in the authority had to move schools at least every five years. By Easter 2007, the last of the teachers and leadership staff who were at the school in 2003 had been transferred. Richardson Primary School—that body of professionals that went to make up the school teaching community and had won national and international recognition for its work—no longer existed.

By October 2007, the total teacher use of the digital instructional technology at Richardson had begun to decline, brought about largely by the policies of the leadership of the local education authority.

NGUNNAWAL PRIMARY SCHOOL, CANBERRA, AUSTRALIAN CAPITAL TERRITORY

Ngunnawal is a government primary school in the Gunghalin region, one of the newer areas of the Australian Capital Territory. It has approximately 450 students, K–6. The school draws from an above-average socio-economic group, in marked contrast to Richardson Primary. (Fuller details on the school can be found at http://www.ngunnawalps.act.edu.au/.)

Figure 17.1 Ngunnawal Primary School (Courtesy Ngunnawal PS)

Ngunnawal chose to introduce interactive whiteboards throughout the school in 2004. In the three years since, the school has witnessed a dramatic change in its teaching. Barbara Muirhead has been the principal since the introduction of the boards. A school leader of many years standing, Barbara has commented that the transformation has been the most dramatic in her 40-plus years of teaching.

There is an excitement in the classrooms these days—from both teachers and students. Students portray their learning through excellent multimedia presentations. The enthusiasm is contagious and new teachers are supported with our team approach to quickly develop their skills.

The principal's decision to move from its traditional computer labs was taken after viewing the boards in use with the students at Richardson Primary.

> Ngunnawal was still the newest ACT school and had been set up with fibre-optic cabling for high-quality ICT. We decided to purchase one or two for the senior units. However, it became very clear that most teachers wanted one in their classroom, so I had to rethink the initial idea of purchasing one or two.

Fortunately, and largely because of the astute financial management of the founding principal, Ngunnawal was able to afford to buy an interactive whiteboard for every double teaching unit, all at the one time. Barbara decided to place an IWB, a sound system, scanner, digital camera and, in time, pods of personal computers in each double teaching unit. If, as she hoped, the boards had the desired impact and teacher acceptance, she would then place an additional IWB in each unit. That the school did in 2007.

Barbara was very conscious of securing total teacher acceptance of the technology and thus ensured from the outset that the teachers were given the time and support needed to become comfortable in using the boards. Of interest was the decision to place an IWB in the teachers' commonroom and allow anyone who was interested or who had a good idea, to share it with their colleagues.

Barbara Muirhead captures the school community's acceptance of the IWBs in this observation:

> Excitement, enthusiasm—and very soon many students possessed sound knowledge about accessing information and were able to trouble-shoot; e.g. 'You need to turn the sound on, Barbara—that button at the bottom of the board!' and 'Just Google it Barbara'! They have learned how to solve their own problems and to find solutions by navigating their way through on-line learning. They appear to have become more interested in their world. Teachers and parents are more than pleased with the learning that takes place.

One of the unintended dividends of the introduction of the IWBs was the improvement they brought in student behaviour.

> Expectations have risen. Student behaviour has improved in senior classrooms, which I believe is a result of the boards providing a strong visual stimulus.

The school's introduction of the boards was unintentionally assisted by the local education authority's decision to provide high-speed broadband access to the school and through the school's fibre-optic network to all the boards.

The teachers and the students, from the very young upwards, embraced the boards from the outset. Ngunnawal had all teachers using the boards integrally in their teaching within a year, and by that stage pressure was mounting for a second board to be installed in each teaching unit. That acceptance was assisted by very astute school leadership that was prepared to provide the teachers with the time, training and ongoing support they required, and to overcome the inevitable hurdles.

The major hurdle is probably the financial obligation and need for technical assistance to maintain and support a strong network.

Ngunnawal, like many others, had to contend with the theft of data projectors, and indeed the removal of part of the ceiling in the process! The promotion of several key staff placed some added pressure on operations, but overall digital take-off was achieved quickly and with much enjoyment. In achieving take-off the school had to markedly rethink the storage and management of its digital teaching materials.

When asked what would happen when she moved on, the principal was of little doubt that the enhancement of the teaching with the digital instructional technology would continue at pace.

[The school] will continue to grow and develop as it is embedded in the teaching and learning culture at Ngunnawal. Our strategic planning takes into account the need to continue to build and develop digital tools to serve the needs of our electronic age students.

INGLE FARM PRIMARY SCHOOL, ADELAIDE, SOUTH AUSTRALIA

Ingle Farm Primary is a government primary school of approximately 510 students located in the northern suburbs of Adelaide, the capital of South Australia. The school is located in an old housing commission area and as such draws upon a low socio-economic community in a similar way as at Richardson.

There are, however, features of the Ingle Farm student population that make the school even more challenging. The core of the student population of around 260 includes approximately 40 Indigenous Australians and a sizeable number of students for whom English is a second language. The school also caters for approximately 250 'new arrival' students—refugees from around the world who have come to Australia speaking little or no English and who are sent to Ingle Farm for eighteen months to learn English. There are, moreover, two special education units.

Ingle Farm's decision to adopt interactive whiteboards throughout emerged out of a serendipitous visit of the principal, David O'Brien, to Canberra and the opportunity to explore the IWB developments taking place at Richardson Primary School. As David indicated when asked why he chose to use IWBs:

> ... gut reaction. One had only to look at the mix of students at the school, the strong ESL and Aboriginal representation to appreciate the potential. Made a lot of sense. 'Blind Freddy' could see the educational opportunities particularly for a school with a large proportion of Indigenous students and students learning English.

David opted to start with three IWBs in 2003, and in so doing chose to start with three teachers who wanted to use the technology. Two had strong ICT skills while the other was a very good classroom teacher. In the opening phase David needed to provide both logistical and hands-on support for those teachers, but in the second year he was able to call upon an experienced teacher-librarian to play the program coordination and support role.

The whole-school use of the technology was the plan from the outset, as was total teacher acceptance of the boards. The implementation strategy therefore factored in getting all teachers on board and providing them with the required ongoing professional development, support, and most importantly the time to explore the many options. Ingle Farm brought to the school the deputy principal from Richardson, Peter Kent, and in turn sent a group of teachers to Richardson to see first-hand the work being done there.

Figure 17.2 SMART interactive whiteboard in use at Ingle Farm Primary School (Courtesy Ingle Farm PS)

The nature of teacher acceptance of the particular technology was such that David had (what had to be a first with instructional technology!) teachers queuing up to get their own board. When asked why the teachers should have been so accepting of the boards, when they had not been of the many earlier instructional technologies, David observed:

> ... the boards fitted with their teaching paradigm. They fit their picture of teaching. The trick is to move them on from there once they are comfortable with the board. They are not complicated.

Ingle Farm funded the acquisition of all boards from its normal recurrent funding. Unlike Richardson it was not in a position to obtain any financial help from its parents. Only around 10–15 per cent of the families have been in the position to make even a very small financial contribution to the running of the school. However, as a school with so many 'special' students it is provided with a level of government funding above that of most other government schools.

By 2006, even with an ever-expanding population, Ingle Farm was able to install IWBs and the complementary digital tools in all 35 classrooms, and provide Internet access in all rooms as well as the requisite ICT support. As with each of the other case studies, the sustained school-wide use of the IWBs was helped along by the school library and a very astute teacher-librarian, who soon came to play a significant teacher support role.

A telling development occurred in 2006 when the then program coordinator was 'head-hunted' by an IWB provider. That loss prompted the school to rethink its teacher support arrangements and adopt a model that could be sustained over time. After a comprehensive mapping of staff networking with their colleagues, the school identified four teachers, each with particular expertise, to provide the ongoing support for the staff. The principal commented that there was so much to do that they needed to spread the expertise.

The impact of the total school use of the digital technology has been pronounced for both students and teachers. The student attainment, like that of Richardson Primary, has risen appreciably since the introduction of the IWBs. Between 2003 and 2005, the school's literacy and numeracy scores moved from below the mean of similar schools and that of the state, to where they were above like schools and the state mean. It is a very significant achievement for the student cohort.

Significantly, again like Richardson and to a lesser extent Ngunnawal, student behaviour improved.

The digital instructional technology is now very much a part of the life of teachers at Ingle Farm, as are visitors wandering through the school to view the teachers' work; in the past year the school had 76 visits. Teachers appointed to Ingle Farm now expect to have their own IWB. When asked about what would happen when he moved on, David believed that there 'wouldn't be any change'. Integral total teacher use of the instructional technology is now fully embedded.

Further information on the school can be found at http://www.ifps. sa.edu.au/.

EMMANUEL COLLEGE, GOLD COAST, QUEENSLAND

Emmanuel College is an independent Christian school of approximately 1300 students on the Gold Coast in Queensland, Australia, with approximately half its students in the primary years and half in the secondary. The school is relatively new, having been established for approximately 25 years, and is still growing and building new facilities. Emmanuel draws upon a predominantly middle-class community. For fuller details, go to http://www.emmanuel.qld.edu.au/.

Emmanuel decided to embark on a major upgrade of its ICT in 2002. The first step was to provide all its teachers with laptops, to network all classes and generally work on having all teachers comfortable with using the technology. That uptake took time—after twelve months there were a significant number of the teachers who were still barely using the laptops.

Figure 17.3 Emmanuel College (Courtesy Emmanuel College)

The school decided to begin installing interactive whiteboards in all classrooms in 2004. In interviewing the principal, Graham Leo, on the reasons for opting for IWBs, he responded:

... believed they would allow the teachers to better cater for the learning style of Generation Y. The students often respond better to an interactive style than they do to the traditional methods.

Of note is that Emmanuel's decision to introduce IWBs throughout was primarily that of the principal and the ICT coordinator, Paul Schnetker. Graham, a very experienced school principal, had a clear vision of what was needed, the implementation strategy he would use and the importance of securing the acceptance of all the teachers.

The school chose to start with a board in each of the year levels, and then throughout Years 1 to 3. The intention was to showcase what was possible while at the same time letting the students and the parents pressure the other teachers into using the boards. As Graham Leo indicated:

the desire was to show the teachers what was possible. Others would watch. The desire was also to put indirect pressure on the teachers, by making their peers successful—recognising it was vital to gain teacher acceptance if the school was to succeed.

Emmanuel consciously opted to get the teachers comfortable using IWBs as soon as possible. Interestingly, it chose not to provide extensive training on the teaching software that came with the boards but to ease teachers in by using existing software like Encarta, the Internet and MS Office. The strategy worked well and within a very short time, as with each of the other case studies, teachers wanted to know when they could have their IWBs.

What all the case studies show is that when the implementation is handled well by the school leadership and teacher acceptance is kept to the fore, the challenge facing the schools will be to find the finance to acquire the technology for all the classrooms.

Emmanuel, again like the other case studies, chose to provide in addition to the boards a surround sound system, scanner, DVD player and digital cameras in all classrooms. It also provided all the primary classes with a digital microscope. The school had little difficulty in financing the fit-out of each room. The College worked on a cost of $5000 per room, or the cost of two or three PCs. As the principal observed, the outlay on the IWBs 'was less than the cost of landscaping'.

Graham Leo, like the principals of all the case studies, was very conscious of the key leadership role that has to be played by the principal if a school is to achieve total teacher usage of the instructional technology.

Unless the principal is behind it, the project will fail.

Only the principal can provide the budget, ensure the appropriate professional development and deflect the inevitable flak.

Emmanuel has placed particular store on the ongoing development and training of its teachers. It has opted for a multi-pronged approach that provides ongoing support for all teachers. Wherever possible, the training and assistance are individualised. Graham was very conscious of the importance of professional development. When asked what the school had provided, he responded: 'a lot—particularly in the first twelve months'. However, in so doing, 'they tried to give small doses frequently … a constant drip feed … It was vital to have the teachers teaching their colleagues.' An excellent indication of the importance Emmanuel has attached to its staff development was its preparedness in 2007 to host Australia's annual national conference on the use of interactive white-boards in teaching.

The impact of the introduction of IWBs throughout the College has been immense. The principal expressed the belief that in 40 years of teaching:

what we have seen at Emmanuel has been one of those quantum leaps. We've seen massive change in the teaching, particularly in the primary school.

Paul Schnetker echoed those sentiments. With the students it was very much '—wow!' The students love using them, and quietly pressure their teachers to constantly make best use of the technology. Interestingly, Emmanuel consciously sought to educate their parents on the use of the boards and ensured that they saw their children using the technology.

The hurdles that had to be overcome were not dissimilar to many larger schools, a key one being getting the ICT support staff to appreciate that their prime responsibility was to provide an infrastructure that would support the classroom teaching. Overcoming the hurdles was helped by the active leadership role played by the principal.

When both Graham and Paul were asked about what would happen when Graham moved on, both were firmly of the view that the whole-school use of the digital technology was so embedded in the life of the school that nothing would change.

ST BERNADETTE'S PRIMARY SCHOOL, CASTLE HILL, NEW SOUTH WALES

St Bernadette's Primary School is a Catholic parish primary school in Castle Hill, a suburb in the northwest of Sydney, Australia. It draws in the main upon an upper middle-class socio-economic population. It has approximately 600 students in K–6.

Prior to embarking on its plan to introduce interactive whiteboards throughout, the school had—as the principal, Ted Langford, so aptly described—'tinkered round the edges' with different types of instructional technology, and in particular digital technology. The school leaders, along with the staff at the school, have a strong belief that it is incumbent upon educators that they prepare students for a high-tech future. They believed the use of ICT in schools must mirror the use of ICT in the business world if we are to prepare students for the future. However, prior to the introduction of IWBs the school had never achieved the stage of a global, integrated solution.

The school—and in particular Ted Langford and the school's curriculum coordinator, Jenny Bellenger—recognised the need to adopt a whole-school approach that would enrich the teaching and learning of all. The desire was to create a dynamic learning environment. St Bernadette's work was made that little bit easier by having the local Catholic education authority fund the networking of the school and the provision of Internet access from all classrooms. Like Emmanuel College, all the teachers at St Bernadette's had their own computers before the IWBs were introduced, and many of the classrooms had data projectors.

The school leadership carefully and purposefully researched the way forward. While it had heard of school-wide successes with the IWBs, it moved deliberately, and in the process sent a sizeable group of teachers to Richardson Primary, to St Catherine of Siena, Preston, and elsewhere to view the boards in action. Following almost three years of research, the school decided to use the boards throughout.

As part of the implementation process the school called for expressions of interest from all teachers. When nearly 90 per cent expressed a desire to have an IWB in their classrooms, the school decided to fit out rooms with an IWB, a laptop for the teacher's school and home use, a surround sound system, a digital camera and printer/scanners. In the history of the use of instructional technology, St Bernadette's, like each of the aforementioned case studies, had the unusual challenge of meeting the teachers' request to have the technology.

The boards were introduced in Term 1, 2006. Ted and Jenny were both of the belief that all teachers were not only comfortably using them within a very short time, but had embraced this technology. Of significant note was the fact that St Bernadette's hosted a national IWB and schooling conference towards the end of Term 3 of the same year, at which many of its teachers presented.

The swift and widespread teacher acceptance and use of the IWBs were undoubtedly aided by the thoughtful groundwork and preparation that had been done prior to their introduction together with the multi-pronged professional development initiatives the school instituted from the outset. The school took advantage of the support provided by the company through which the boards were purchased, fostered the concept of a whole-school learning community, allocated two coordinators to provide formal and informal support, and utilised grade buddies and cross-grade teams.

St Bernadette's continues to be conscious of the centrality of ongoing professional development and of assisting teachers new to the school to be trained in the effective use of the IWBs.

When asked why the teachers were so accepting of this technology, both Ted Langford and Jenny Bellenger commented on the importance of the teachers recognising the educational value of the technology, and with that recognition teachers would break their backs if they believe it will help the kids.

Students must always be the focus of the learning process, not the technology. Technology should be selected based on its suitability for the learning task as well as its ability to engage the learner. Staff wanted to create an environment where student learning was challenging, stimulating, exciting and fun.

In detailing the progress made with the technology, examples were cited from all manner of teachers—from the infant grades to teachers at the end of their career who pushed themselves in order to make the most effective use of the available technology, and even casual teachers who were at the school for only a few days at a time. Ted made the observation that the teachers were just 'swept along; caught on the wave—not wanting to miss out'.

The students and the parents matched the teachers' acceptance of the boards and related digital tools. While the school worked to introduce the boards to the parents, most were 'amazed at what they saw the children doing'.

Interestingly, Ted Langford noted that 'while the school had never had a significant student behaviour problem, the introduction of the boards made classroom management that much easier'. The other significant impact was on the students' reading due to the visual nature of the boards— a feature also noted by the parents of Richardson Primary School.

When asked where to from here, both Ted and Jenny commented on how far the teachers have travelled in such a short time, saying that they have 'come a long, long way. Teachers are always trying to reach for a higher bar … always wanting to learn. We are at the stage of consolidating what has been learned and as our main focus at St Bernadette's is to provide high-quality education for all students, we are endeavouring to deepen the learning and encourage students to become more critical thinkers due to the enormous amount of information at their fingertips. Another focus is incorporating the use of Web 2.0 with the IWBs.'

When questioned about what would happen with the digital technology when he moved on, the principal was sure that the school would continue to grow, in that the technology was now embedded. While Ted and Jenny believe there is still immense energy among the staff, there is also recognition of the need to consolidate the gains made. One of the questions the school continually asks itself and the community is the kind of teaching the students will encounter when they move on to the secondary schools.

St Bernadette's, like Richardson in its heyday and Ingle Farm Primary, receives numerous school visits from other staff and leadership teams, with more than 60 visits since the boards' introduction.

COMMENTS

One of the vital but unheralded features of all the case studies was that they are normal suburban schools whose focus is very much on providing the best possible teaching and improving the learning of their students. None were showcase schools specifically constituted or funded as 'technology schools' or 'schools of the future'.

In all the schools the everyday use of the digital instructional technology had been normalised and embedded into everyday teaching in the same way as pens, paper and the traditional teaching boards. In many respects, the best test one can use in ascertaining the whole-school use and acceptance of the digital instructional technology is to ascertain the extent to which it has become a normal part of everyday teaching. Indeed it is from that normality of the case study schools that so much is to be learned by schools worldwide.

The experiences of all five schools were remarkably similar, except for the outside intervention at Richardson. All in a very short period had their teachers expressing the desire to use, and then using, the technology in their everyday teaching. Decades of non-use of the latest technology changed overnight. Not only had the supposed 'Luddites' disappeared, but also suddenly teachers were clamouring to use the technology.

All the principals had the pleasant but unusual challenge of finding the monies to buy the technology to meet the teachers' requests; rather than, as previously, forcing the teachers to use a technology most didn't want. All five schools addressed the implementation as part of their overall school development program and not as separate ICT plans. These normal schools, from a range of socio-economic situations, were able to finance the fit-out of the total school in a relatively short time from their normal funding.

Multi-pronged, ongoing teacher development programs characterised each of the case studies. Professional development was central to each.

In all studies the students, the parents and the teachers embraced the boards and the related digital technology. And interestingly, all the schools reported—with no prompting—an improvement in overall student behaviour.

Significantly all but one believed they had reached the point where the total teacher use of the technology had become embedded and as a total staff they were looking to ways to make even better educational use of the tools.

What has not been mentioned is that the five schools used a variety of IWBs, and both Windows and Mac back-end computers. It made no great difference. Ironically the first question usually posed by schools contemplating using IWBs is: Which do we buy, and do we use Macs or PCs? It is the human element that is important.

On reflection, what the five case studies highlight is the relative ease of achieving total teacher usage of instructional technology in everyday teaching, provided the school pays due regard to a few key variables. A school needs to be well led, focus on enhancing the teaching, choose appropriate technology that can be readily integrated into the teaching, pay due regard to the school-wide implementation of the technology, and provide ongoing professional learning and development to all the teachers.

18

THE LIFE CYCLE OF INSTRUCTIONAL TECHNOLOGY

It should now be abundantly evident that the life cycles of all the instructional technologies have been remarkably similar and provide decision makers with an invaluable insight for future planning and procurement. All of the technologies have a finite life, characterised by six key stages. While the life cycles vary in duration, and while the general inclination is for most of the life cycles to become ever shorter, it will always be important to note the exceptions. Ultimately, however, all the instructional technologies will be superseded by what the consumers deem to be a superior instructional technology.

Surprisingly, while the key elements of the life cycle have been apparent for many years (Cuban, 1986, p. 5), school and education authorities would appear to have learned little from them and rather have chosen to repeat history and make the associated mistakes.

STAGES OF THE LIFE CYCLE

The instructional technology used in schools up until 2008 moved through the following stages.

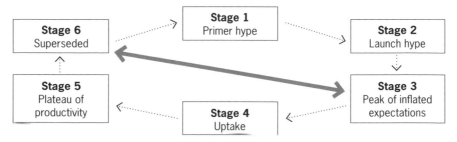

Figure 18.1 Life cycle of instructional technology (Courtesy Lyndall Mealy)

1 Primer hype

The opening stage with each component of the technology was the priming of the market for the widespread acceptance of the new technology.

Over the past century the sophistication of the 'primer' marketing has grown, as have the monies invested. The aim was to titillate the market and to prepare it for the product launch. Invariably there has been a working of both the trade and general media, and a readying of the distributors and the general consumer market for the launch of the product.

Behind all the launches have been major corporations with significant marketing funds and expertise. One has only to note the primer hype in 2007 associated with Microsoft's Vista or Apple's iPhone to appreciate the sophistication and effectiveness of their marketing arms, but that kind of primer hype was evident in 1920 and 1960, as much as it was in 2008.

This type of hype has always been apparent, particularly in the trade journals. It has always been vital to prepare the resellers and to have them on board, ready for the product launch. The claims made for the new product were invariably inflated, with no mention being made of any shortcomings. From the mid 1990s and the emergence of the networked world one saw the 'spy' websites and mailing lists adding to the hype and intrigue. Unlike the trade journals, the 'spy' sites enjoyed revealing technological glitches, but also reflected on the beauty of the technology.

By the latter 1980s it was commonplace to the use of beta software releases for both marketing and product development purposes. Microsoft in particular became highly skilled in capitalising on the early adopters to test and refine its product, as well as to promote the product well before its release.

All major technology companies have invariably worked in a 'commercial in confidence' mode with the complementary technology providers to ensure that the peripheral technology was available at the release of the core product, and have worked with them in the 'primer marketing'. The major applications software companies have, for example, worked since the latter 1970s with the relevant software developers and the computing printer companies to ensure that the appropriate peripherals and content were available for the product launch. It is easy to forget that some of the earliest alliances were between Microsoft and Apple, involving both Bill Gates and Steve Jobs (Wikipedia, 2008i).

Since the 1980s it has not been uncommon in the primer hype phase for the technology companies to work in confidence with pathfinding education authorities and individual schools to both 'test' the technology before release and ready the school to feature in future product advertising. It takes a strong decision maker to say no to the acquisition of the latest technology, even before its launch.

2 Launch hype

The second stage is the product launch and the immense hype and exaggerated claims associated with it. The desire has been to alert potential buyers to the new offering. As mentioned, all the new technologies were forecast to revolutionise teaching. The intention at this point, as with all new products, is to generate significant media coverage and to convert the hype into sales as soon as feasible. In brief, the manufacturers are seeking to engage the potential purchasers and convince them to forego the old and acquire the new technology.

The marketing focus has always been very much on the benefits of the technology, with little comment being made about price or any technical shortcomings. One has only to note the way in which Microsoft and Apple launched their products from the 1990s onwards, with the respective CEOs fronting major promotional campaigns, to appreciate the sophistication and impact of the major technology launches.

The 1990s and the online world brought a significant variation to the traditional high-profile product launch. It came with Netscape's decision in 1995 to 'launch' its web browser free of charge and to secure its income from supplementary products and advertising. Google, YouTube, MySpace and Skype all followed suit and, like Netscape, relied on the global use of email and 'word of mouth' to promote their products. In essence, the latter companies let their product sell itself. In so saying, when these web-based services were sufficiently robust the marketers were brought into play. Seemingly overnight the services 'were found' and their income-generation facilities activated.

3 Peak of inflated expectations

The third phase accords with what the international business company Gartner Consulting describes in its five-stage 'hype cycle' as the 'peak of inflated expectations', where a 'frenzy of publicity typically generates over-enthusiasm and unrealistic expectations' (Gartner Consulting, 2008). Gartner rightly indicates 'there may be some successful applications of a technology, but there are typically more failures' (ibid.).

This is the stage when not only the major technology providers promote the product but so, too, do the providers of the peripheral technology and the resellers. And this is also the period when the sales teams seek to capitalise on the hype generated. Sales targets have always driven sales teams. To achieve their targets the sales people have often been more concerned about the moment rather than the successful long-term use of the technology. In brief, they have done and will continue to do their utmost to secure the sale. If they need to use a little hyperbole, they will.

Further, this is the stage when the technology companies have typically featured the pathfinding schools and the 'noted educators' in their publicity.

In looking back at the efforts made to introduce all the major technologies—with the possible notable exception of the IWB—it bears noting the following:

a The focus in the hype period is very much on the capability and the positives of the individual piece of technology, and discussions with those interested in acquiring the technology. Invariably little attention has been paid in the hype phases to the human variables that will impact on the effective long-term use of the technology by teachers. Few hard questions are asked about the intended and desired use of the technology in teaching. In part, that lack of attention to the human change variables has had to do with the industries' preoccupation with the wider market place and the focus on the financial decision makers, as well as the concentration on selling the particular technology.

b The teachers—that is, the potential users of the technology—were left out of the decision making. Indeed, in the 1950s through until the 1970s there was the very strong view among educational administrators and tertiary educators that teachers simply did not understand what was best for schooling, particularly if teacher productivity was to be increased.

c The initial versions of the technologies were expensive, limited in facilities, relatively heavy and usually beset by technical glitches.

Once the technology gained market acceptance the price dropped, the sophistication and reliability of the technology grew, and the weight dropped. For example, when released in the later 1970s, the initial VHS video recorders sold in Australia for approximately $A1100. They came with mono sound, two recording heads and mechanical controls. In 2007, stereo VCRs with six heads were retailing for a mere $A120—a fraction of the initial cost when inflation is factored into the comparison. And anyone who bought a digital camera in the early 2000s will appreciate the drop in price and the increase in sophistication and power within five years.

4 Uptake

The fourth phase, all going well, is when the schools take up the new technology in volume. History shows that the uptake of all the technologies—except for the IWB in some situations—has been slow and limited. Traditionally schools have not embraced any technology with gusto, invariably only acquiring a small amount of the technology and then only when the initial price dropped. Nonetheless, there has always been a small group of early adopting teachers and schools that have been prepared to try the technology, be it educational TV, OHPs, video recorders or laptop computers.

Notwithstanding the limited uptake, the education authorities have invariably provided figures that show how much has been spent on the technology and how widely it is being used in its schools. Expressions like 'at least one in every school' have been and are still being used.

Gartner refers to the take-up stage as the 'trough of disillusionment' in that this is the period when most companies look for the return on their investment. In the school's market many companies over the past century have not secured the desired return on their investment. One has thus seen—as will undoubtedly be the way in the future—technology companies at this stage not achieving the desired uptake and withdrawing their technology from the schools' market. The authors had first-hand experience with this phenomenon with interactive whiteboards, where a number of Dutch, British, US and Chinese producers of IWBs found it impossible to compete with those IWB companies that provided comprehensive interactive multimedia teaching applications with their boards.

5 Plateau of productivity

This is the stage where a technology reaches the 'plateau of productivity' as its benefits become widely demonstrated and accepted. The technology becomes increasingly stable and evolves in second and third generations. The final height of the plateau varies according to whether the technology is broadly applicable or benefits only a niche market (Gartner Consulting, 2007).

The teaching board—be it the black or subsequent green or white versions—has been the instructional technology that probably best exemplifies this phase. It was accepted by all and gradually refined over the years. The VHS video recorder is, however, an excellent example of a technology that has found a niche as an instructional technology within virtually all primary and secondary schools, and where schools have acquired second and third generations of the technology. Many schools have been using the technology for near on 30 years to supplement the teaching.

Another two good examples of instructional technology finding a niche and long-term acceptance are the 16-mm projector and the slide projector. The 16-mm film projector with an anamorphic lens was very well used in film studies in the 1970s, 1980s and indeed 1990s until such stage as video could be economically projected onto a large 16:9 ratio screen. The same occurred in secondary art and geography lessons where the photographic slide projector was integrally used for nearly 40 years with little fanfare until the ready availability of data projectors.

6 Superseded

All instructional technology eventually reaches the point where it is superseded by the new. Even the amazing blackboard is reaching the stage in its life cycle in the developed world where it will soon be totally superseded.

The superseding of the instructional technology is a phenomenon that many school and educational authority decision makers are only slowly coming to appreciate and to factor into their choice of technology, their budgeting and indeed their accounting. Depreciation is a very real issue, as is the disposal of hundreds of dated personal computers and their peripherals.

CONCLUSION

The lesson for all educational decision makers to observe in considering and costing instructional technology is to appreciate the likely duration of its life cycle, the value for money it provides and when it is best to buy into the life cycle.

CHAPTER 19

THE LESSONS TO BE LEARNED

It is apparent that many school and educational authority leaders have learned much from history—particularly since the mid 1990s. But for many there is still much to be learned.

TOTAL TEACHER USAGE

The first and most important of the lessons to be taken on board is the challenge of getting all teachers to use the appropriate instructional technology wisely and effectively in their everyday teaching.

For over a century, schools, education authorities and governments have striven to achieve that usage. While in 2008 there were significant pathfinding situations across the developed world that had shown what was required to secure that sustained total usage, and indeed the vital catalytic impact of that development on the nature of schooling, those situations were still very much in a minority. The importance of the challenge was underscored by the seeming propensity of the pathfinders to move ever further into the digital world at pace and to continually widen the gap between them and the paper-based schools and education authorities.

In the Introduction chapter, the authors commented on the relative ease of astute school leaders achieving total teacher usage of the instructional technology if the schools simultaneously addressed a suite of key variables. The featured case studies attest to the validity of that call, but they do not reveal the challenge of sustaining and enhancing the effectiveness of that total use in a time of increasingly rapid and uncertain change and sophisticated and integrated digital technology across a total education authority, let alone a nation.

Total teacher and, in turn, student use of the appropriate instructional technology should be the goal of every government, education authority and school—small and large, rich and disadvantaged, rural and urban. A far more telling performance indicator than the computer-to-student ratio is the percentage of the nation's teachers using the appropriate instructional technology in their everyday teaching.

SHAPING VISION AND STRATEGY

Central to the realisation of that total usage and, in turn, the development of digital schools, is the school, education authority and—in particular—the national government being proactive, having a vision for schooling in a networked world and implementing a comprehensive, appropriately funded strategy that will assist in providing the desired education and ultimately enhancing national productivity. The astute governments have long recognised the fundamental importance of educating their young for a digital future, linking education with national productivity and putting in place a comprehensive national strategy to achieve that goal.

All governments and education authorities need to appreciate the importance of that vision and its associated shaping strategy and face the reality that they are going to fall increasingly further behind the path-finders and relegate their education to a lower standard division if they don't. In 2008, the deleterious impact of not being proactive and mounting a national strategy to educate the young for a digital future using the educative power of the technology was clearly evident to the more astute, but apparently not to the leaders in many schools and education authorities.

The contrast between the proactive and reactive was apparent in all the developments since the 1990s. However, the contrast becomes even more pronounced when comparing the key attributes of each that were apparent in 2008, as shown in Table 19.1. Each of the developments that flow from having or not having a shaping vision and well-conceived holistic implementation strategies is clear for all to see, and for teachers to experience. While one can imagine the spin doctors shaping their counter-arguments, one needs only to listen to the concerns of the teachers in the reactive environments—let alone ask for objective research data on key performance indicators—to appreciate the extent of the growing divide.

While, as mentioned, it is appreciated that the situation will not always be as black and white as portrayed; nonetheless many of you will be able to relate to the scene painted.

It is important to stress that this comparison was the state of play that the authors found in mid 2008. With the ever-increasing pace of technological development and the impact of the second-generation iPhone, Google's moves with OpenSocial, and Facebook's decision to adopt an open development platform yet to be experienced (Quittner, 2008), many of the elements of the comparison are likely to change within a year or two.

The lesson that should be apparent is that unless schools and governments adopt a proactive approach very soon and begin educating for a digital future, the kind of differences identified in Table 19.1 are going to intensify at pace.

Table 19.1 Attributes of proactive and reactive schools, education authorities and governments

PROACTIVE	REACTIVE
Educational vision for networked world/ digital future	Belief in traditional schooling, with the technology existing to enhance it
Nexus between education for digital future, national productivity and funding	Disjointed, reactive responses to key technological developments
Positive outlook to using the emerging digital technology wisely to enhance schooling	Negative attitude to the emerging digital technology, and preference for traditional ways
Holistic developmental strategy for implementing desired vision that addresses human and technological variables over time	Policy seemingly developed 'on the run', reacting to media pressure Use of discrete ICT plans
Development strategy given priority funding	Regular complaints re the lack of adequate funding; blame always accorded others
Concern to provide appropriate network infrastructure, bandwidth and network support	Inadequate infrastructure and support, with major shortcomings Low-speed and low-level teaching room connectivity to the Web

>>

PROACTIVE	REACTIVE
Use of market position to choose or to have developed digital technologies and solutions that facilitate the attainment of the desired educational requirements	Use of a series of short-term, high-profile initiatives that focus on the 'in' technology, with little attention to infrastructure and human change Marked propensity to go with the market in the choice of instructional technology
Recognition of the lead role to be played by the school principals and education authorities	Minimal development provided to existing or potential leaders to lead digital schools
Focus on enhancing teaching and learning	Focus on the technology, with a continued reliance on the use of personal computers
Teacher acceptance and involvement central to the wise use of digital instructional technology	Teachers disenfranchised
Appropriate digital technology placed, or scheduled for placement, in each teaching room	Digital technology concentrated in specialist rooms, with controlled access
Significant support provided to assist in the development and teacher acquisition of interactive multimedia teaching materials	ICT perceived by most staff as the prime responsibility of the ICT teachers Interested teachers obliged to acquire their own digital teaching materials, as cheaply as possible
High-level, if not total, teacher and student use of a suite of digital instructional technologies in everyday teaching	Low-level teacher and student use of digital technology in everyday teaching Teaching boards, pens and paper remain the most commonly available technology in most teaching rooms
Importance attached to and funding provided for ongoing teacher and leadership development	Little or no school-based funding for the development of teachers' digital competencies
Digital technologies being increasingly used and integrated in all school operations	Limited digital integration Extensive use made of dated technology
Prime role of network and digital support staff is to assist the prime purpose of education—the provision of desired education	Network managers have major responsibility for network use by students, teachers and school leaders Inadequate ICT support, usually provided by the teachers

>>

PROACTIVE	REACTIVE
Increasingly wider educational use of the Web, and in particular the Web 2.0 facilities encouraged, with minimal access constraints	High-profile publicity of and warnings on the negative features of the Internet Significant constraints imposed by authorities and network managers on student access to and use of Web 2.0 facilities
Digital take-off, shift to digital operational paradigm and development of digital schools Ever-rising teacher, student and parent expectations of the digital technologies Responsiveness to rapid change	Inflexibility and difficulty of the schools and bureaucracy in accommodating rapid change Schools continue to operate within traditional paper-based mode
Recognition accorded the educational importance of digital technology in the home and potentially disadvantaged students	Schools continue to operate as largely stand-alone entities with little recognition of the use and educational impact of digital technologies in the home upon the young
High expectations placed on whole school and staff, supplemented with regular monitoring of performance	Minimal or unrealistic expectations placed on the school's or teachers' use of digital instructional technologies
Increasing dependence on quality information services and information management	Low status or abolition of teacher-librarians Inadequate or ineffectual information management systems
Strong total school community acceptance of the use of digital and networked technologies	Growing frustration and alienation among students and teachers wanting to take advantage of emerging technologies
Extensive research undertaken and published on the use and impact of the digital technology Development builds ongoing research, evaluation and professionalism of the educators	Little, if any, research undertaken and published on the impact of digital instructional technology Reliance on PR spin to secure political advantage

ONUS ON THE SCHOOL

While it is imperative that national governments and education authorities adopt comprehensive programs and provide the favourable climate for development, ultimately the onus is on each school to achieve total teacher and student usage, and digital take-off. The authorities can only do so much. In the end, each school community has to adopt an implementation strategy appropriate to its particular situation.

It will be evident that each of the featured case studies achieved total technology uptake by teachers with little or no support from their local education authority. While that is relatively simple for the more astute school leaders, if nations are to achieve digital take-off in all their schools they will need to not only provide the desired direction and support, but place high expectations on all school leaders and pressure on those lagging.

FUNDING

National strategies need to be appropriately funded. When governments link education with national productivity they tend to provide the appropriate funding well above that allocated in the traditional paper-based model of school recurrent funding. The pathfinders had provided substantial ongoing supplementary funding to support all the technical and human facets of the national digital strategies. The bottom line is that governments have to be prepared to allocate the necessary monies if they want to successfully use the digital instructional technology to ultimately enhance national productivity.

We discuss below what might be done.

CRITICAL MASS

The work of the pathfinding schools and education authorities has reinforced the importance of reaching the 'critical mass' stage in the provision of the appropriate technology, and in the percentage of teachers in each school and across the nation using that technology in their everyday teaching. The research that the authors undertook on the introduction of IWBs into schools revealed the profound impact on the students, the teachers and parents when a critical mass of around 60–70 per cent had been reached with the installation and use of the boards. The expectations of the students (and parents) of the non-using staff when that level was reached were telling.

The same critical mass of technology—and teachers using that technology—is needed if nations are to begin enhancing the national productivity. In the same way that if only a small proportion of early adopting teachers in a school are using the technology one would not expect any significant impact on student learning, so it will be at the national level. It may well be that the critical mass stage at the national level is slightly lower than that at the school level. When, for example, the UK had just over 50 per cent of the nation's classrooms with an IWB, the impact on British schooling—and indeed the wider society—was immense.

STAGED DEVELOPMENT

The other reality that has emerged from the pathfinder situations is that in the initial stages of digital take-off the digital instructional technology was—as anticipated by John Naisbitt in *Megatrends* in 1984—used primarily to perform the tasks of old. It should be no surprise to note that the overview of the research undertaken on the impact of ICT on European schools by Balanskat, Blamire and Kefala in 2006 found only early signs of significant improvement. Moreover, that improvement was linked in the main to the large-scale teacher use of IWBs and broadband in the UK.

Becta, in reflecting on its developments in 2007, made a similar observation.

> *ICT is currently used more frequently for whole-class activities in schools than by small groups or pupils working on their own. Developments in the use of technology to support more personalised learning are evident, but are at an early stage. Schools are beginning to provide access to their networks from remote locations for staff and pupils.*
>
> *Communications technologies provide obvious opportunities for collaboration and sharing, but practice is at an early stage. Schools have yet to make significant use of Web 2.0 and social networking technologies to support learning.*
>
> (Becta, 2007, p. 54)

It stands to reason that a significant enhancement in total student learning and national productivity will only come when the technology is being used by a critical mass of teachers across the nation in 'new activities, processes and products' (Naisbitt, 1984, p. 19). It will not be until the technology is being used integrally like it is in the home that one should expect any pronounced improvement in the appropriate student learning. As suggested, in many situations that could take years.

Naisbitt's proposition was supported by the research conducted by the Illinois Institute of Design (ID), which in 2007 observed:

> [Schools] are following the pattern of what other organisations do when faced with disruptive technology. Time and again, the standard pattern is for organizations to initially ignore disruptive technology, claiming it is not relevant to their core needs. Then they adopt it, using it at first as a faster and better way of doing an existing function. Schools are now in the middle of this first stage of adoption, in which they are using digital media to transform the creation and delivery of information and skills.
>
> (Illinois Institute of Design, 2007)

However, they go on to conclude:

> Ultimately schools will not be improved if they only transform the medium of delivering content while ignoring the changes in how organizations work and what society needs.
>
> (ibid., p. 51)

DEVELOP FROM A RESEARCH BASE

An important lesson for all governments, education authorities and schools to take on board is the vital importance of using research to shape the way forward.

Of note is the considerable funding allocated in the national strategies of the likes of the UK and Singapore on all manner of research, and the use made of that research to refine the developmental strategy. The contrast with the more reactive situations is pronounced. One notes in them a strong inclination to rely on industry-sponsored research or the efforts of government 'spin doctors' to validate the latest announcement.

While individual schools might not have the time, expertise or funds to conduct extensive in-house research, they have highly competent educators on staff capable of using their professional expertise to identify what is and what is not working.

HISTORY'S LESSONS

What else can education learn from the history of the use of instructional technology in schools? What other factors need to be addressed to get all their teachers and students wisely using the tools of the contemporary digital world?

The first of the findings relate to the use of digital technology in the home, and the role the school library has and should play. While neither is necessarily central to the sustained whole-school use of digital instructional technology, they do need to be borne in mind in that quest.

The technology of the home

- The quality, quantity and use made of the technology in the average home have always exceeded that available in the average classroom.
- All the instructional technology introduced in the century was—with one major exception—designed originally for home or office use.
- Students not only have greater access to the technology at home but also generally have greater freedom over the use of that technology.
- Young people, for the last 20 years at least, have developed their ICT and general technological competencies primarily at home, and not in the classroom.
- There is a strong correlation between the students' ICT and general technological competencies and the availability of the technology in the home.
- The signs are that within the 1995–2008 period young people developed in the home a wide set of key technological skills, many of which were not addressed or were barely considered within the classroom. By 2008, there was a wide and growing divide between the extent of the digital technology and its use in the home and the classroom. Schools and education authorities had largely chosen to ignore the technological development of the young in their homes, particularly in the period 1995–2008, and have rarely

factored that development into any holistic or networked educational development. Schools and education authorities have invariably continued to work on the assumption that the only 'real' education occurs in the classroom.

- Those students who lack web access within their homes have their life chances diminished when compared with those that have.
- The moves by the likes of the UK, Singapore and New Zealand that sought to enhance the life chances of the young by providing the requisite web access in the home for all young people should bear careful consideration.
- While further research is needed, the young in their homes appear to favour a chaotic, constructivist style of learning that places a strong emphasis on play, in contrast with the more formal educational style favoured by schools and authorities.
- The students' perception of the key competencies and skills for life in the digital world would appear to be at significant variance to those identified and assessed by education authorities.
- Today's youth want to use the contemporary technology in their learning.
- All schools and education authorities should give greater recognition to the learning that young people are experiencing in their homes, to factor that learning into the overall education of their students, and to shape it and give it due recognition as the situation arises.

Role of the school library and teacher-librarians

- School libraries and astute school librarians have played a central and invariably leading role in achieving and sustaining total teacher usage of instructional technology.
- Quality school libraries and school librarians have probably undergone greater change in the past 30 years than any teaching group within schools, with the signs suggesting that that change will intensify in pace.
- While the nature of the school library will continue to change at pace, the growth of digital schooling should oblige schools to place ever-greater store on the professional handling of information and the importance of integrated, whole-school information management and information services.

Achieving total teacher usage of instructional technology

One of the more important lessons to emerge from the analysis of the last century is that there are nine interrelated variables that need to be addressed simultaneously to achieve total, ongoing teacher and student usage of the appropriate instructional technology. These variables are:

1   Teacher acceptance
2   Working with the givens
3   Teacher training and teacher developmental support
4   Nature and availability of the technology
5   Appropriate content/software
6   Infrastructure
7   Finance
8   School and education authority leadership
9   Implementation.

1   Teacher acceptance

The fundamental importance of securing teacher acceptance is hopefully clear for all to appreciate.

Technology after technology one notes the preoccupation with the power of the technology—the implied assumption being that by making the technology available teachers would use it and the students will benefit. In virtually every instance the challenge of getting all teachers to accept the technology for use in their everyday teaching was not considered. Indeed, as noted with radio, educational television and computer-assisted learning, there were many who believed it would be best to leave the teachers out of the decision making and to 'teacher proof' both the curriculum and the use of the technology.

It is not until the 1990s, and more so the latter 1990s, that one starts to see the pathfinding education authorities and schools beginning to pay serious attention to selecting instructional technology that all the teachers would use.

What is now apparent is that to get all teachers to accept the everyday use of instructional technology, teachers need to:

* believe their use of the technology will enhance their teaching and improve student learning
* feel comfortable using the technology
* be able to use the technology integrally in their everyday teaching

- have the technology readily available in each teaching room
- have tools that will also assist, when required, in the management and administration of their classes.

In brief, teachers want digital instructional technology that will assist their teaching, not tools that oblige them to change their teaching to suit the nature of the technology.

In its 2007 Review, Becta makes the very telling point when referring to the rapid teacher acceptance of IWBs:

> *What characterises these technologies is that they link closely to, and support, current educational practice. Adoption of technologies which enable educational practice to develop and change follows a very different pattern, requiring culture change and focused local leadership and management to drive adoption and embedded use.*
>
> *Delivering change to ensure technology supports the extension and empowering of learning, as well as enhancing and enriching it, is challenging. For this reason, demonstrating transparent benefits from related technologies, and bridging the 'natural' use of technologies that support current practice with those which challenge it, are likely to be important strategies.*
>
> (Becta, 2007, p. 66)

As the research regularly attests, the most important factor by far in improving student learning is the teacher, not the technology. Teachers will readily use tools that assist their teaching, and time and time again have demonstrated they will not use those instructional technologies that oblige them to change their pedagogy to suit the technology.

There is a very old expression that once a teacher closes the door to his or her room, he/she is in total control. That was as true in 2008 as it was in 1957.

> *Although there has been much talk of respecting teacher expertise, recognising exemplary teachers, and appointing occasional teachers to blue ribbon commissions most teachers historically have had little say in designing and implementing technology plans.*
>
> (Cuban, 2001, p. 183)

The teacher is the gatekeeper who has to be convinced. In fact, it is every teacher, whether working full-time or part-time in the school, who has to be convinced.

Use of instructional technology by early adopting teachers is not enough. There have always been early adopting teachers who have been prepared to go out of their way to use the new technology and who have used it to enrich the learning of their students. The use of a technology by early adopter teachers should not be taken as a sign that other teachers will follow. Rather, all teachers have to be comfortable using the technology, and not as has been the norm for the past 50 years where only the early adopters used the technology.

2 Working with the givens

Teaching throughout the developed world, be it in Germany, the UK, Hong Kong, the US or Australia, has always had to work with a number of fundamental givens. They are so basic that they are often forgotten.

- All efforts to get all teachers and students in a school using digital instructional technology have to appreciate and work within or around the givens.
- Traditionally schools have been organised around class groups, both in the primary and secondary years. Teachers have been allocated class groups of anywhere from ten to 50 students to teach, to manage and often to administer. While efforts have been made throughout the past century to personalise teaching, the vast majority of schools in 2008 were still organised around classes.
- Invariably teachers have had the task of teaching those classes in an allocated room or two.
- The teaching room has contained the instructional tools that the teachers use integrally in their teaching, with a black, green or white teaching board as the centrepiece at the front of virtually every teaching room. Teachers will work with and shape their teaching around the tools they know they can use every lesson. Unwittingly, one of the structural impediments to the widespread use of personal computers, and in particular the use of PCs as part of the digital toolkit, has been the concentration of the digital technology in specialist rooms and leaving all the other rooms with but the traditional pens, paper and board.
- The size and nature of those teaching rooms have largely determined the nature and extent of the instructional technology that could be used. Space was limited, particularly in the secondary schools. Most teaching rooms were never designed to accommodate desktop computers. Teachers soon found they could only shoehorn three or

four desktop computers and a printer into the average classroom. The security of the technology in the classroom has always been a factor, particularly when the technology was young in its life cycle and attractive to thieves.

- Teachers have limited time each day, and indeed each year, to teach what over many decades has been considered a crowded curriculum. The concerns about the fullness of the curriculum were as evident in the 1970s as in the 2000s. Teachers have always been concerned about the limited teaching time at their disposal, and any who have been a school principal will be aware of the flak forthcoming if the school dares to include an activity that takes away teaching time. That shortage of time and the pressure to 'complete the program' have always made most teachers reluctant to 'waste' time by taking a class to technology in a specialist room. It was even worse when the technology did not work.

- Teachers want to create their own lessons, or at least place their professional stamp on the lesson. While most will use a variety of source material, and may well use packaged resources, they will still want to attune the material to fit with their teaching style. While thus far lesson preparation has been universally time consuming, and one would have to suggest highly inefficient, each teacher's ownership has been central. The digital 'cut and paste' facilities, particularly those provided with the better IWBs, enable the ownership to be maintained while producing lessons more efficiently.

- Teachers will want—as always—to use a suite of instructional tools to enrich their teaching. It is important for school and educational leaders to reject any manufacturer's claim that their particular technology will be schooling's magic panacea. Teachers will for many years continue to use their voice, their theatrics, paper, books, teaching boards and a range of other facilities in addition to the digital technology available.

- Teachers are expected to manage their own classes. In the eyes of many school administrators classroom management is more important than the quality of the teaching! If the technology consistently fails and the teachers have to manage the class at the same time as fixing the technology, that instructional technology will be little used by most teachers.

Larry Cuban, in *Oversold and Underused* (2001), sums up the situation succinctly when he observes:

Without attention to the workplace conditions in which teachers labour and without respect to the expertise they bring to the task there is little hope that new technologies will have more than minimal impact on teaching and learning. (p. 197)

The vital point that many appear to have missed is that teachers want instructional technologies that will aid their teaching. Like the aforementioned tradesman, they want to be able to select and use the appropriate tools for the task at hand. It continues to surprise to still hear calls for teachers to change their teaching to suit the use of personal computers.

3 Teacher training and teacher developmental support

Closely allied to the teacher acceptance and the need to work within the givens is the necessity of instituting an appropriate, holistic, ongoing teacher training and teacher development and support program that is normalised within the school's operations. It is far more than some incidental professional development (PD); rather, it is woven into the life and ongoing development of the school. The focus needs to be on the teaching and not on the technology as such. The key would appear to be an effective, ongoing, multifaceted program that is appropriate to the school and its context, and caters for each teacher's needs.

Probably the key element is the provision of time in the everyday workings of the school when teachers—individually, in groups or with support—can explore how best to apply the ever-emerging, ever-improving digital tools in their teaching. The comment was aptly made that teachers need time to 'play in the sandpit'. As mentioned with the 'givens' the teachers' days are full. Time is needed to reflect and reorient.

Release time costs, but it is a cost that should be factored into both the initial implementation and the ongoing enhancement strategies. The experience thus far would suggest that most of the training and support is best provided within the school, and in context, although many of the schools examined made good use of occasional external expertise and sending groups of teachers and leadership staff regularly to conferences and other schools.

By according due recognition and resources to teacher development, schools are proclaiming the importance they attach to their teachers, to quality teaching, and indeed involving their teachers in the acceptance of the appropriate instructional technologies.

The teacher training and support should be tailored and, over time, attuned to the changing scene within the school. In the initial stage, significant specific training could be required in leading to digital take-off, but after take-off ongoing curriculum and pedagogical support should probably be accorded greater emphasis. Any such program should accommodate staff turnover and casual teachers. Of note was the different successful models used in the various schools studied, strongly suggesting that a 'one model fits all' approach should be avoided.

- An appropriate, whole-school teacher developmental support model is fundamental to sustaining the effective total teacher use of the instructional technology.

If schools are to embed the use of an ever-changing digital technology in the teaching and take advantage of the new educational opportunities appearing virtually every week, they will have to provide effective professional assistance. Today, no one teacher can hope to stay abreast of the emerging teaching materials without quality support. Interesting was the number of the situations studied where the lines between training, teacher support and collaborative lesson development were blurred.

History unfortunately consistently highlights the failures of governments and educational leaders to allocate the desired funding for any meaningful staff development. It was still rare in 2008 to see an education authority allocating significant funding for teacher development when new technology was announced. It has also not been uncommon for the new programs to be funded only for a short period in the misguided belief that 'seed' funding will generate sustained development. Nor has it been uncommon for the teacher development budget to be the first cut removed when authority savings were required.

A major concern noted in many countries was the scant preparation provided for trainee teachers in the everyday use of digital instructional technology. The authors were regularly informed of the dearth in the availability and integral use of interactive whiteboards and the digital toolkits in tertiary institutions.

4 Nature and availability of the technology

The importance of selecting and indeed developing an appropriate suite of instructional technology is now clear for all to see. In brief, teachers want instructional technology they believe will enhance teaching and learning and can use integrally in their everyday teaching. They also want technology that will allow their students to develop their own digital work in both the classroom and at home.

The technology has to be:

- readily available in all the teaching rooms
- able to be integrated into the everyday teaching
- comfortable for all teachers and students to use, from kindergarten upwards
- highly reliable
- relatively inexpensive
- interactive
- multimedia capable
- able to be used in conjunction with a suite of digital tools, both hard and soft.

There needs to be a piece of instructional technology that can act as the hub for the digital toolkit and integrate all the other digital tools.

The chosen instructional technology should also:

- assist in enhancing the teacher's efficiency and help to maintain, if not reduce, the teacher's workload
- help in class management
- interface with the school's learning, administration and communications systems
- assist personalised teaching.

In analysing the introduction and the use of each of the major instructional technologies over the century it is apparent that schools and education authorities have largely gone with the market in their selection of the main instructional technologies. Indeed it is not until the 1990s and the ever-growing body of technology available that one begins to see educational leaders taking responsibility, asking the hard questions, undertaking genuine trials of the various technologies and, most importantly, seeking to shape the development of the desired instructional tools. Up until that stage schools had basically made do with the latest major releases of the technology corporations. While the education authorities were meticulous in their choice of the 'best' brands, there was little apparent questioning of the appropriateness of the technology for use in classrooms.

It should thus come as little surprise that so much instructional technology over the last century was so little used, and the outlay basically wasted.

It was still difficult in 2008 to find examples of proactive educational leaders working with technology companies to develop tools specifically for teaching. While it has been common in other areas of endeavour for the major clients to work with the research arms of major corporations to develop the desired hardware and software, and while that has happened to a degree with the school administrative systems, it is not readily apparent with instructional technology until the 1990s.

In the 1990s one finally begins to see a few education authorities and schools exercising greater control, using their market strength and specifying what they want from the technology companies. Sometimes it was simply the development of an educational variant of a mainstream product, but increasingly it was the case of the education authority wanting a new entity.

The same pathfinding governments and education authorities extended that work into the 2000s, and by 2008 one could see instructional technology being chosen that was appropriate for classroom teaching by all.

5 Appropriate content/software

Related to the nature and availability of the technology is the importance of teachers and students having appropriate, quality-content teaching programs and, in more recent years, applications software to use with the instructional technology.

In the early years of film, radio and television the availability of 'software' was a major issue, both in terms of there being appropriate programs and schools being able to readily access them. When teachers had to book months ahead for the desired film, wait for it to be delivered and work with the return-by dates, only the enthusiasts used the facility. Video and audio recorders with their facility to time shift programs represented a breakthrough, but teachers still had to contend with the other shortcomings of those technologies.

Computing software remained a significant issue for most teachers and students until the 1990s and early 2000s and the advent of the GUI interface and the gradual introduction of a suite of user-friendly multimedia development tools. The work in recent years by Microsoft, Apple and Adobe and the various interactive whiteboard hardware and software companies has given teachers and students a plethora of multimedia software with which to work. From the mid 1990s onwards, the Internet opened an immense and unparalleled mixed bag of teaching materials, but it was of use only to those teachers who had the requisite facilitating and accessing technology in their classrooms and authorities willing to allow it to be used to advantage.

One of the issues to be addressed far more fully at the national and international level is how schools can transfer quality content they have purchased to the emerging medium. While instructional technologies will come and go, history has shown that quality content will always be wanted. Provision thus needs to be made on high—probably at governmental—level to facilitate the ready transfer of the content from an old to a newer medium. It was, for example, apparent in 2008 that many schools were at the point of wanting to transfer their extensive VHS libraries to a digital format; however, at the same time vested industries were being very successful in tightening their control over moving pictures and instituting legal blocks to the transfer of 'their' content to different media.

6 Infrastructure

The importance of having in place the often mundane arrangements to ensure that the instructional technology could be used to best advantage in each classroom is often overlooked. However, one has only to experience sitting with a restless class waiting for ten minutes while one page of the learning platform loads, or encounter a school where the electricity is off for two days, or inform a teaching staff that all of their teaching resources on the intranet had been lost and that the backup had failed, to appreciate the importance of appropriate infrastructure.

From the 1940s to the 1970s, the infrastructure included the film delivered by train and courier, the radio reception and, in turn, the TV signal. In our interviews we were regularly reminded of the challenges facing the use of electronic instructional technology outside the major cities. Many schools had only one 'dodgy' television antenna outlet. With video, it was getting the program into the classroom, either via a reticulated setup or a portable VCR. U-matic VCRs were most assuredly not portable. With the digital technology, and the surging use being made of the networked world, the infrastructure included the increasingly sophisticated network access, hosted solutions, appropriate databases, the need for ever-greater capacity, the data-presentation facilities and the information management and storage systems, together with the surety that the technology would be functioning all the time.

By now it will be obvious that the effectiveness of the infrastructure entails not only the technical aspects but also the many human and managerial variables that will allow the infrastructure to be used to best advantage, funds to pay for its use, removal of unnecessary constraints on access, and the forward planning required to ensure the infrastructure is able to handle the surge in use in a digital school. In 2008, a significant number of classrooms in the developed world still did not have ready, well-maintained, broadband access to the Internet. Without that access teachers' use of the digital toolkit was markedly constrained.

- The sustained total teacher use of instructional technology can only be achieved with the appropriate infrastructure and technical support.
- The importance of that infrastructure and associated technical support is growing at pace, particularly in the larger schools. Without it the digital instructional technologies simply cannot be used or be used to their capacity.
- History has shown the provision of high-speed network access to every classroom has markedly assisted the successful whole-school use of instructional technology. While it is difficult to say at this stage exactly how important it has been, it is of note that the networking of many classrooms from the beginning of the 2000s coincided with the general moves by teachers to use IWBs, the various parts of the digital toolkit and the networked teaching opportunities. The study by Balanskat, Blamire and Kefala (2006) on the impact of ICT on European schools in 2006 noted:

Broadband is a major factor in increasing collaboration between teachers.

Embedded, reliable and high-capacity broadband in the classroom increases the quality and quantity of educational activities that can be undertaken. (p. 7)

The challenge in the smaller schools mentioned earlier is one requiring particular attention. Becta, in its 2007 Review, noted that despite the immense efforts made in the UK over the past decade the smaller school infrastructure shortcomings were still a concern.

Smaller institutions especially require ongoing support and help to recognise and address technical and technology-related issues. There is a strong argument for promoting more 'wrap-around' services to schools, possibly linked to local partnerships and/or contractual arrangements with the commercial ICT sector. These should not only aim to lift the burden of technology implementation and support from institutions or providers with limited capacity, but also integrate technology planning with more general business and improvement planning.

(Becta, 2007, p. 68)

7 Finance

In 2008, the time is surely due for governments and education authorities to adopt a model of recurrent school funding appropriate to the digital era. The traditional, paper-based model has long passed its use-by date.

Schools can no longer be expected to find the growing requisite funding from the current minuscule recurrent funding, parent contributions or even the kind of ongoing supplementary funding enjoyed by the pathfinders. With a change in government that latter funding can disappear—as the US found with the demise of the Clinton–Gore government. A fundamental rethink of school financing is required, with governments needing to develop a funding model that befits digital schooling. The rethink should review the current school funding allocations and the often strict funding divisions, and take into serious consideration the vast and successful investment parents are already making in digital technology, more and more of which will be mobile and personal.

Schools, education authorities and governments need to develop funding arrangements appropriate for a networked world, and no longer for the 'stand-alone' schools of a bygone age.

In an era of increasingly sophisticated technology—and when the international research such as Barber and Mourshed's seminal work (Barber & Mourshed, 2007) is questioning the educational folly of further reducing class sizes and lifting staffing levels and, in turn, the proportion of the total budget allocated to teaching staff—it is time to begin shifting monies in the existing recurrent funding. As a former 'architect' of a Year 11/12 secondary college system established 30-plus years ago to provide senior students with greater flexibility in their learning, Mal Lee would contend that teaching and learning in the post-compulsory years could benefit from not obliging 17- and 18-year-olds to attend school every moment of the school day, making far greater and wiser use of appropriate instructional technology in the school and home, and using a few less teachers.

While the focus of this study is on the use of the instructional technology, it needs to be appreciated that much of that technology should rightly be integrated into all the operations of the networked school community. In 2008, it made little sense to have separate technology budgets for education, information services, administration and marketing operations of a school.

Related is the need for national authorities to identify which parts of the school's infrastructure costs should best be borne by the school, the education authority or the whole of government. Increasingly nations are wisely moving to integrated national broadband networks that cater for all parts of government, be it for schooling, health care, libraries or local government. What is required is a closer examination (even with school-based management, or SBM) of which facilities should be funded in a networked environment by whom, rather than simply leaving it to the schools to cobble together a solution.

That need to take advantage of the technology in the home has been apparent for some time, but the dramatic changes of the last five years, in particular, and the escalating digital divides that are now transpiring make it vital.

In a 1996 article titled 'The Educated Home', Mal Lee flagged the need for schools to cease trying to duplicate the burgeoning digital technology of the home (Lee, 1996). Chris Dede in 1998 extended that thinking and advocated the adoption of what he then termed a 'distributed learning' model that took into consideration the very substantial digital 'instructional technology' in the home (Dede, 1998). In the last decade the desirability of all nations—developed and developing—fundamentally rethinking the model used to fund the digital technology in the school has grown by the day as the divide between the home and the school has widened, and as the home has become an ever-more important part of networked learning communities. As the administrators of Central Okanagan School District found from bitter experience, it is both an educational and financial irresponsibility for nations to seek to replicate the resources of the home in the classroom, knowing it cannot and should not be done.

In *Leading a Digital School*, Dr Roger Hayward, the principal of one of the early schools in Australia to adopt a student laptop program, points to the folly in 2008 of schools investing vast monies in the acquisition and support of laptops at a time when a $15 USB drive can provide the ready access of students' work from home to school (Lee & Gaffney, 2008, pp. 86–87). The second-generation iPod, or an equivalent multifaceted facility as mentioned earlier, had the very real potential to be as widely used by the young across the developed world as the cell phone in 2008. Why should schools and governments seek to replicate that kind of inexpensive, immensely powerful, portable instructional technology knowing full well that young people will acquire it, and that historically the technology in the classroom has never been able to match that in the home?

Thus far these kinds of suggestion to capitalise on the technology of the home have gained little acceptance. The failure by the authorities to rethink the funding should be no great surprise in an area of endeavour still characterised by its retention of the ways of the past and limited vision.

8 School and education authority leadership

Historically it has been the technology companies that have basically determined the choice of the instructional technology, with the school and education authority leaders generally supporting that choice. While, as mentioned, there were pathfinding schools and education authorities taking control of the choice and use of the instructional technology, the vast majority were still going with the flow and relying on the wisdom of the major technology providers.

- If schools and education authorities want all teachers and students to use the contemporary instructional technology integrally and wisely in all classrooms, they need to lead and take responsibility.
- The bottom line is that the school principal is central to the ongoing total teacher usage of instructional technology in the classroom. The principal can 'make or break' the whole-staff use of instructional technology.

In the same way in which there have been the early adopting teachers making good use of the instructional technology, so too have there always been the early adopting school principals who have sought to use the technology wisely throughout the school. Many of the early adopting principals have had a strong macro understanding of the instructional technology and have been able to marry that awareness with that of organisational change in order to bring about the significant school-wide use of the instructional technology. Invariably those leaders have grown their understanding of the technology by themselves. However, increasingly over the last 20-plus years, there has been another group of early adopting school leaders who have appreciated the importance of making wise use of the instructional technology but have lacked the requisite understanding of the technology and had to rely on 'expert' staff for guidance.

- Schools must have educational leaders—educational architects— with the knowledge to make the best use of the digital technology available.

One of the major shortcomings in the use of instructional technology has been the almost total absence of training or development programs that prepared school and authority leaders to best harness the ever-developing technology. None of the existing or former school leaders interviewed had ever had access to appropriate training. The post-graduate programs and the authors' search for appropriate, practical education authority unearthed few of value. Kathryn Moyle's national study, undertaken in 2006, of the ICT awareness of Australia's school principals supports this finding (Moyle, 2006). There are highly theoretical educational technology programs but few that provide current or potential school principals or educational administrators with the requisite up-to-date macro expertise.

As the sophistication and complexity of both the instructional technology and the associated enabling arrangements and implementation strategies grow at pace and the vital role of the leadership is understood, it is essential that the key decision makers are given the requisite ongoing professional development.

Historically the teaching profession has for many generations been great at discussing 'future schooling'. Virtually every year, from the 1950s onwards, one can find educators somewhere in the world conducting a major conference on the shape of future schooling. Invariably the use of technology was featured at each, and very often a major sponsor was one of the larger technology companies. What the authors found far more difficult to identify were forums, particularly involving educational leaders, that addressed the practicalities of getting all teachers to use the appropriate instructional technology wisely.

For school and education authorities to lead and, most importantly, to take responsibility for the use of instructional technology in schools, one is going to need leaders in each school with the know-how required to lead a digital school. While the focus traditionally is on providing the teachers with the expertise, it should at the same time ensure that the school and education authorities have the expertise to lead.

In 2008, many in the school and education authority leadership were of a generation that had little association with sophisticated instructional technology. While the scene was gradually changing (as mentioned elsewhere), the challenge is growing at a pace that necessitates a dramatic shift in the education of the leadership. The sustained enhancement of digital schools will depend largely on knowledgeable school and education authority leaders being prepared and able to control the use of the digital technology. Gone are the days when educational leaders simply took their lead from industry. Educational leaders, as the architects of educational development, do need—at the very least—a macro understanding of the technologies that are now so central to the operation of schools, and an in-depth appreciation of the major variables required for success. Similarly, those leaders need to take prime responsibility for the total and sustained effective use of the digital instructional technology by their teachers and students.

The UK, in reflecting on the effectiveness of its national initiative over the past decade, noted in its 2007 Becta Review:

> *Schools that have made best progress with ICT have senior managers who are involved in developing a whole-school strategy, focused on how ICT enhances teaching and learning (Ofsted, 2004). Professional development for school leaders is a key factor in developing institutional e-maturity and implementing new ways of working with ICT (Ofsted, 2004; PwC, 2004a).*

> (Becta, 2007, p. 21)

> *Schools that saw ICT as a tool for raising standards were generally those where senior managers had a clear overview of the quality of provision across the school. Managers ensured there was an ongoing debate about how ICT was used, and how it engaged learners and benefited learning and teaching. They also involved subject leaders or heads of department to ensure that ICT played a full part in the teaching and learning of each subject. In the most effective practice, new staff are inducted and supported as they develop an understanding of the school's expectations of ICT (Ofsted, 2005a).*

> *A complex set of changes is needed to implement ICT effectively. School leaders consulted in 2006 regarded their role as a change manager, addressing the 'human factors' associated with the implementation of ICT (Twining et al., 2006).*

> (ibid., p. 22)

In retrospect, the move made in many education authorities in the 1980s to shift to school-based management (SBM) and to devolve significant responsibility for the use of ICT to the schools did not help many schools and education authorities to take the lead in the holistic use of digital instructional technology. At a stage when the technology was developing at pace and where expert direction and support were desired, there were few in the schools and the education authorities able to provide that direction. Many of those authorities rightly contended that under a devolved model of school management the responsibility for all the technology rested with the school. One thus saw—as mentioned in Chapter 13—throughout the 1980s and 1990s, and even the 2000s, many schools trying to do the 'right thing' making unwise, often amateur decisions that resulted in considerable waste.

The reality, as evidenced in nations like the UK, Singapore and New Zealand, is that there are many decisions particularly relating to networking and bandwidth that are best negotiated and funded on high, and many other areas where the highest authority is best placed to leverage the major technology providers and set the parameters for its schools. It is imperative that all education authorities display the desired leadership, and in a manner befitting their context. It is also vital that both the school and education authority leaders—and indeed the faculties of education, also—address the many and diverse ramifications of schools operating within a digital paradigm, and attune their operations accordingly.

The challenge for many education authorities is immense. Globally they have over many years demonstrated a pronounced inability to synchronise the operations of bureaucrats when it came to implementing authority-wide instructional technology programs. Stories abound of schools having to overcome major hurdles imposed by different sections of the bureaucracy. The segmentation that besets the secondary school invariably abounds in most central offices, with wars between the empires as dramatic as those in the schools. To provide the requisite high-level leadership, that should not continue.

9 Implementation

Historically one has to conclude that the instructional technology implementation strategies used by schools and education authorities have been in the main ineffectual, or even abject failures. The vast majority have been simplistic in nature and not striven to understand or system-atically address the human and technical variables associated with any major organisational change. When one has school and education authority leaders lacking a macro appreciation of the technology and its implementation, the political desire to capitalise on the swift rollout of the latest technology and middle managers whose concern is primarily with getting the technology working, the chances of the holistic being successfully addressed are significantly reduced.

While, as mentioned, there have been notable exceptions, it is only in the last decade—helped undoubtedly by the confluence of the factors identified by Friedman (2006)—that one begins to see the adoption in schools and education authorities of comprehensive, well-reasoned implementation strategies others can build upon. A thoughtful, holistic implementation strategy that addresses the kind of variables described is essential if schools are to achieve ongoing total teacher use of the digital instructional technology.

Implementation of the instructional technology in the 1940s through to the 1970s was primarily left to the early adopting teachers who wanted to use the technology. They invariably handled the rollout, conducted the training of interested staff, and were generally involved in the operation and support of that technology. In the 1970s, with the emergence of school library resource centres and the appointment of A/V support officers, the responsibility shifted to the library—a role many libraries were to play for the next 30-plus years. The introduction of computers invariably again saw the early adopting teachers handle their implementation and use, and indeed much of the everyday technical maintenance— often well into the 1990s. Throughout the 1940s to the early 1980s, few principals played a major part in the implementation of the instructional technology other than in facilitating its acquisition and promoting its value to the school.

By the mid 1980s, with the growing appreciation of the importance of integrating computers across the curriculum and indeed the increasing sophistication of the digital technology, schools and education authorities moved to the use of computing and, in time, IT and ICT plans. Like most other school policies they tended to be developed and implemented in isolation and invariably were focused on the technical. Like the other 'strategic' school planning of the period, schools were expected to specify the desired outcomes three to five years ahead, even though the technological developments were happening at a pace and with an uncertainty few could anticipate.

That pattern continued well into the 2000s with many schools and education authorities, with the education authority bureaucrats increasingly mandating the nature of the plans and unwittingly reinforcing the idea of ICT usage being a discrete entity with little relationship to the whole-school development. The plans themselves were invariably concerned with the quantity and power of the personal computers being provided, forgetting that history had shown the mere existence of a quantity of instructional technology—even when it is 'state-of-the-art'—did not mean it would be used, or used well. The 2005 OECD analysis of the efforts by the member nations reflects the continuing preoccupation with the quantity of instructional technology, and stands in antithesis with the 2006 and 2007 Becta Reviews that address all the variables.

History has consistently demonstrated the importance of education authorities:

- having a high-level understanding of how digital technology can be used wisely and efficiently by its schools
- regularly researching major societal and technological trends
- constantly attuning their operations to fit with the emerging technologies, and
- providing their schools with the direction setting and support they require.

Sadly in 2008 that kind of capability was still rarely seen. The norm after 50 years is that most education authorities are well behind where the technology is at, and that they will react only after the technology companies, pathfinding schools and authorities have shown the way.

Both schools and education authorities would do well to genuinely review the effectiveness of their instructional technology strategies. The implementation track record of educational authorities has left much to be desired over many years. The existence of 'in-depth', objective studies of the effectiveness of government-initiated technology programs are notably lacking. It is time for them to evaluate the effectiveness of their instructional technology rollouts, addressing both the educational and the political value.

Many schools across the developed world have spent considerable scarce monies on instructional technology—and ICT in particular—with scant teacher usage, but, as with the education authorities, there are few concerted analyses of their implementation strategies.

In the latter 1990s, the more astute school and education authority leaders appreciated the growing importance of digital convergence, the all-pervasive digital technologies in all school operations, the rapid shift to digital integration, the blurring of and indeed need to remove the old segmented operations in schools, and have moved to use whole-school and whole-system planning capable of accommodating rapid and uncertain change.

The schools featured in the case studies in Chapter 17 have all opted for the whole-school approach that focused primarily on enhancing the teaching and simultaneously addressed a range of variables as part of their whole-school development.

By the mid 2000s it was apparent that the level of digital integration in schools and the surge in the sophistication of the instructional technology were such that schools had to use very well-conceived and appropriate whole-school development strategies if they wanted to achieve the ongoing total teacher usage of the instructional technology.

> *ICT implementation at a school level should be viewed in the context of school improvement plans and not simply as a technical issue. Problems that the school faces should be identified, strategies for overcoming these problems designed, and progress indicators designated. The highest returns on ICT in education appear to come when ICT is seen as part of a strategy for solving an important problem rather than as an end with itself.*
>
> (Venezky & Davis, 2002, p. 46)

The history shows that most schools have moved—like the technology itself—from a very rudimentary level of implementation in the 1960s and 1970s to the point in the 2000s where they needed highly complex and appropriate implementation strategies if they were to harness the increasingly sophisticated technology. The sophistication of the implementation strategy basically had to grow at a pace to match the sophistication of the instructional technology.

Any contemporary whole-school implementation strategy needs to bear the following in mind:

- Once a critical mass of teachers in a school or education authority use predominantly digital teaching materials, the fundamental nature of teaching changes, the teachers very soon recognise the immense opportunities opened by the digital technology to enrich their teaching and their expectations keep growing at pace.
- When schools achieve digital take-off and have all the teachers using predominantly digital teaching resources, then that development in turns impacts on the school's other operations and serves as a catalyst to shift the school's total operations from a paper-based to a digitally

based operational paradigm. Once schools begin operating digitally, they then become conscious of the many implications and the changes that need to be made.

- It is important to factor into the implementation strategy the education of the key stakeholders on the reasons for the move. Those stakeholders include the bureaucracy and the relevant government ministers.
- The creation and funding of schools designed to showcase the use of instructional technology—be they television schools, schools of the future or technology schools—have not stimulated wider whole-school uptake of the particular instructional technologies.
- The schools that have impacted on others are those normal schools whose pathfinding work can be applied to any other school.

The test of how well an instructional technology is accepted is that its use has becomes normalised—and largely forgotten—as has happened with pens, paper and the traditional teaching boards.

THE CHALLENGE TO LEARN FROM HISTORY

The messages are there for all to see.

There were, in 2008, schools and education authorities that have shown what is required to get all teachers and students using the appropriate instructional technology integrally in everyday teaching in every classroom. There were, however, many that were continuing with the ways of old, making the same mistakes, wasting immense resources, and—most importantly—not using the undoubted power of the digital technology to help provide all their students with a better and more appropriate education, and therefore not enhancing national productivity.

It is appreciated that the challenge is immense and is growing. If, however, schooling is to be relevant in the contemporary world, it needs to accept the challenge.

APPENDIX

THE RESEARCH METHODOLOGY

In setting out to explore the use of the various instructional technologies in classrooms over the last century, and in particular to identify the lessons that should have been learned, it was soon apparent that remarkably little research had been undertaken or indeed written on the subject. This was particularly so of the twentieth century. The extent and nature of general teaching of the various technologies appeared not to be an issue.

Over the last ten to fifteen years there has been a burgeoning of research in most developed nations on the impact of technology on teaching and learning in both the classroom and the home, and a sub-stantial body of data and research that could be used when examining teacher usage, but still little on the reasons for the lack of teacher and, in turn, student usage of the various digital technologies. It was as if the matter had become a concern of the late 1990s and 2000s, and only then in the more astute schools and education authorities and with the more prescient governments.

Of particular note is the contrast between the extent and nature of the research undertaken on this issue by the UK, one of the aforementioned proactive nations, and the US, which under the Bush administration has in many respects become one of the significant reactive situations. What is significant in the US after the Clinton–Gore era is the lack of any sense of national vision for a digital era, comprehensive national strategy or associated nationally sponsored research.

In reflecting on the technologies of the past 50 years and their class-room use, the authors have been able to draw upon their own extensive classroom use of or consultancy experience with virtually all except the most recent of instructional technologies, and to use that professional understanding to validate the ever-growing body of historical material available on each of the technologies with the free online encyclopaedia, Wikipedia. Special mention needs to be made of the use of Wikipedia, a source still questioned by many traditionalists. The authors increasingly found Wikipedia to be an invaluable, ever-more important and indeed unparalleled source of information on the history of all the technologies, particularly when used in conjunction with the authors' own under-standing. None of the traditional sources can match the currency of Wikipedia, particularly on the newer and emerging technologies.

(Note that in quoting from Wikipedia the authors have included the hyperlink citations when provided.)

As indicated previously, little has been written on the use of various technologies in the twentieth century, other than in the US. The authors have nonetheless drawn extensively on the writings of Paul Saettler and his *The Evolution of American Educational Technology* (1990) and Larry Cuban's seminal work, *Teachers and Machines*, published in 1986. While Saettler provides a very good insight into the evolution of various technologies, he does not address the disinclination of teachers to use those technologies. That was left to Cuban, both in his 1986 work and in *Oversold and Underused*, published in 2001.

What was also surprising (a point also noted by Cuban, 1986) was the limited amount of data collected on the level of school and classroom use of the technologies. The vast majority of the existing data is simplistic in nature, of dubious validity, and was used by governments and education authorities for political purposes to imply the extensive use being made of the particular technology. As Cuban indicates, much of the US data was compiled by school principals for superintendents to make such profound observations as 'each school in the state has a television set or 16-mm projector'. The authors' own analysis of the limited Australian and twentieth-century UK data confirmed that propensity and they had difficulty securing in-depth objective research until the last decade. The 'spin doctors' have been in play for many, many years.

The situation changes appreciably in the more astute, proactive nations from the mid 1990s onwards, with virtually all researching their significant investment in a digital future. That research has been used extensively in both the analyses of the 1990s and 2000s and in the clarification of the issues needing to be addressed.

To help redress the shortcomings of reliable information on teacher usage before the 1990s, and to secure a working knowledge of recent developments, the authors chose to interview the following groups:

1   an extensive cross-section of former school principals and educational administrators from Australia, New Zealand and the UK;

2   a cross-section of people to the fore in the introduction of ICT and in particular IWBs into schools, many of whom had been ICT coordinators and teachers who then moved into educational technology businesses; and

3   experienced teacher-librarians. The authors reasoned that teacher-librarians were probably the best placed school personnel to comment

professionally on the actual use made of the various instructional technologies since the 1960s, conscious of the fact that it was the library that invariably controlled the lending of much of the technology and its 'software', be it film, audio tapes, videos or computer applications.

The authors also opted to use the major international teacher-librarian mailing lists to seek out the recollections of experienced teacher-librarians. A summary of those recollections can be found at http://awinzenried. bigpondhosting.com/Library/Lib_tech.htm.

As indicated previously, the authors undertook a series of research exercises that explored the variables associated with the whole-school use of interactive whiteboards and the associated digital technologies. Aware as they were of the number of schools across the world that had succeeded in getting all the teachers to use IWBs, the authors chose to supplement their earlier research with five case studies. While all five were Australian, they could just as readily have been selected from the UK, Hong Kong, New Zealand, South Africa or the US, and the same lessons would become apparent. Two of the schools chosen were of low socio-economic standing, while the others were drawn from more affluent situations. The schools were variously state, Catholic and independent.

In examining and identifying the life cycle of the instructional technologies, particular acknowledgement needs to be given to both the ground-breaking thinking of Professor Larry Cuban and the Gartner Consulting work (2007) on its now renowned 'hype cycle'. While not identifying a life cycle as such, Cuban (1986) identified many of the commonalities of the developments with the instructional technologies he examined. The authors' own analyses of all the major technologies confirmed in their minds a common finite life cycle among all the technologies. That thinking was supported by the research and consultancy experience of Gartner Consulting. While designed to assist in analysing the likely uptake of all emerging technologies, the Gartner analysis has carry-over implications for the instructional technology.

CONCLUSION

By comparing and contrasting the data gained from the literature, the case studies and the wide range of interviews, the authors found the same messages coming to the fore.

BIBLIOGRAPHY

Note: A growing number of websites can only be accessed by members. Some of the websites below fall into that category. While all the hyperlinks worked on the date indicated you might need to go to the home page and become a member before accessing.

AAPT. (2007). Research finds new technology is challenging the Australian family. Retrieved March 31, 2008, from http://home.aapt.com.au/At_AAPT/What_s_news/2007/Research_finds_new_technology_is_challenging_the_Australian_family.html.

Anderson, R.E., & Becker, H.J. (1999). Teaching, learning and computing: 1998 national survey. University of California and University of Minnesota: Center for Research on Information, Technology and Organizations.

Atkinson, M., Lamont, E., Gulliver, C., White, R., & Kinder, K. (2005, March). *School funding: A review of existing models in Europe and OECD countries.* LGA Research Report, Slough: NFER.

Australian Broadcasting Commission. (1979, July). *The role of ABC educational broadcasting.* Unpublished report of a sub-committee of the ABC Federal Educational Broadcasts Advisory Committee, Australia.

Australian Communications and Media Authority. (2007, December). *Media and communications in Australian families.* Canberra. Retrieved July 16, 2008, from http://www.acma.gov.au/webwr/_assets/main/lib101058/media_and_society_report_2007.pdf.

Austrom, L., Kennard, R., Naslund, J., & Shields, P. (Eds.). (1989). *Implementing change: A co-operative approach.* Vancouver, BC: British Columbia Teacher-Librarians' Association.

Balanskat, A., Blamire, R., & Kefala, S. (2006, December 11). *The ICT impact report: A review of ICT impact on Schools in Europe.* Retrieved July 16, 2008, from http://ec.europa.eu/education/doc/reports/doc/ictimpact.pdf.

Barber, M., & Mourshed, M. (2007). *How the world's best performing school systems come out on top.* McKinsey & Company. Retrieved July 16, 2008, from http://www.mckinsey.com/clientservice/socialsector/resources/pdf/Worlds_School_Systems_Final.pdf.

Becker, H.J. (2000, November 15). Findings from the Teaching, Learning, and Computing Survey: Is Larry Cuban Right? *Education Policy Analysis Archives.* Retrieved July 16, 2008, from http://epaa.asu.edu/epaa/v8n51/.

Becta. (2005). *The Becta Review 2005: Evidence on the progress of ICT in education.* British Educational Communications and Technology Agency. Retrieved January 2, 2008, from http://www.becta.org.uk/page_documents/research/becta_review_feb05.pdf.

Becta. (2006). *The Becta Review 2006.* Retrieved July 16, 2008, from http://publications.becta.org.uk/display.cfm?resID=25948.

Becta. (2007). *Harnessing technology review 2007: Progress and impact of technology in education: Summary report.* Retrieved July 16, 2008, from http://publications.becta.org.uk/display.cfm?resID=33980.

Becta. (2008). *What is a learning platform?* Retrieved July 16, 2008, from http://schools.becta.org.uk/index.php?section=lv&catcode=ss_lv_lp_03&rid=12887.

Bennetto, E. (1991, August). The school library and the VCE. *School Library News*, 15–16.

Berger, P., & Kinnell, S. (1994, October). Educational CD-ROMs: A progress report for the disc orientated. *School Library Journal, 119*(16).

Breeding, M. (2007). *Library Technology Guides.* Retrieved July 16, 2008, from http://www.librarytechnology.org/automationhistory.pl.

Center for the Digital Future. (2008). *2008 digital future report.* University of Southern California: Annenberg School Center for the Digital Future. Retrieved 16 July, 2008, from http://www.digitalcenter.org/pages/current_report.asp?intGlobalId=19.

Chalmers, A., & Slyfield, H. (1993). *Contributions to learning: Libraries and New Zealand schools.* Wellington: National Library of New Zealand, Research Unit.

Coley, R.J., Cradler, J., & Engel, P. (1997). *Computers and classrooms: The status of technology in US schools.* Educational Testing Service.

Coulson, A. (2006, December 14). The Cato Education Market Index. *Policy Analysis, 585.*

Cuban, Dr. L. (1986). *Teachers and machines: The classroom use of technology since 1920.* New York: Teachers College Press.

Cuban, Dr. L. (1993). *How teachers taught: Constancy and change in American teaching.* Columbia University: Teachers College Press.

Cuban, Dr. L. (2000a). Taking stock: What does research say about technology's impact on education?. *techLearning*, New Bay Media. Retrieved July 16, 2008, from http://www.techlearning.com/db_area/archives/TL/062000/archives/cuban.html.

Cuban, Dr. L. (2000b). *So much high-tech money invested, so little use and change in practice: How come?* Retrieved July 16, 2008, from http://www.edtechnot.com/notarticle1201.html.

Cuban, Dr. L. (2001). *Oversold and underused: Reforming schools through technology, 1998–2000*. Cambridge, MA: Harvard University Press.

Dede, C. (Ed.). (1998). Six challenges for educational technology. *Learning with technology*. Alexandria, VA: Association for Supervision and Curriculum Development.

Department of Education (DoE). (1998). *Learning technologies in Victorian schools 1998–2001*. Melbourne: Victorian Department of Education.

DfES. (2005). *Harnessing technology: Transforming learning and children's services*. London. Available from http://www.dfes.gov.uk/publications/e-strategy/docs/e-strategy.pdf.

Dillon, K. (Ed.). (1997). *School library automation in Australia*. Wagga, New South Wales: Charles Sturt University.

Dutton, W.H., & Helsper, E.J. (2007). *Oxford internet survey 2007 report: The internet in Britain.* Oxford University: Oxford Internet Institute.

Ely, D.P. (1982, November 1). The role of the school media specialist: Some directions and choices. *Journal of Research and Development in Education, 16*(1).

eSchool News. (2007, August). Educators assess iPhone for instruction. *eSchool News*. Retrieved June 30, 2008, from http://www.eschoolnews.com/resources/mobile-computing/mobile-computing-articles/index.cfm?rc=1&i=51131;_hbguid=3797aed1-6fa7-4e22-9d26-db5f61e68127.

Ewing, K., & Hauptman, R. (1995). Is traditional reference service obsolete? *Journal of Academic Librarianship, 21*(1).

Friedman, T. (2006). *The world is flat* (2nd Ed.). New York: Farrar, Straus Giroux.

Futuresource Consulting. (2008). Interactive displays/ICT products market. *Quarterly Insight, State of the Market report*, Quarter 1, 2008. Unpublished presentation.

Gartner Consulting. (2008). Understanding hype cycles. Retrieved November 19, 2008, from http://www.gartner.com/pages/story.php.id.8795.s.8.jsp.

Gee, J.P. (2006). Literacy, learning and video games. *EQ Australia*, Winter 2006.

Gee, J.P. (2007). *What video games have to teach us about learning and literacy* (2nd Ed.). New York: Palgrave Macmillan.

Gerstner, L.V, Semerand, R.D, Doyle, D.P., & Johnston, W.B. (1995). *Reinventing education: Entrepreneurship in America's public schools*. New York: Penguin.

Goodlad, J. (1984). *A place called school*. New York: McGraw Hill.

Gore, A. (1994). 'Super highway' speech. Retrieved July 16, 2008, from http://artcontext.com/calendar/1997/superhig.html.

Haycock, K. (Ed.). (1997). *Information rich but knowledge poor?* Vancouver, Canada: International Association of School Librarianship.

Healy, S. (1998). *Knowledge management at Tintern: Creating new ways of working.* Unpublished manuscript.

Her Majesty's Inspectors of Education. (2005). *The integration of information and communications technology in Scottish schools.* Retrieved July 16, 2008, from http://www.hmie.gov.uk/documents/publication/EvICT%20Final%2018%20Oct.html.

Herring, J. (2007). Teacher-librarians and the school library. In S. Ferguson, *Libraries in the twenty-first century.* Wagga, New South Wales: Charles Sturt University.

Higgins, S., & Moseley, D. (2002). Raising achievement in literacy through ICT. In M. Monteith, *Teaching primary literacy with ICT.* Buckingham: Open University Press.

Honey, M., & Henriquez, A. (1993a). *Telecommunications and K-12 educators: Findings from a national survey.* New York: Bank Street College of Education, Center for Technology in Education.

Honey, M., & Henriquez, A. (1993b). Initial findings from a national survey on K-12 educators' use of telecommunications. *Information Searcher*, 5(3).

Illinois Institute of Design (ID). (2007). *Schools in the digital age.* Illinois Institute of Technology. Retrieved July 16, 2008, from http://www.id.iit.edu/635/documents/MacArthurFinalReport1.pdf.

IWBNet. (2004) *Digital hubs.* Retrieved November 18, 2008, from http://www.iwb.net.au/advice/digital-hubs/1-intro.htm.

IWBNet. (2008). *Richardson Primary 2003: Whole-school adoption of IWBs.* Retrieved July 16, 2008, from http://www.iwb.net.au/advice/casestudies/richardson/1-intro.htm.

Jaber, W.F. (1997). *A survey of the factors which influence teachers' choice of computer-based technology.* Unpublished PhD dissertation. Faculty of the Virginia Polytechnic Institute and State University. Retrieved November 19, 2008, from http://scholar.lib.vt.edu/theses/available/etd-71997-02347/unrestricted/WJABER2.PDF.

Jackson, P. (1968). *Life in classrooms.* New York: Holt, Rinehart and Winston, Inc.

Johnson, S. (2006). *Everything bad is good for you: How today's popular culture is actually making us smarter.* London: Penguin Books.

Kennan, A., Willard, P., & Wilson, C. (2006, March). What do they want? A study of changing employer expectations of information professionals. *AARL, 37*(1).

Kitchen, S., Finch, S., & Sinclair, R. (2007). *Harnessing technology schools survey 2007*. Coventry: Becta. Retrieved July 16, 2008, from http://partners. becta.org.uk/index.php?section=rh&catcode=_re_rp_02&rid=14110.

Kodak. (2008). *History of Kodak*. Retrieved July 16, 2008, from http://www. kodak.com/US/en/corp/kodakHistory/index.shtml.

Lai, Kwok Ling. (1996). *Words have wings*. Dunedin: University of Otago Press.

Layton, T. (2000, September). Digital learning: Why tomorrow's schools must let go of the past. *Electronic School*. Retrieved July 16, 2008, from http://www.electronic-school.com/2000/09/0900f1.html.

Lee, B., & Boyle, M. (2004). The teachers tell their story. *IWBNet*. Retrieved July 16, 2008 from http://www.iwb.net.au/advice/research/documents/ TeachersStory1.pdf.

Lee, M. (1996). The educated home. *The Practising Administrator, 3*.

Lee, M. (2000). Chaotic learning: The learning style of the 'Net Generation'. In G. Hart (Ed.), *Readings and resources in global online education*. Melbourne: Whirligig Press.

Lee, M. (2006). Managing the school's digital teaching resources and assets. *Australian Educational Leader, 3*.

Lee, M., & Boyle, M. (2003). *The educational effects and implications of the interactive whiteboard strategy of Richardson Primary School: A brief review*. Retrieved July 16, 2008, from http://www.richardsonps.act.edu. au/interactive_whiteboard_initiative.

Lee, M., & Boyle, M. (2004, March). Richardson Primary School: The Richardson Revolution. *Educare News*.

Lee, M., & Gaffney, M. (Eds.). (2008). *Leading a digital school.* Melbourne: ACER Press.

Lee M., & Winzenried, A. (2006), Interactive whiteboards: Achieving total teacher usage. *Australian Educational Leader, 28*(3), 22–25.

Looker, E.D., & Thiessen, V. (2003). *The digital divide in Canadian schools: Factors affecting student access to and use of information technology*. Retrieved July 16, 2008, from http://www.cesc.ca/pceradocs/2002/papers /EDLooker_OEN.pdf.

Lyneham High. (1998). *Between the lynes*. Lyneham High Year Book. Canberra: Lyneham High School.

MacKenzie, J. (2003). The true cost of ownership. *From Now On*. Retrieved July 16, 2008, from http://fno.org/mar03/truecost.html.

Measday, B. (2004, October). Viva La Revolution! *IWB News*. Available from www.ifps.sa.edu.au/Viva%20La%20Revolution.pdf.

Meredyth, D., Russell, N., Blackwood, L., Thomas, J., & Wise, P. (1998). *Real time: Computers, change and schooling*. Canberra: Department of Education, Training and Youth Affairs.

Moyle, K. (2006). *Leadership and learning with ICT: Voices from the profession*. Retrieved July 16, 2008, from http://www.appa.asn.au/CMS/uploads/articles/leadership%20and%20learning%20with%20ict.pdf.

Naisbitt, J. (1984). *Megatrends*. London: Futura.

National Centre for Education Statistics (NCES). (2008). *Digest of Education Statistics 2007*. Retrieved July 16, 2008, from http://nces.ed.gov/programs/digest/d07/.

National School Boards Association (NSBA). (2007). *New study explores the online behaviors of US teens and tweens*. Retrieved July 16, 2008, from http://www.nsba.org.

Negroponte, N. (1996). *Being digital*. New York: Hodder and Stoughton.

New Zealand Digital Strategy. (2008). *Digital strategy: Glossary of key terms*. Retrieved July 21, 2008, from www.digitalstrategy.govt.nz/templates/Page____60.aspx.

Oblinger, D.G., & Oblinger, J.L. (2006). *Educating the Net Generation*. Educause. Retrieved July 16, 2008, from http://www.educause.edu/educatingthenetgen.

OECD. (2005). *Are students ready for a technology-rich world? What PISA studies tell us*. Paris, France: OECD Publishing Programme for International Student Assessment. Retrieved July 16, 2008, from http://www.oecd.org/dataoecd/28/4/35995145.pdf.

OECD. (2006). *Modernising school education: Main messages 5.1 School Management*. Retrieved July 16, 2008, from http://ec.europa.eu/education/policies/2010/doc/progress06/modernschool_en.pdf.

OECD. (2008). *Households with access to the Internet 2003–06*. Retrieved May 21, 2008, from http://www.oecd.org/document/23/0,3343,en_2649_342 23_33987543_1_1_1_1,00.htm.

Papert, S. (1980). *The gears of my childhood*. Retrieved July 16, 2008, from http://www.papert.org/articles/GearsOfMyChildhood.html.

Papert, S. (1996). *The connected family*. Atlanta: Longstreet Press.

Passey, D. (2002). *ICT and school management: A review of selected literature*. Lancaster University: Department of Educational Research. Retrieved July 16, 2008, from http://partners.becta.org.uk/page_documents/research/ict_sm.pdf.

Peake, D. (1996, December). The heroic age of Australian library automation and its immediate aftermath. *LASIE, 27*(4), 4–17.

Perelman, L. (1992). *School's out*. New York: Avon Books.

Prensky, M. (2001, October). Digital natives, digital immigrants. *On the Horizon, 9*(5). NCB University Press. Retrieved November 30, 2007, from http://www.marcprensky.com/writing/Prensky%20-%20Digital%20 Natives,%20Digital%20Immigrants%20-%20Part1.pdf.

Prensky, M. (2006). *Don't bother me Mum, I'm learning*. St Paul, Minnesota: Paragon House.

Quittner, J. (2008). 'Who will rule the new Internet? *Time, 23*. Retrieved July 16, 2008, from http://www.time.com/time/business/article/0,8599, 1811814,00.html.

Raitt, D. (Ed.). (1999, December 7–9). *23rd International Online Information Meeting proceedings*. Oxford: Learned Information Europe.

Raitt, D., & Jeapes, B. (Eds.). (1995, December 5–7). *19th International Online Information Meeting proceedings*. Oxford: Learned Information Europe.

Raitt, D., & Jeapes, B. (1996, December 3–5). *20th International Online Information Meeting proceedings*. Oxford: Learned Information Europe.

Rose, T. (1996). The future of online education and training. In D. Raitt, & B. Jeapes (Eds.), *Online Information 96 Proceedings*. Oxford: Online Information Europe.

Rowand, C. (2000). Teacher use of computers and the Internet in public schools. *Education Statistics Quarterly, 2*(2), 72–75. Washington DC: US Department of Education, National Center for Education Statistics.

Saettler, P. (1990). *The evolution of American educational technology*. Connecticut: Information Age Publishing.

Sandery, P. (1982). *The future role of computers in education*. Unpublished paper given to the Institute of Public Affairs, New South Wales, Australia.

Schramm, W., Nelson, L., & Betham, M. (1981). *Bold experiment: The story of educational television in American Samoa*. Stanford: Stanford University Press.

Scott, C., & Tierney, G. (1996). Learning for the future: Developing information services in Australian schools. *School Libraries Worldwide, 2*, 95–103.

Secondary Futures. (2006). *Students First*. Wellington, New Zealand. Available from http://www.secondaryfutures.co.nz/pdfs/Students_ First.pdf.

Secretary for Education and Manpower. (2005). Electronic credits scheme. *Education Bureau Circular Memorandum No. 25.* Retrieved July 16, 2008, from http://www.edb.gov.hk/FileManager/EN/Content_2306/cm25_2005_english_up.pdf.

Shears, L. (Ed.). (1995). *Computers and schools.* Melbourne: ACER Press.

SMART Technologies. (2008). *Company history.* Retrieved July 2, 2008, from http://www2.smarttech.com/st/en-US/About+Us/News+Room/Media+Kits/Corporate+Media+Kit/History.htm.

Starr, P. (2002, November 30). Computing our way to educational reform. *The American Prospect.*

Statistics New Zealand. (2007). *Household use of information and communications technology: 2006.* Retrieved July 16, 2008, from http://www.stats.govt.nz/products-and-services/hot-off-the-press/household-use-of-information-and-communication-technologies-survey-2006/household-use-ict-2006-hotp.htm.

Tapscott, D. (1996). *The digital economy: Promise and peril in the age of networked intelligence.* New York: McGraw Hill.

Tapscott, D. (1998). *Growing up digital.* New York: McGraw Hill.

Tapscott, D. (2007). *Wikinomics.* New York: Atlantic Books. Available from http://21centuryconnections.com/learning.

The Greaves Group. (2006). *America's digital schools 2006 report.* Retrieved July 16, 2008, from http://ads2006.net/ads2006/pdf/ADS2006KF.pdf.

Tyack, D., & Cuban, L. (1995). *Tinkering towards Utopia: A century of public school reform.* Cambridge, Mass.: Harvard University Press.

UK Treasury Briefing Paper. (2007, July). Unpublished handout. Retrieved July 16, 2008, from http://schools.becta.org.uk/index.php?section=oe&catcode=ss_es_opp_02&rid=13420.

University of Bath. (2008). *Web publishing at the University of Bath: Glossary.* University of Bath: Department of Marketing & Communications. Retrieved July 1, 2008, from internal.bath.ac.uk/web/cms-wp/glossary.html.

Vancouver Sun. (2008, May 26). District wakes up from laptop dream. *Vancouver News.*

Venezky, R., & Davis, C. (2002, March). *Quo Vademus? The transformation of schooling in a networked world.* OECD/CERI.

Warner, D. (2006). *Schooling for the Knowledge Era.* Melbourne: ACER Press.

White, S. (2005). *A brief history of computing: Complete timeline.* Retrieved July 1, 2008, from http://trillian.randomstuff.org.uk/~stephen/history/timeline.html.

Wikipedia: The free encyclopedia. (2008a). Chalkboard. FL: Wikimedia Foundation, Inc. Last edited 13.30, February 11. Retrieved June 30, 2008, from http://en.wikipedia.org/wiki/Chalkboard.

Wikipedia: The free encyclopedia. (2008b). Whiteboard. FL: Wikimedia Foundation, Inc. Last edited 18.33, June 25. Retrieved June 30, 2008, from http://en.wikipedia.org/wiki/Whiteboard.

Wikipedia: The free encyclopedia. (2008c). Public broadcasting. FL: Wikimedia Foundation, Inc. Last edited 15.15, June 23. Retrieved June 30, 2008, from http://en.wikipedia.org/wiki/Public_broadcasting.

Wikipedia: The free encyclopedia. (2008d). Reversal film. FL: Wikimedia Foundation, Inc. Last edited 17.15, April 19. Retrieved June 30, 2008, from http://en.wikipedia.org/wiki/Transparency_(photography).

Wikipedia: The free encyclopedia. (2008e). Overhead projector. FL: Wikimedia Foundation, Inc. Last edited 12.25, June 8. Retrieved June 30, 2008, from http://en.wikipedia.org/wiki/Overhead_projector.

Wikipedia: The free encyclopedia. (2008f). Compact cassette. FL: Wikimedia Foundation, Inc. Last edited 21.19, June 28. Retrieved July 1, 2008, from http://en.wikipedia.org/wiki/Compact_Cassette.

Wikipedia: The free encyclopedia. (2008g). U-matic. FL: Wikimedia Foundation, Inc. Last edited 4.48, 20 June 20. Retrieved July 1, 2008, from http://en.wikipedia.org/wiki/U-matic.

Wikipedia: The free encyclopedia. (2008h). VHS. FL: Wikimedia Foundation, Inc. Last edited 01.30, June 29. Retrieved July 1, 2008, from http://en.wikipedia.org/wiki/VHS.

Wikipedia: The free encyclopedia. (2008i). Macintosh. FL: Wikimedia Foundation, Inc. Last edited 02.58, June 30. Retrieved July 1, 2008, from http://en.wikipedia.org/wiki/Macintosh.

Wikipedia: The free encyclopedia. (2008j). Windows. FL: Wikimedia Foundation, Inc. Last edited 13.49, June 30. Retrieved July 1, 2008, http://en.wikipedia.org/wiki/Microsoft_Windows.

Wikipedia: The free encyclopedia. (2008k). Super 8mm film. FL: Wikimedia Foundation, Inc. Last edited 17.25, June 26. Retrieved July 1, 2008, from http://en.wikipedia.org/wiki/Super_8_mm_film.

Wikipedia: The free encyclopedia. (2008l). History of video games. FL: Wikimedia Foundation, Inc. Last edited 04.42, June 24. Retrieved July 1, 2008, from http://en.wikipedia.org/wiki/History_of_video_games.

Wikipedia: The free encyclopedia. (2008m). Internet protocol suite. FL: Wikimedia Foundation, Inc. Last edited 10.08, June 8. Retrieved July 2, 2008, from http://en.wikipedia.org/wiki/Internet_protocol_suite.

Wikipedia: The free encyclopedia. (2008n). History of Google. FL: Wikimedia Foundation, Inc. Last edited 10.31, June 28. Retrieved July 2, 2008, from http://en.wikipedia.org/wiki/History_of_Google.

Wikipedia: The free encyclopedia. (2008o). Electronic Learning. FL: Wikimedia Foundation, Inc. Last edited 16.55, July 1. Retrieved July 2, 2008, from http://en.wikipedia.org/wiki/E-learning.

Wikipedia: The free encyclopedia. (2008p). MySpace. FL: Wikimedia Foundation, Inc. Last edited 15.05, July 1. Retrieved July 2, 2008, from http://en.wikipedia.org/wiki/MySpace.

Wikipedia: The free encyclopedia. (2008q). YouTube. FL: Wikimedia Foundation, Inc. Last edited 09.53, July 1. Retrieved July 2, 2008, from http://en.wikipedia.org/wiki/YouTube.

Wikipedia: The free encyclopedia. (2008r). Facebook. FL: Wikimedia Foundation, Inc. Last edited 09.53, July 1. Retrieved July 2, 2008, from http://en.wikipedia.org/wiki/Facebook.

Wikipedia: The free encyclopedia. (2008s). iPod. FL: Wikimedia Foundation, Inc. Last edited 18.58, July 1. Retrieved July 2, 2008, from http://en.wikipedia.org/wiki/IPod.

Wikipedia: The free encyclopedia. (2008t). Digital cameras. FL: Wikimedia Foundation, Inc. Last edited 21.05, June 24. Retrieved July 2, 2008, from http://en.wikipedia.org/wiki/Digital_camera.

Wikipedia: The free encyclopedia. (2008u). Calculator. FL: Wikimedia Foundation, Inc. Last edited 18.03, June 29. Retrieved July 2, 2008, from http://en.wikipedia.org/wiki/Calculator.

Wikipedia: The free encyclopedia. (2008v). Video projector. FL: Wikimedia Foundation, Inc. Last edited 20.43, June 17. Retrieved July 2, 2008, from http://en.wikipedia.org/wiki/Video_projector.

Wikipedia: The free encyclopedia. (2008w). iPhone. FL: Wikimedia Foundation, Inc. Last edited 04.09, July 2. Retrieved July 2, 2008, from http://en.wikipedia.org/wiki/IPhone.

Williamson, A. (2006, October). Computers in homes. *Literature Review*. Prepared for The 2020 Communications Trust, Wairua Consulting Limited. Retrieved July 18, 2008, from www.2020.org.nz/docs/2020.CiH.Lit%20review-1.0.pdf.

Winzenried, A. (1996a, August). Imagine the possibilities. *The Electronic Library*.

Winzenried, A. (1996b). Future information provision: burnout, boom or bust? In D. Raitt, & B. Jeapes, *2nd Asian Online Meeting Proceedings, Hong Kong, April 8–10, 1997*, 23–31. Oxford: Learned Information Europe.

Winzenried, A. (1998). *Towards the next millennium*. Paper presented at ASLA XVI Conference 'Bytes, Books and Bollards by the Bay', January 1999.

Winzenried, A. (2002). *Staffing the library of the future*. Unpublished PhD thesis, Charles Sturt University, Wagga, New South Wales, Australia.

Woolles, B., & Loertscher, D. (Eds.). (1986). *The microcomputer facility and the school library media specialist.* Chicago: American Library Association.

INDEX

home–school nexus 223–4
hosted solutions 144–5, 156
Hughes, Phillip xi, 166, 167
hyperlearning 4

IBM computers 26, 77–8, 80
    5150 computer 77
ICT infrastructure 136, 152, 231,
    233–4, 242
    bandwidth 155–6, 180, 233
    computer platform 117, 128
    connectivity costs 138, 183
    designing for school's core
        business 176, 180, 225, 231,
        232–3
    funding 106, 183, 195, 220, 244
    hosting, internal/external 144–5,
        156
    mobile storage 164–5
    network 117, 127, 132, 138, 141,
        152, 180, 193, 217
    storage 192
ICT support 136, 182, 190, 199, 201,
    204
    nature of help 182, 201, 206
    training 172–3, 195, 199, 200, 203,
        206, 208
ICT usage 186–8, 220
    achieving total teacher usage 136,
        186–8, 198–9, 220, 230–1, 237–8
    critical mass 220, 243
    reflecting business world 205
    student access 81, 186, 221
    student use practices 156, 186, 221
    teacher acceptance 225–6, 242–3
Ilford 26, 57
Illinois Institute of Design 4, 22, 112,
    150, 222
    Schools in the Digital Age 150
Industrial Revolution, the 1
information superhighway 9, 123–5,
    130–1

Ingle Farm Primary School (SA) 196,
    199–202, 207
instructional technology 8–9
    appropriate content 163, 183
    appropriate technology 164, 180,
        231
    consonance with educational goals
        95, 206, 231
    life cycle 7, 152, 209–14, 228
    research base 205, 222–3, 226
    role of educational leaders in
        choice 172, 183, 197–8, 230
    teacher acceptance 10–11, 119, 123,
        173–5, 186–8, 203, 208
    teacher understanding 173, 242
    teacher usage 114, 123, 186–8,
        192–208, 215–6
    visioning 171, 216–7
    within students' homes 3, 195
Intel 26
interactive whiteboards (IWBs) 2, 8,
    12–3, 16, 41, 94, 158–9, 162, 166–84
    and Indigenous students 199–200
    and parents (of students) 177, 186,
        194, 196, 204, 206
    and student behaviour 177, 194,
        198, 203, 208
    and student engagement 187
    and student retention 189
    and teacher retention 187, 199
    and theft 199
    as digital hubs 120, 176, 178, 182
    costs 146, 187, 195, 201, 203, 207
    impact on learning 159–177, 189,
        190, 193, 199–200
    impact on teaching 119, 175, 194,
        196, 201, 222
    in China 171
    in France 32, 171
    in Hong Kong 171, 187
    in Ireland 187
    in Mexico 32, 171, 174